Irish prehistory:
a social perspective

Irish prehistory: a social perspective

Gabriel Cooney
Eoin Grogan

WORDWELL
Dublin

First published 1994
Wordwell Ltd
PO Box 69
Bray
Co. Wicklow
Republic of Ireland

ISBN 1869857 11 9

British Library Cataloguing-in-Publication Data
A catalogue record for this book
is available from the British Library

Printed by Colour Books Ltd
Typeset by Wordwell Ltd

CONTENTS

LIST OF FIGURES

CHAPTER 6

CHAPTER 7

ACKNOWLEDGEMENTS

In writing a book like this the first and most important debt we have to acknowledge is to the many archaeologists, past and present, whose work forms the basis of the interpretation of Irish prehistory presented here. Of course, the interpretations we have given may in some cases be at variance with those of the original works but that is in the nature of the reassessment which we are attempting. Our greatest individual debt is to Nicholas Maxwell, who encouraged us to write this book, was willing to to publish it, and was patient with our failure to meet deadlines. Professor Richard Bradley of the University of Reading read the entire text in draft and we have benefited greatly from his comments. We are also very grateful to Sarah Cross and Finola O'Carroll for useful comments on the text. We would like to acknowledge several people who allowed us to refer to unpublished work namely; Arthur ApSimon, John Bradley, Edward Bourke, Tom Condit, Peter Danaher, George Eogan and Helen Roche, and Finola O'Carroll. Emer Condit copy edited the manuscript and we are indebted to her for all her hard work and for putting some sense and style into our initial text. Mary Davies compiled the index and we are very grateful for the clarity which she brought to that task. Catherine MacConville designed the book cover, which splendidly interprets our concept of the intermeshed nature of archaeological evidence.

The book heavily relies on an integration of text and illustrations and we are very grateful to Sarah Cross for all the time and effort she gave to generating the illustrations, and for her assistance in compiling the bibliography. We would also like to thank Henrik Kiær for his work in bringing the illustrations to their final form. We would like to thank the Faculty of Arts, University College Dublin, for invaluable financial assistance at a critical time, and the Department of Archaeology, University College Dublin, who provided the resources and support which enabled us to write this book.

1 INTRODUCTION

The first question the reader may well ask is 'Why another book on Irish prehistory?', following on the recent publication of volumes by Harbison (1988) and O'Kelly (1989) which cover the same ground and which were intended as an update on the book by Herity and Eogan (1977). The approach in these texts can in turn be linked back to that of Raftery (1951), Ó Ríordáin (1946) and Mahr (1937). There is no doubt that Harbison and O'Kelly both cover a lot of the new information that we have gained about Irish prehistory in the last fifteen years or so, and with their differing approaches — Harbison emphasising a narrative, historical–cultural view and O'Kelly examining the component parts of the prehistoric record — add important new perspectives to our view of the first seven thousand years of human settlement in Ireland. But in many ways they differ little in their methodology from Herity and Eogan. In all three cases examination of the detail of the archaeological evidence is taken to be of paramount importance. The incomplete and varied nature of this evidence is taken to imply that there are areas of prehistoric life and society that we cannot hope to reconstruct. Thus Harbison in the Epilogue to *Pre-Christian Ireland* commented that our knowledge of prehistoric people is a 'very incomplete story' and that aspects such as the number of people involved in the construction of Newgrange or the likely population numbers at given times in prehistory are impossible to predict (1988, 195). This seems to indicate a certain reluctance to go beyond a treatment of the technical and economic aspects of the evidence, a trait which is shared by the other two books. Where speculation is made about social or ritual aspects of the evidence the basis on which inferences are made is not clearly defined. The view propounded by C. F. C. Hawkes (1954) and Smith (1955), that there is a scale of inference that can be applied to archaeological data and that one gets on increasingly dicey ground as topics such as ritual, religion and social organisation are discussed, seems to hold sway. The concept expressed in these volumes on Irish prehistory seems similar to that put forward by Smith, namely that 'archaeological evidence when it is confined to material remains demonstrably supports only a limited range of conclusions about human activity' (Smith 1955, 7).

Much of the recent writing about Irish prehistory demonstrates a restricted interest in or concern with the debate which has been going on more widely in archaeology since the 1960s (e.g. Hodder 1991; Trigger 1989) on the extent to which this pessimistic view of the ability of prehistoric archaeology to tackle social questions can be refuted. Indeed, one has the impression that the term 'New Archaeology' is seen by many Irish prehistorians as a catch-all phrase to cover theoretical developments in the discipline over the last twenty to thirty years without the realisation that this term itself has become dated and is regarded as reflecting archaeological orthodoxy. It can be seen to embody only one of a possible range of approaches (e.g. Hodder 1986; Shanks and Tilley 1987a; 1987b; Whittle 1988; Malina and Vasicek 1990). Broadly speaking, two different perspectives have emerged which for varying reasons deny the idea that there are any essential limitations to our knowledge of the past. The systemic/processual approach to archaeology espoused by Clarke (1968), Binford (e.g. 1983), Renfrew (e.g. 1979) and others is based on the argument that all aspects of human behaviour are interrelated and that it is possible to construct meaningful relationships between material remains and other parts of a cultural system. Binford (1971), for example, related the form and structure of the burial practices of a society which the archaeologist can recover to the form and degree of complexity of the organisational characteristics of the society itself, for which, of course, we may have no direct evidence. In contrast, the post-processual approach espoused by Hodder and others, such as Shanks and Tilley, stresses that while there may be principles of meaning or symbolism underlying material culture, 'There can never be any direct predictive relationships between material culture and social behaviour because in each particular context symbolic principles and general tendencies for the integration of belief and action are rearranged in particular ways as part of the strategies and intents of individuals and groups. The whole is particular, dependent on context' (Hodder 1982, 217).

Both of these perspectives offer critical insights into the understanding of prehistoric societies and are utilised in this review of Irish prehistory. This work differs from previous studies in taking the question of the nature of society as a fundamental one to be addressed as a central theme in attempting to understand the nature of human settlement in prehistoric Ireland. Whether one views the nature of material culture from a systemic or a contextual standpoint, what both approaches agree on is the impossibility of considering human activity and the material remains that result from it without considering the social context in which it occurs. For example, the nature of subsistence economies cannot be understood in isolation from the societies which practised them as the two are inseparable (Champion *et al.* 1984, 5). It is very frequently the case, however, that reports on the faunal remains from prehistoric sites presume that these can be read off as a simple economic equation without taking into account the nature of the site or the associated human activity.

It follows on this view that all aspects of the material evidence have to be seen as interrelated and relevant to attempts to understand what was actually happening in prehistory. It is important as well to get away from the image of the archaeological record as an incomplete jigsaw waiting for the archaeologist to come along and solve it. Material culture cannot be read straight off; it has been influenced by a variety of formative processes and post-depositional factors which greatly affect the nature of the archaeological record. In the case of the former, it is a commonly held assumption, for instance, that stray finds have in most cases been lost accidentally unless they show signs of having been hidden. But frequently the context of the find, such as a bog or river, may indicate a deliberate purpose behind the original deposition of the object which offers an insight into the role that artifacts had in society. A variety of natural and human processes, for example erosion and deposition, and agricultural and antiquarian activity, have greatly affected our knowledge of the prehistoric past. Unless account is taken of those factors which have been operating since the archaeological material was deposited in the ground, we cannot hope to gain a realistic, critical understanding of how the archaeological record reflects the past from which it is derived.

Given the emphasis on understanding the nature and organisation of the human activity that produced the material culture, it is our intention to try to integrate as much as possible the various aspects of the archaeological data that characterise different periods. The fact that these strands of evidence may occur in apparently unrelated contexts should not be looked on as a problem but perhaps as a key to understanding contemporary society. Thus for example the paucity of links, frequently referred to, between the burial record and metal artifact evidence in the Bronze Age (e.g. Harbison 1973; Eogan 1983) is not an attempt by prehistoric people to foil archaeologists in attempting correlation between ceramic and bronze artifact typologies, but rather a deliberate separation reflecting the way that individuals and social groups viewed the relationship between these two aspects of their lives.

A consequence of this emphasis on understanding the relationships between aspects of the evidence is our concentration on a study of its spatial dimension. This applies at the level of both understanding different activities on individual sites and looking at the relationship between sites of the same and differing functions and their setting in the landscape. We also try to integrate the record of stray finds and known archaeological sites to better understand human activity in the landscape. It should be clear that, as today, people were not restricted to discrete dots on a map indicating their residential, work and other activities but that these locations were linked by a web of human activity across the landscape. This is being shown by projects such as those at Céide, Co. Mayo (Caulfield 1983; 1988), Glencloy in Co. Antrim (Woodman 1983) and Bally Lough in Co. Waterford (Zvelebil *et al.* 1987; Green and Zvelebil 1990), which indicate that prehistoric archaeological sites showing a concentration of human endeavour for residential, ritual or other reasons are set against a background of archaeological remains across much of the landscape. This background indicates the presence of the wider human activity that linked specific places and locations.

In understanding how and why prehistoric societies changed over time and in examining the relationship between people and the landscape, it is being increasingly realised that a regional approach offers considerable advantages (e.g. Cooney 1987; Grogan 1989; Mallory and McNeill 1991). By decreasing the size of the area examined it is possible to assess in more detail different facets of the evidence and to interpret behavioural and social patterns. By applying this approach in the same region over a long period it is possible to utilise one of the major features of Irish prehistory, namely its long duration, to gain insights into the processes of cultural and social change in the past. A regional perspective is also of value in reminding us that we should not necessarily expect all parts of Ireland to exhibit similar patterns of development. Indeed, at a time when one might expect people's primary identification to have been with their own locale (Evans 1981, 16) it seems likely that distinctive regional differences would have emerged.

The themes touched on above will form a continuing focus in examining the evidence from the main cultural and chronological blocks in Irish prehistory. A feature of these chronological blocks that has often been noted is that the nature and range of available evidence is variable. While this clearly poses problems it is also an important aspect of the record that may in fact tell us as much about people in the prehistoric past as the surviving evidence itself. The continuity of the thematic approach will also help to set the evidence from any one period against the perspective of long-term trends and developments in Irish prehistory. The text has been written within a structure which examines these major periods — the Mesolithic, Neolithic, Early, Middle and Late Bronze Age and Iron Age — but which also concentrates attention on the transitions between them, as these are critical in examining the reality of cultural and social continuity and change in Ireland during prehistory. In the illustrations there is a deliberate focus on interpreting the archaeological evidence as opposed to presenting drawings of objects and plans of sites. By using the same range of graphic illustrations throughout the work, particularly distribution maps, topographical cross-sections of site locations and bar charts, we have tried to maintain a continuity in our examination of different periods and different kinds of archaeological evidence.

Finally, neither the text nor the illustrative material of this book should be seen as a comprehensive review of Irish prehistory. The recent texts on Irish prehistory by Harbison (1988) and O'Kelly (1989) and Mallory and McNeill's (1991) presentation of the archaeology of Ulster offer up-to-date assessments of the evidence produced by recent archaeological research. While both new material and alternative assessments of existing data are utilised in this work, what we are concentrating on is a presentation which interrogates this evidence to reach a better understanding of people and society in the prehistoric past. Attention has been paid recently to the concept of archaeology as text (e.g. Hodder 1988; Thomas 1991, 3–6). This can mean different things, but a central element of this phrase is the implication that archaeology is written in the present by archaeologists attempting to reconstruct the past. We have no doubt that our view of the Irish prehistoric past is imperfect and will be superseded in the future, but we hope to make a contribution to changing and broadening the agenda for research and understanding.

2 THE FIRST SETTLEMENT OF THE IRISH LANDSCAPE: FORAGERS IN A FORESTED LANDSCAPE

The beginnings of human settlement

Despite the irony that we still have no actual physical evidence of people in the form of burials from the first 4000 years of human settlement in Ireland, one of the most dramatic changes in Irish prehistory over the last twenty years or so concerns our understanding and interpretation of settlement and society during this first phase of human settlement. Although people living in the Mesolithic period (Middle Stone Age) are often referred to by the generic title of hunter-gatherers, this term suggests the primacy of hunting as a subsistence strategy, which would not appear to have been the case in Ireland. Indeed, because of the generally better preservation of bone on archaeological sites, compared to that of plant foods, it may well be that the importance of hunting in temperate Europe has been overestimated (Clarke 1976; Price 1987). Within this broader European context it is clear that the general course of settlement and society in Ireland took on a distinctive character from a very early stage.

It appears that groups of hunter-gatherers originally came to Ireland from the western shores of Britain sometime before 7000 BC. They may well have been guided by the mountain peaks along the eastern coastline that would have been visible from the other side of the then-narrower Irish Sea (Woodman 1981) (Fig. 2:1). This human movement can be seen in the context of the post-glacial colonisation of Ireland which saw the arrival in stages

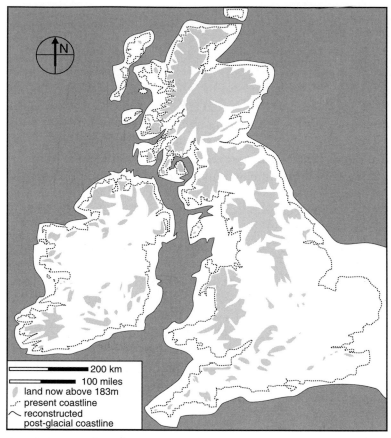

Fig. 2:1—*Overlay of reconstructed early post-glacial shoreline on modern topography of Ireland and Britain (after Woodman 1981).*

of a distinctive insular fauna and flora more restricted than those in Britain and even more so compared to continental Europe (van Wijngaarden-Bakker 1985a; Wheeler 1977). These restrictions are due to a variety of ecological filtering factors. Once Ireland became an island, as it may have been from very early in the post-glacial period (but see Mitchell 1986, 71–5), the opportunities for colonisation would have greatly decreased for animal and plant species.

Since the early part of the twentieth century there has been interest in the question of whether people might have been present in Ireland during the Ice Age or Pleistocene (see discussion in Woodman 1978, 199–205; 1986a; 1992, 297–9). At present there is still no definite evidence for this, despite various attempts to identify what would be a Palaeolithic or Old Stone Age beginning for the human settlement of Ireland. The few Palaeolithic implements known from the country, such as the hand-axe found near Dun Aonghus on Arainn, Co. Galway (Murphy 1977), and the struck flake from Mell near Drogheda, Co. Louth (Mitchell and Sieveking 1972), can be dismissed as the result of modern human import and of transport by natural agencies. This is itself an interesting comment which we should perhaps remember in treating the archaeological evidence from periods when the influence of these factors would not normally be considered. On the other hand, the possibility of a human presence in Ireland during the latter stages of the Pleistocene and in the Late Glacial cannot be dismissed as there would have been ice-free areas in the south of the country potentially suitable for settlement.

From the environmental record it is clear that the post-glacial period, or the Littletonian period as Mitchell has termed it (1976; 1986), started as a clean sheet in ecological terms as the final cold snap that marked the end of the Ice Age also effectively brought an end to much of the Pleistocene fauna and flora (Stuart 1985). It would seem that people first appeared in the Irish landscape when it had become covered in pine, hazel and birch forest. Breaks in this forested landscape would have taken the form of forest glades, the banks of rivers and lakes and coastal areas. Over the next couple of thousand years the composition of the forest changed gradually until it was dominated by oak, elm and alder. It is likely that these and other environmental changes, such as the altering balance between land and sea in coastal areas (Devoy 1983; Synge 1985), would not have been noticeable to particular human generations, but the cumulative effects would have been an important influence on people whose lifestyle was built around the natural resources they used for food.

Corresponding broadly with these environmental developments there is a change in the character of the stone tools and the waste (debitage) resulting from the working of flint, chert and other stones. On the basis of these changes in the lithic industry a distinction can be made between an Early and Later Mesolithic period (Woodman 1978). The question of whether this change in technology is linked to those in the environment already mentioned and whether it had social and settlement consequences will be discussed below.

The Early and Later Mesolithic

It was only in the early 1970s (see Woodman 1973/4) that major changes in the developmental sequence for the Irish Mesolithic put forward by Movius (1942; 1953) and elaborated by Mitchell (e.g. 1970) became apparent. Primarily through the work of Woodman it was realised that preceding the tradition of working flint to produce large leaf-shaped flakes, which had been recognised by Movius as being distinctive of the Irish Mesolithic, there was a lithic industry centred on the production of microlithic or small stone implements which would normally have been used in numbers in composite tools. This microlithic industry is very much in character with the nature of the lithic traditions in European Mesolithic societies and provides a firm basis on which to explain the background to the beginning of human settlement in Ireland.

The nature of the Early and Later Mesolithic industries has been set out in detail by Woodman (1978), but there are a few general points about the relationship between the two industries that are important to note. It appears that the change-over from microliths to large blades took place sometime around 5500 BC, although there is no site that shows evidence for this transition. The character of the microlithic industry at the earliest known Mesolithic sites at Mount Sandel, Co. Derry, and Lough Boora, Co. Offaly, has been described by Woodman (1985a, 171–2) as already having some distinctly Irish features. This suggests, as one might expect, that these sites probably do not represent the activities of the first generations of settlers. Early Mesolithic material is known from a more restricted number of locations than the Later Mesolithic lithics (see Figs 2:2 and 2:3) but in contrast to the latter it usually occurs in undisturbed contexts. Much of the Later Mesolithic flint comes from disturbed contexts

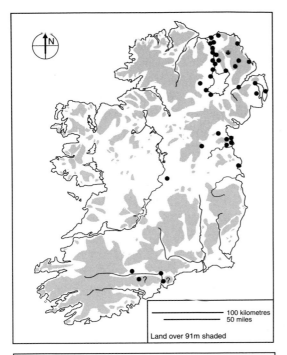

*Fig. 2:2—
Distribution map of
Early Mesolithic
material in Ireland
(after Woodman
1989).*

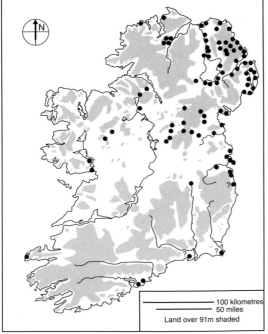

*Fig. 2:3—
Distribution map of
Later Mesolithic
material in Ireland
(after Woodman
1989).*

in coastal deposits, and the virtual absence of Early Mesolithic material in coastal locations may reflect rising sea-level during the period of the Mesolithic and the consequent submergence of the Early Mesolithic coastline (Fig. 2:1), particularly in the north-east of the country. In comparing the pattern of distribution of lithics from the two periods, not only do environmental factors have to be taken into account but also the nature of the material, as it is likely that Early Mesolithic microliths will only be recognised by deliberate strategies of field-walking and excavation whereas, because of their larger size and leaf-shaped forms, Later Mesolithic flakes are much more easily recognised and collected.

The surviving evidence from the Irish Mesolithic lithic industries appears to indicate that they were geared, either directly or indirectly, towards the procurement and processing of food, and this was clearly a central concern of hunter-gatherers in Ireland as elsewhere. In his study of forager subsistence and settlement patterns Jochim (1976, 12, 50–1) suggested that there were three interlinked components: firstly the range or schedule of resources that were available and how these could be used, secondly the location of settlement to best exploit the resource range, and thirdly the demographic arrangements adopted by groups. This latter component may of course have been influenced not only by the balance between the food supply and the number of mouths to feed but also by social factors such as the occurrence of group ceremonies and the need to acquire marriage partners. Because resources are often only available on a seasonal basis a lot of discussion of Mesolithic settlement and society centres around the way in which people adapted their settlement pattern to this variable resource base. Two related lines of approach enable us to say something about these issues: firstly an examination of the location of the sites and secondly a look at the known sites in terms of food sources represented, the human activities carried on and the organisation of those activities.

The location of Mesolithic sites

Woodman (1978) compiled a gazetteer of over 170 sites where Mesolithic material had been found up to the mid-1970s, ranging from single finds of a diagnostic artifact type to large lithic

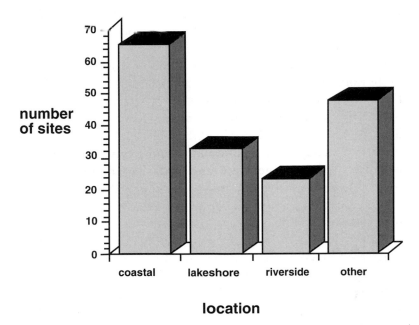

Fig. 2:4—Locational trends of Irish Mesolithic sites (based on informa-tion in Woodman 1978).

assemblages sometimes associated with other cultural material. Analysis of the location of these sites in the landscape (Fig. 2:4) makes it clear that the majority (72%) are in coastal, lakeside or riverside locations. The dominance of 'close to water' locations (see Fig. 2:5, showing the topographical location of Later Mesolithic sites in north Leinster) may in fact be even greater than suggested by Fig. 2:4 as the 'other' category includes both sites where it is not possible to determine the location from the known details and the relatively small number of known sites in more upland locations, such as those from the Antrim Plateau, and in the Kevin/Rotherham lithic collection from the Loughcrew hills in Co. Meath. It is interesting on the other hand that Dillon's (1990) recent research on the latter material has demonstrated that there is both Early and Later Mesolithic material present there.

Discoveries of Mesolithic material since the late 1970s,

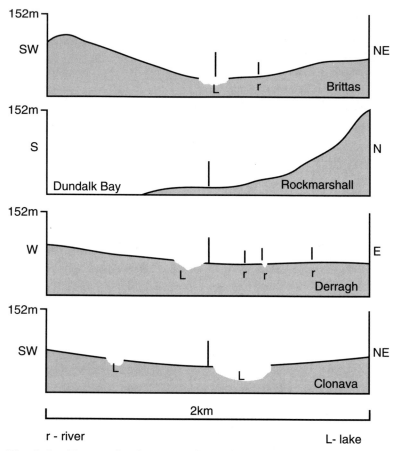

Fig. 2:5—Topographical transects illustrating the location of Later Mesolithic sites in north Leinster: Brittas (Moynagh Lough), Co. Meath; Rockmarshall, Co. Louth; Derragh (Lough Kinale), Co. Longford; and Clonava (Lough Derravaragh), Co. Westmeath.

particularly in Munster, have been in areas that could have been predicted, as the material has turned up mainly in coastal areas, close to lakes or in river valleys (e.g. Anderson 1991; Woodman 1984; 1989; Woodman *et al.* 1984; Green and Zvelebil 1990). These indeed are the areas that would have been most attractive to foragers in the earlier post-glacial. As Clarke (1976) pointed out, these zones are rich and diversified in food resources. They have a high annual productivity compared to other areas and a large amount of this is potentially edible. There was a range of plants, fish and wild fowl, and in coastal areas additional resources, such as molluscs and crustaceans, would have been available. The presence of open water and the adjacent vegetation would have attracted mammals to come out of the predominantly forest-covered terrain. In the specific context of Ireland it could be argued that the attractiveness of these zones would have been greater because of the restricted range of mammals available.

Looking at the methods by which this material has been found, however, urges caution in dismissing the possibility of finds outside these zones. It is clear that in north Leinster at least (Fig. 2:6) much of the Mesolithic evidence has been found through deliberate search strategies, such as field-walking and bulk collection of exposed material. Hence there has been a

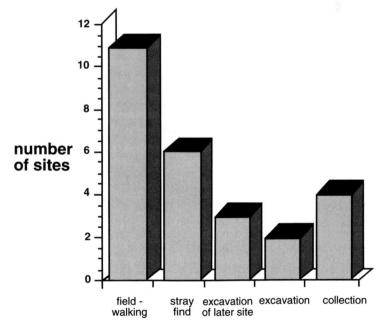

Fig. 2:6—Circumstances of recovery of Mesolithic material in north Leinster.

reinforcement of apparent locational trends through fieldworkers concentrating on known areas of occurrence. It should also be said that the known pattern of location and distribution (Figs 2:2 and 2:3) is in many ways an incomplete one. The areas where Mesolithic material turns up are those which have been most prone to environmental change since the earlier post-glacial period. Processes such as changing sea and freshwater levels, erosion, alluvial deposition and the build-up of peat in raised bogs may distort or mask our knowledge of Mesolithic settlement patterns (Mitchell 1986, 91–6).

Woodman (1986b, 15) has pointed to an apparent contrast in that the Later Mesolithic material tends to be more low-lying than that of the Early Mesolithic. This raises interesting questions about possible differences between the two periods. It could reflect important locational differences in activity between the Early and Later Mesolithic. On the other hand, it may reflect alluviation in the lower parts of river valleys masking what were the land surfaces in both the Early and Later Mesolithic, in the same way that flooding of coastal areas has removed evidence for Early Mesolithic coastal settlement. Indeed, Woodman (1989, 123) has suggested that this coastal zone may have been the major area exploited during the Early Mesolithic. However, it is also relevant to reiterate the practical difficulties of seeing and recovering Early Mesolithic microlithic material as against the typical large flake implements of the Later Mesolithic. In comparing the number of known sites belonging to the two periods (Figs 2:2 and 2:3) we suggest that this is an indication that events in Ireland followed general European trends where the density of settlement increases during the course of the Mesolithic (Price 1987; but see Woodman 1985c; 1986b, 13–14, for a different view, discussed below). However, the environmental and recovery bias towards greater knowledge of the Later Mesolithic must always be borne in mind. Woodman and Anderson (1990, 387) have pointed out that many Later Mesolithic artifact types can be regarded as woodworking tools and that the major change between the Early and Later Mesolithic was not so much a shift in economic base as an alteration of procurement strategies whereby much more emphasis was placed in the Later Mesolithic on making facilities such as traps, particularly in fishing.

Activities on Mesolithic sites

Out of the couple of hundred of known Mesolithic 'sites' only a small number have been excavated and/or produced anything other than lithic material. Without going into the detail already well documented by Woodman (1978; 1985a) and van Wijngaarden-Bakker (1985a; 1985b), it is clear that a range of food resources were utilised, with an emphasis on salmonids and eels, plant foods (especially hazelnuts), shellfish and pig, with some evidence for exploitation of smaller mammals and wild birds. Individual sites have evidence for a number of food resources and this should be seen in combination with the general and deliberate location of Mesolithic sites in areas where a variety of food sources could be obtained.

Most of the evidence for human activity on these sites centres around the procurement and processing of food and the working of lithic material. Obviously the latter activity would also have been intimately connected with the food quest. The only houses known are the series from Mount Sandel, each about 6m across, apparently representing replacement over time. The evidence at this site suggests that activities were carried out in an organised manner, with a flint-working area distinct from the main residential focus (Woodman 1985a, 137–47). Hearths and pits, in which a lot of the food and artifactual material turned up at Mount Sandel, are also present at the Lough Boora Early Mesolithic site (Ryan 1980a). Hearths or spreads of charcoal are a common feature, and at the Later Mesolithic coastal site at Sutton, Co. Dublin (Mitchell 1956; 1972a), excavation revealed four pits and a hearth under a shell midden. At Glendhu, Co. Down, a line of paired post-holes over 10m in length of possible Later Mesolithic date may have held the uprights of drying racks or some other outdoor facilities (Woodman 1985d). At Newferry a stone edging was laid down at one stage, apparently to stabilise the sandbank on which Later Mesolithic activity was taking place (Woodman 1977, 163). At Moynagh Lough in Co. Meath it appears that material may have been laid down to serve a similar function at a site that was on two low knolls in lake shallows (J. Bradley 1982/3, 15; 1991, 7–9).

On many of the sites there is the impression of a restricted range of activities. Does this reflect the nature of Mesolithic settlement or are we seeing sites that are largely marginal to the main focus of settlement? One can contrast Mount Sandel with every other Mesolithic site in Ireland, with the possible exception of Lough Boora, in terms of the range and organisation of activities concentrated there. These differences are central to the question of the pattern of settlement in Ireland as it appears that they represent the difference between a base camp, occupied for a substantial part of the year or perhaps all year round, and an array of sites with a more restricted and more specialised use (e.g. Binford 1980). The question that must be asked in looking at Mesolithic settlement and society in Ireland is whether Mount Sandel should be seen as representative of the core of the pattern of settlement in the Irish Mesolithic or as a unique site.

Settlement and society in the Irish Mesolithic
Up to the 1970s there was the view that hunter-gatherers in prehistory had led a very difficult marginal existence. This is perhaps exemplified in the description of the people of the Irish Mesolithic as 'strandloopers'. Archaeological and anthropological research indicates that this view is incorrect and that, while the quest for food was a central activity, the range and plentifulness of food resources meant that food could be secured by hunter-gatherers without in any way consuming all their time and effort. Sahlins (1974) has characterised people in this type of situation as belonging to the 'original affluent society' (see also Bird-David 1992). While this view in turn may oversimplify the possible resource difficulties that foragers might have to face at particular times it is of value as a reminder that hunter-gatherers had the capacity to organise a regular supply of food and that food-gathering may have been embedded in an array of other cultural activities. In some areas hunter-gatherer communities developed a considerable degree of social complexity (e.g. Price and Brown 1985).

In the first detailed interpretation of the settlement pattern in the Irish Mesolithic Woodman (1978, figs 60–1) saw Mesolithic groups as concentrating in coastal areas in spring, at inland riversides and lake shores in the summer and early autumn, and possibly moving to slightly higher ground in the later autumn and winter. This was based on the location of Mesolithic material and the known range of resources exploited. Many of these resources are seasonal in nature and so it seems probable that at different times of year a varying combination of resources would have been in use. Hence Woodman (1978, 176–81) suggested that coastal resources may have been predominant in the spring and early summer, with the focus then shifting to the exploitation of salmon and eel migrations, and that the autumn and winter diet may have been based on pig and other meat supplemented by hazelnuts. This model also fitted in with the then-dominant view of forager settlement as following an annual pattern of movement orientated around a number of base camps strategically placed to exploit seasonally abundant resources. It was one of the two general patterns of hunter-gatherer subsistence–settlement systems defined by Binford (1980). He contrasted the seasonal mobility associated with a 'foraging' strategy with the more restricted movement and strategic placement of base camps in a 'mapping-on' or 'collector' strategy.

As discussed above, however, there is only one definite base camp known from the Irish Mesolithic — Mount Sandel. In this context it is difficult to assess the degree of seasonality in settlement. Most of the identifiable sites would appear to be either specialised-function sites or transitory camps. These would be expected to occur within the exploitation range or territory of a base camp. For example, the Later Mesolithic material found by Mitchell (1972b) at Clonava, Lough Derravaragh, Co. Westmeath, would fit into the category of being the result of the exploitation of a chert source and a favourable location for fishing. But it was located on the periphery of what would have been a dry island of glacial till in a wetland landscape which would have had potential as a more substantial base for settlement (Fig. 2:7). Mount Sandel itself could have been occupied for a substantial part of the year on the basis of the food resources exploited, and in some cases stored, by the inhabitants

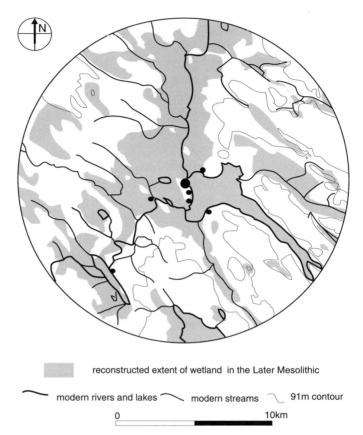

reconstructed extent of wetland in the Later Mesolithic

modern rivers and lakes ⁀ modern streams ⁀ 91m contour

0 ———————————— 10km

Fig. 2:7—Territory within 10km of the Later Mesolithic site at Clonava, Lough Derravaragh, Co. Westmeath, with reconstruction of extent of wetland in Later Mesolithic period.

(Woodman 1985a, 167). Woodman has suggested, on the basis of the size of the houses there, that it is likely to have been the base for a (family?) group of, at maximum, ten people. This figure is substantially below the estimate of 25 that Wobst (1974) considered viable for a hunter-gatherer social band or group composed of a number of families, and it is likely that one or two other sites in the vicinity of Mount Sandel were occupied contemporaneously (Woodman 1985a, 155–6). The latter suggestion points to the likelihood that the band or group was a flexible demographic and social arrangement. Families or perhaps even specific subgroups were capable of operating on their own in conditions of lower densities of resources or in cooperation where necessary or possible under optimum conditions. Mount Sandel, then, clearly does not solve the problems regarding Irish Mesolithic subsistence–settlement patterns, but it does suggest that a model based simply on seasonal mobility is insufficient. The presence of the specialised-task and short-stay camps that dominate the evidence for the Irish Mesolithic is reminiscent of the array of sites that Binford saw as characteristic of a 'collector' strategy where these sites are operating to serve the near-sedentary residential camp. Perhaps in the Irish Mesolithic it is not unreasonable to expect that in the vicinity of the known specialised sites there were more permanent camps which would have acted as the bases for a variety of subsistence strategies.

This would seem to fit well with the increasing appreciation that European Mesolithic hunter-gatherers had a more complex subsistence–settlement strategy than had previously been suggested (e.g. Bailey 1983). Rowley-Conwy (1983) in examining the Ertebølle culture in the Danish Mesolithic suggested that in locations, particularly coastal ones, where a range of migratory species appear close to each other at different times of the year, these and other resources could have been exploited from a single home base, with a variety of briefly occupied special-purpose camps being used. In a review of the evidence Price (1987, 286) suggests that year-round occupation of limited territories may have been the norm, particularly in the coastal areas of western Europe, during the later part of the Mesolithic. In Ireland the majority of Mesolithic sites similarly occur in the best locations to exploit resource-clustering on a year-round basis. It seems plausible to suggest that a sedentary pattern of settlement might have been at the core of Irish Mesolithic society.

Looking at this question from a chronological perspective, Woodman (1985c; 1986b, 13–15) has suggested that there may have been a shift from a more sedentary lifestyle in the Early Mesolithic to a highly mobile economy in the Later Mesolithic. Again it has to be stressed that this view stems from the example of an Early Mesolithic base camp at Mount Sandel and the lack of a definite base camp in the archaeological record for the Later Mesolithic. On environmental grounds it can be argued that there may have been higher productivity of resources in the Atlantic conditions of the Later Mesolithic compared to the Boreal-type conditions of the Early Mesolithic (see discussion in Woodman 1985b, 257–8) and that this is likely to have provided a basis for more permanent settlement. As Woodman (1986b, 13) has pointed out, because of changes in procurement strategy in the Later Mesolithic with the emphasis on specialised sites, base camps in this period could have a much lower visibility than other kinds of sites. Taking into account the difficulties of assessing what is, after all, a very partial record, it does seem likely that the general trend in Ireland, as in western Europe, was for more sedentary settlement, particularly in coastal areas, towards the end of the Mesolithic.

Related to the question of the system of settlement and subsistence that was in use is the number of people that had to be fed. Anthropological studies suggest that many 'modern' hunter-gatherers live, or lived, at densities of around one or less than one person per 10km^2. This would give a notional figure of around 7,000 people or less living in Ireland at any time during the Mesolithic. Clearly this is only a guess which indicates the likely scale of population and does nothing to tell us about the development of population numbers from the start of the Mesolithic. The population was made up of the bands or groups discussed above, composed of a number of families. Kinship in this type of society is the basis of all social and economic relationships and the family is the primary unit of production and consumption, but work is also carried out communally. Division of labour and status would have been by age and sex, and positions of authority may have been attained through individual merit (e.g. Service 1971; Clark and Neeley 1987), although more complex social structures are known amongst some hunter-gatherers (Bender 1978; Layton 1986).

Because of the lack of base camps apart from Mount Sandel, it is very difficult to assess the extent of the area that such groups would have exploited on a regular basis. One frequently used estimate is that the major area of resource exploitation would have been within two hours of a base camp (Higgs and Vita-Finzi 1972). Again this is not to be seen in any way as an absolute figure but as one which gives an indication of the size of territory we should be thinking of. Researchers in Britain (Jacobi 1979) and in north-west Europe (Gendel 1987; 1989) have looked at regional differences in terms of both artifact assemblages and individual artifact types which might suggest a level of social integration between groups within a region and an identifiable contrast with other regions. While the evidence is not easy to interpret, it does suggest that in the Later Mesolithic regional social territories may have emerged. In Ireland, by contrast, one of the interesting points about the Later Mesolithic is that despite the use of different materials a series of implements were being produced to a 'definite template', as Woodman (1987, 144; see also Woodman 1989) has put it. Similarly, in the Early Mesolithic Woodman (1987, 140) noted a unity in the range and type of microliths used on different sites. On stylistic grounds, then, one could suggest that there was little sense of regionalisation in the Irish Mesolithic, although Ireland was itself a very distinct region within the wider context of the west European Mesolithic.

People from different bands or groups would clearly have come into contact with one another either accidentally or deliberately for partners, social contact and information. One way in which the archaeologist might find tangible evidence of this is through the presence of non-local materials being used for implements. Woodman (1987) has explored this question but looked at it primarily from the perspective of the strategy that Mesolithic people used to procure lithic materials from outside the immediate vicinity of their area. He suggested that in the Early Mesolithic this was achieved through obtaining raw materials in the course of ordinary hunting or foraging trips — what is referred to as an embedded procurement strategy. By contrast, he suggests that in the Later Mesolithic such materials may have been obtained during deliberate trips by small task groups to procure raw material. Woodman cites the presence of sites in the Bann Valley without industrial waste and industrial sites on the Antrim coast with few retouched tools as evidence of this transportation of raw materials to areas of extensive settlement. It could be argued, however, that this view underestimates the potential importance of exchange. This may be indicated in the presence of, for example, the occasional chert microlith at Mount Sandel and flint microlith at Lough Boora, in each case occurring well away from any possible source area, and this pattern continues on Later Mesolithic sites (Woodman 1978, 144–6). Given this evidence, it seems plausible to suggest that contact between different groups may have had a more important role in the procurement of raw materials, particularly in the form of reciprocal gift exchange (Mauss 1954; Renfrew and Bahn 1991, 309–13). A range of items, of which lithics may be the only durable element left in the archaeological record, could have been exchanged between groups, and the act of making these exchanges would have served to create contacts and social ties through the obligation to return in an equivalent kind any gifts accepted. This contact is certainly suggested by the uniformity across the country of both the Early and Later Mesolithic lithic industries which suggests little sign of regionalisation or the development of social territories. Particularly in the Later Mesolithic what is striking is that the island as a whole can be set in contrast to the character of contemporary lithic traditions in Britain and on the Continent. This contrast could be taken to indicate that people in Ireland were living in comparative isolation, or alternatively that they deliberately maintained a separate cultural identity and successful lithic technology despite contact with groups who were making stone tools in a very different way. This question of the relationship of hunter-gatherers in Ireland to the wider west European context is a vital one in looking at the transition in Ireland from a very long-established foraging lifestyle to the beginnings of farming.

3 THE FORAGER–FARMER INTERFACE

When and how did the transition to agriculture occur?
It is against the background of the independent development and insular nature of the Later Mesolithic in Ireland that we begin to get evidence of a new type of subsistence activity in the form of the cultivation of domesticated crops and the herding of domesticated animals sometime around 4500–4000 BC. The ambiguity expressed in this wide date range illustrates one of the problems there are in discussing the beginnings of farming in Ireland. Another basic question that must be asked is who brought about these changes in subsistence activity? As Whittle (1990, 223) has stated in a recent review of this topic, 'neither the date of transition nor the nature of communities during transition are well known'. In the past, given the minimal role and importance ascribed to hunter-gatherers in this process, it was assumed that they were gradually assimilated by a spread of farming communities who brought in farming and an associated new culture and technology (e.g. Case 1969a; 1969b). More recently it has been realised that hunter-gatherers were well adapted to their environment and that in parts of western Europe during the later phases of the Mesolithic period communities appear to have been developing an internal social complexity. This, allied to the varied chronology of the establishment of farming in western Europe, has led to a very positive role being given to hunter-gatherers in many areas in the initiation of farming, which hence is seen as emerging in the indigenous context of the local Mesolithic (e.g. Dennell 1985; Price 1987; Zvelebil and Rowley-Conwy 1984; 1986). Of course farming

constitutes only one element of the Neolithic, which is said to be
characterised also by more or less permanent settlement, a range
of burial and ceremonial sites and a distinctive set of material
culture. Looking at this broader context of the
Mesolithic–Neolithic transition, it may have been brought about
by foragers choosing to take on all or part of an economic,
technological and/or social package for a number of different
reasons, or it may have been the result of the expansion of
farming communities, or indeed a complex mixture of both these
processes (Whittle 1990, 209–15). The debate about the
beginnings of farming and the Neolithic in Ireland must be set
against the background of a general spread of agriculture from
south-east Europe and the presence of well-established Neolithic
communities in parts of western Europe (see Whittle 1985, fig.
6.1).

The nature of the transition in Ireland
What makes Ireland an interesting case in this question is firstly
that it is an island and secondly that the Later Mesolithic shows
little evidence of external contacts. Because of its island character
most of the basic elements of a farming subsistence strategy, such
as the domesticated cattle, pig and sheep and the wheat and
barley cereal crops, had to be physically transported across the sea
by somebody, and there are very few visible signs of a network of
contact and exchange between Ireland and adjacent areas in the
Irish Sea zone through which Mesolithic people could have
gained access to the new knowledge, a novel subsistence system,
associated technology and artifact styles. In contrast to Britain,
where some continuity can be seen in the use of resources,
exchange patterns and regional differences from the Mesolithic to
the Neolithic (R. Bradley 1984, 11–15), in Ireland the
established view is that the lithic industry of the Neolithic is quite
distinct from that of the Later Mesolithic (Woodman 1976; 1987,
144–5), the distribution and location of Mesolithic and Neolithic
material in the landscape is complementary (Cooney 1987/8, 8),
and one of the major features of the Neolithic is evidence for
regional patterns in economy and society emerging for the first
time. In general terms these three statements are still borne out

by the archaeological evidence, but the distinction between the Irish Mesolithic and Neolithic may not have been as clear on the ground as they would suggest. For example, Woodman and Anderson (1990, 378) argue that in terms of the size of blades and flakes Later Mesolithic and Neolithic lithic industries may be similar. The work of the Bally Lough Project around Tramore Bay and Waterford Harbour suggests that there during both the Mesolithic and Neolithic the coastal and estuarine areas were the focus of residential activities and that utilisation of the locally available lithic materials showed considerable continuity (Green and Zvelebil 1990, 83–4; Peterson 1990, 97–8). At the same time there are some signs of a broader continuity across the foraging–farming interface, as, for example, in the continued use of mudstone as a raw material for stone axes (Cooney 1989, 155).

How are we to explain these patterns of change and continuity? If it was the indigenous hunter-gatherers who introduced farming then we should not be surprised by the continuity. On the other hand, if people arrived in Ireland from Britain or continental Europe as pioneer farmers with their own cultural identity then distinctions between the newcomers and the natives might be expected. Clearly the first step in this process was the importation of the new species of plants and animals and new knowledge onto the island. But what we have in the archaeological record is the next stage in the process, the occurrence of evidence for farming for the first time within Ireland itself. For example, at a limited number of Later Mesolithic sites, such as Sutton (Mitchell 1972a) and Dalkey Island (Liversage 1968), there are signs of contact with farming in the form of domesticated animal remains. Given the lack of evidence we have for processes that might have motivated Later Mesolithic people in Ireland to a change in lifestyle, such as climatic change, technological innovation, changes in social networks (see below) or the appearance of new plants and animals (Layton *et al.* 1991), the balance of argument still appears to favour some input from new people. Evidence such as the presence of domesticated cattle bone at Later Mesolithic sites seems best explained not by hunter-gatherers importing what would have been to them a strange and exotic mammal species but by hunting-gathering communities coming into contact with people obtaining food from farming who had become established in Ireland and who had cattle to exchange, lose or be stolen. To put it another way, the foraging–farming frontier had moved to within Ireland. It seems most likely that when new settlers came they would have arrived in small numbers from the western shores of Britain or possibly directly from continental Europe. Given that this movement is likely to have been small-scale in nature and that contacts with hunter-gatherers are likely to have taken place in Ireland from a very early stage, our difficulties in separating out these two elements in the population of the fifth millennium BC are not surprising. It may well be the case that at least initial contact between hunter-gatherers and farmers consisted of foragers utilising the new large mammals that were brought in and which may have escaped from early farming settlements. More formal contact would have begun with the expansion of the population and settlement area of farming groups. Indeed, as Thomas (1988a, 63–4) has suggested, it may have been the material and ideological aspects of the Neolithic that were attractive to hunter-gatherers rather than farming itself, which, at least in the short term, may not have seemed a very attractive alternative to a subsistence strategy based on foraging.

Recognising the nature of change and continuity from the Mesolithic to the Neolithic

Farming by its nature suggests an attachment to the land, especially through the growth of cereal crops, and this sense of belonging and permanent commitment stretching back through previous generations is something that has been contrasted with the timeless perspective of the hunter-gatherer (Meillassoux 1972). It is also argued to be the basis for much of the character of the social and economic developments that we see in the Neolithic and forms the context for the emphasis on monumental burial places in the landscape. But is this differentiation of perspective on time and the landscape too simplistic a view? It was suggested in the previous chapter that Later Mesolithic settlement in Ireland may have been organised on a near-sedentary basis. Elsewhere in Europe it has been argued that this type of settlement pattern may be the catalyst for, or the result of, growing social complexity, as measured for example by the occurrence of Mesolithic cemeteries (Chapman 1981, Clarke and Neeley 1987; Larsson 1989). The use of a formal area for the dead clearly implies a long-term attachment to a specific location. In the case of Ireland it has been suggested by Burenhult (1984, 142–6), on the basis of his work at the Carrowmore passage tomb cemetery in Co. Sligo, that the first use of megalithic tombs there may have occurred in a Mesolithic context. This proposition is based primarily on the late fifth-millennium BC radiocarbon date from a simple tomb structure (Grave 4 at Carrowmore). However, there is a problem with the reliability of the date as relating to the construction of the tomb, and no Mesolithic artifacts are known from any of the Carrowmore excavations (Caulfield 1983, 206–13). Nevertheless it is important to bear in mind that the complex associations between people and the landscape implied in the concept of a sacred place probably existed long before the beginnings of farming in Ireland.

An aspect of the relationship between people and the land that might be viewed more from a practical perspective is the act of making clearances in the predominantly forested landscape. In this type of landscape one would expect that early farmers would have had to open up land for cultivation purposes at least. Our knowledge about the human impact on the environment in earlier prehistory is based largely on the history of vegetation derived from the study of pollen in peat bogs or lake sediments. The very restricted and equivocal evidence for forest clearance prior to the mid-fifth millennium BC in Ireland (see Edwards 1985, 192–5; Preece *et al.* 1986) seems to fit in with the exploitation of food resources from predominantly open environments seen on Mesolithic sites and should provide a clear baseline against which to judge the beginnings of human interference for agricultural purposes in the pollen record. It is now clear that the traditional event in vegetational history based on pollen analysis which was seen to mark the onset of farming, the so-called elm decline around 4000 BC, was not itself primarily the result of human activity but in all probability was caused by disease and was pre-dated by opening up of the forest

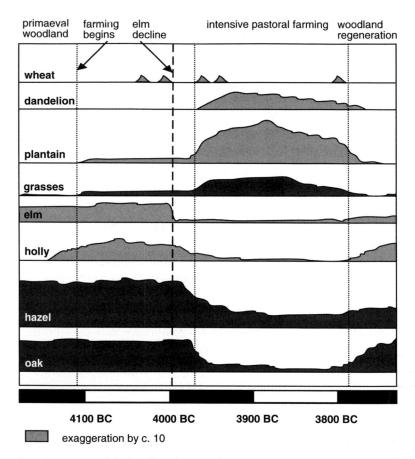

primaeval farming elm   intensive pastoral farming woodland
woodland   begins   decline   regeneration

wheat

dandelion

plantain

grasses

elm

holly

hazel

oak

4100 BC   4000 BC   3900 BC   3800 BC

exaggeration by c. 10

*Fig. 3:1—Simplified pollen diagram from Lough Sheeauns,
Connemara, Co. Galway, showing main trends in selected pollen curves
before and after 4000 BC (after Molloy and O'Connell 1987).*

cover for farming purposes. For example, at Lough Sheeauns near
Cleggan, Co. Galway, Molloy and O'Connell (1987) have
shown that farming began about a century before the elm decline
with the opening up of the forest cover and the occurrence of
small quantities of cereal pollen (Fig. 3:1).

The question of how much earlier than the elm decline
farming began is, however, a difficult one. It relies very much on

the identification of pollen grains of cereals such as wheat and
barley associated with clearance episodes (e.g. Williams 1989).
Clearly cereals had to be introduced into Ireland, and unlike
other plant indicators in the pollen record they can be linked
directly to a farming context. The recognition of even one or
two cereal pollen grains in the vegetational sequences recorded in
profiles from peat bogs or lake sediments is of major importance
because of the very localised dispersal of such pollen around its
growing site (Vuerola 1973). Several authors (e.g. Lynch 1981;
Groenman-van Waateringe 1983; Edwards and Hirons 1984;
Williams 1989) have argued that such clearances are in evidence
in small numbers from at least 4500 BC. One of the best
examples is at Cashelkeelty, Co. Kerry (Lynch 1981), where two
clearance phases, both including evidence of cereal pollen, pre-
date the elm decline, and the earlier of the two clearances began
before 4600 BC (Fig. 3:2). But O'Connell (1987) has queried the
reliability of the cereal pollen grain identifications on which this
view of the beginnings of agriculture is based, principally because
of his recognition of pollen that would otherwise have been
accepted as of cereal type in a deposit dating back to 6000 BC,
pre-dating any possible introduction of cereals to Ireland by over
a millennium. One archaeological backup that is frequently
quoted in support of the earlier fifth-millennium BC date for the
beginnings of farming is the Neolithic site at Ballynagilly, Co.
Tyrone, where the initial occupation has been dated to *c.* 4600
BC (ApSimon 1976), although the excavator has more recently
suggested that the features so dated may be younger by a factor of
a number of hundreds of years, and this would be far more in
keeping with the background of the archaeological material on
the site. The pottery, for example, clearly has a Continental
background, but the earliest dates for this type of pottery on the
European mainland are *c.* 4000 BC (ApSimon, pers. comm.;
Kinnes 1988, 6; Thomas 1988a, 61).

It seems at the moment, then, that two views can be suggested
on the date of the beginnings of farming in Ireland. It may have
begun very tentatively sometime before 4500 BC, with a long
pioneer phase involving small-scale settlement and limited
landscape impact. This would have formed the background to

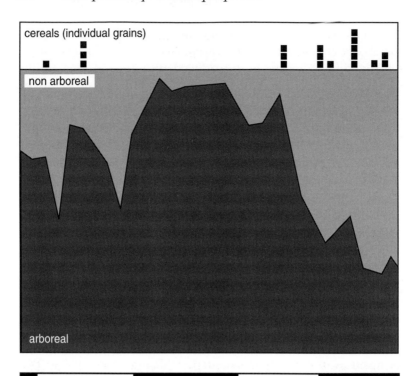

Fig. 3:2—Simplified pollen diagram from Cashelkeelty, Co. Kerry, showing the changing proportion of arboreal (tree) to non-arboreal pollen and the occurrence of pollen of cereals during the earlier prehistoric period (after Lynch 1981).

well-established agricultural communities transforming the landscape and becoming very visible in the archaeological record from around 3800 BC on (e.g. Fowler 1983, 3–5). Alternatively, farming may have commenced only shortly before the elm decline, as at Lough Sheeauns (Fig. 3:1). This would suggest a much quicker build-up to the stage when people brought about a significant transformation of parts of the Irish landscape through their agricultural activities and settlement.

It is perhaps appropriate to end by returning to the question of who was responsible for this transformation. As we have suggested above, on balance the admittedly problematic data favour the partial retention of the traditional explanation, namely the arrival of new people. It is true that the colonisation model has been one of the most overplayed and under-evaluated themes in Irish prehistoric studies (see Waddell 1978); however, as Anthony (1990) has argued, where the evidence indicates a process of human migration it should not be ignored simply because it is not currently fashionable as an explanation for change in the archaeological record. If the argument for a beginning of farming in the earlier fifth millennium BC is accepted, it would allow for a considerable chronological overlap between early farmers and hunter-gatherers. If, on the other hand, a date in the later part of that millennium is preferred, this overlap is removed and the transition from foraging to farming would appear to have been a more abrupt process. In the course of the fifth millennium BC major changes occurred in the Neolithic of western Europe with the breakup of a widespread cultural uniformity, the Linearbandkeramik (LBK), and the emergence and expansion of regionally diverse communities who shared traits such as plain bowl pottery and the construction of monuments for the activities of the living and the dead. The expansion of settlement that accompanied these changes could provide the dynamic process to explain the migration of people to the offshore islands of Britain and Ireland (Whittle 1990, 222), while the altered Neolithic package represented a lifestyle and set of ideas which may have been more attractive to hunter-gatherers (Thomas 1988a, 64–5; Sherratt 1990).

4 WILDSCAPE TO DOMESTICATED LANDSCAPE: EARLY FARMERS AND THEIR LIFESTYLE

Space, material culture, burial and food

There are many definitions of what constitutes the Neolithic and how it was brought about. Ironically, one of the aspects of this period for which we have least evidence is the food sources that people used. It is other aspects of this period, such as the burial monuments, the material culture that people had and the way in which they organised their settlements, that have been the focus of attention (e.g. Thomas 1991). It is the combination of these four elements — food, space, burial, and material culture — that we can use to reconstruct the lifestyles of the period. All of these elements were linked: the use and control of the land for food production, the construction of substantial houses for the living and the dead, and the occurrence of the same kinds of objects in different contexts. These features remind us that the activities of Neolithic people were part of an integrated whole and cannot be understood unless viewed in this light.

Neolithic subsistence patterns

At first glance it would appear that our knowledge of what subsistence patterns were like in the Neolithic is one of the better-known and more clearly defined aspects of the period. Any general treatment of this topic will tell the reader that cattle were the predominant domesticated animal, followed by pig and sheep/goat (the latter amalgam arising because of the frequent difficulty of distinguishing between the faunal remains of sheep and goat). The domesticated animals, particularly cattle, appear to have been the major element in the farming economy, with the main cultivated cereals, emmer wheat and barley, playing a subsidiary role. Small quantities of wild plant foods and bones of wild animals, fowl and fish attest to their role of supplementing the food supply provided by farming practice (Herity and Eogan 1977, 51, 72–3, 91; Harbison 1988, 30–2; O'Kelly 1989, 33–7). The character of this subsistence pattern has been portrayed as the foundation for the enduring pastoral nature of Irish rural life and as an adaptation to the Irish environment, which is seen as being more conducive to producing rich grass to feed cattle than to providing the conditions for large-scale cereal production (e.g. Evans 1981, 38).

However, when looked at more critically this scenario can be seen to be based on limited evidence and on a number of assumptions which need to be evaluated in any attempt to reconstruct the nature of subsistence in the Irish Neolithic. Regarding the nature of the evidence, both van Wijngaarden-Bakker (1974, 320–3) and McCormick (1985/6, 37) have drawn attention to the paucity in quantity and quality of the faunal assemblages from Irish Neolithic sites. Interestingly some of the best assemblages come from burial sites (McCormick 1985; 1985/6), and the major known assemblage comes from towards the end of the period, dating to around 2500 BC at the Final Neolithic occupation at Newgrange (van Wijngaarden-Bakker 1974; 1986). The Lough Gur, Co. Limerick, settlement complex at Knockadoon was excavated (see Ó Ríordáin 1954) before the development of the methodology to extract a wide range of information from animal bones, and subsequent study of the small surviving sample (van Wijngaarden-Bakker 1974, 323) of the original very large faunal assemblage from the various Knockadoon sites could do little more than amplify the general statements made in the original site reports (see Grogan and Eogan 1987, 484–7).

Appreciation of the possibility of extracting surviving plant material from deposits on archaeological sites is also a development that has only been applied to any great extent over the last twenty years. Jessen and Helbaek's pioneering work (1944) was largely based on the grain impressions surviving on the surface of

pottery vessels, while modern work concentrates more on the
range of plant remains that may occur in suitable deposits, such as
the fills of pits on settlement sites (e.g. Monk 1988). In an important review of palaeobotanical evidence for prehistoric crop husbandry in Ireland Monk (1985/6) emphasised the problems of the
low survival rate of plant remains on many archaeological sites,
the difficulties of interpreting the surviving evidence and the
problems of working in a situation where so few sites have been
adequately sampled to see if palaeobotanical material actually sur-
vives. Given these difficulties we should perhaps give greater
weight to the evidence for crop husbandry in the Neolithic than
has been the case in many previous studies. It has been shown
that in Europe during the Neolithic period the type of farming
systems that were most widely used were mixed, with the animal
and crop components being integrated to ensure efficiency of
land use and resources and a varying but significant use of wild
plants and animals (Rowley-Conwy 1981, 94–5; Barker 1985,
28–54). The picture of a low status for cereal crops in Ireland
may have been overemphasised in the archaeological literature
because of the present dominance of pastoralism in the Irish agricultural economy. This, however, fails to take account of both
the historically documented higher acreages for cereals in the past
and the better environmental conditions during much of the Irish
Neolithic when temperatures were about 2–2.5°C warmer than
today. This temperature would have had a number of knock-on
effects vital to cereal-growing, such as the warming of the soil
and the number of sunny days (see Caulfield 1983). So we should
not automatically reduce the role of cereal crops to that of a
minor subsidiary of the pastoral resource. For example, during
the excavation of the smaller of two early Neolithic rectangular
houses at Tankardstown, Co. Limerick (Gowen 1988, 26–42;
Gowen and Tarbett 1988; 1989), a large sample of charred
emmer wheat grain was found along with hazelnuts and what
appear to have been dried crab apples (Monk 1988). Animals represented in the bone remains on this site included cattle, sheep,
pig and possibly red deer (McCormick 1988a) (Fig. 4:1).

In fact the first traces of agriculture that we have in the environmental record are for cereal production. As discussed in the

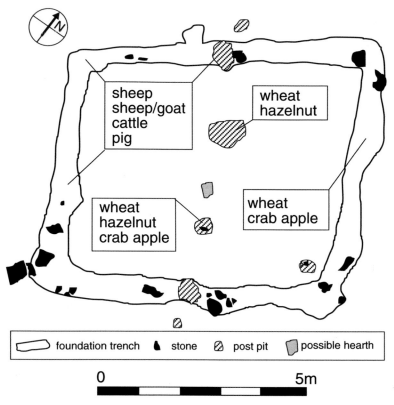

Fig. 4:1—Range and location of subsistence resources found in the smaller Neolithic house at Tankardstown South, Co. Limerick (based on information in Gowen 1988).

previous chapter, much of the argument about when the Neolithic actually began in Ireland centres on the question of the reliability of the recognition of the pollen grains of cereals. Whatever about discussion of the point at which cereals can first be recognised in the pollen record, what is important for the present discussion is the recognition of the widespread if restricted occurrence of cereals in recorded pollen analyses in different parts of Ireland (e.g. see Edwards 1985). The very restricted quantity is explained by the very low rate of dispersal of cereal pollen away from the actual growing site of the crop and this, combined with the large number of occurrences of cereal pollen, emphasises that the pollen record indicates the widespread growing of cereals as an aspect of subsistence. Ironically this suggestion is being made here at a time when the importance of cereal crops in the British Neolithic is being questioned (Moffett *et al.* 1989; Thomas 1991, 19–21). This latter view can be tied in with an emphasis on mobility in the Neolithic settlement pattern and the use of wild resources (Thomas 1991, 27–8), both of which could be seen as indicating continuity from pre-farming subsistence strategies. In Ireland by contrast we can argue that the evidence suggests a farming system which involved a sedentary lifestyle through which radical transformation of society and the landscape occurred during the course of the Neolithic.

It is, for example, becoming increasingly clear from the archaeological record that field systems were utilised during the Irish Neolithic. These may have been to keep animals in or out, to protect crops, to improve the soil and to define property (Fowler 1981, 28). They may have been built in some cases as a protection for the soil resource (Groenman-van Waateringe 1981, 287). It is likely, however, that layout of these fields was also an important social statement in what had previously been wildscape, and that in the case of large-scale systems with one main axis of orientation, so-called coaxial systems, we are seeing a reflection not only of the functional requirements of the fields but also of the scale and type of social organisation involved (e.g. Fleming 1987, 195–8). The surviving field systems, most notably in north-west Mayo (Caulfield 1983; 1988), are covered by blanket bog. Field boundaries dating to this period have been located in several areas such as Valentia Island, Co. Kerry (Mitchell 1989, 94–5), and Connemara in Co. Galway (Gibbons and Higgins 1988). There are also fragments of what may be field boundaries protected by monuments, as in the case of the wall at the unusual megalithic tomb at Millin Bay, Co. Down (Collins and Waterman 1955, 8), and the walls pre-dating the Bronze Age site complex at Beaghmore, Co. Tyrone (Pilcher 1969, 89). This raises the question of the extent of field systems elsewhere in the Irish landscape, particularly in areas that we know from other evidence, such as burial sites or scatters of Neolithic lithic material on the surface, to have been used during the Neolithic. One

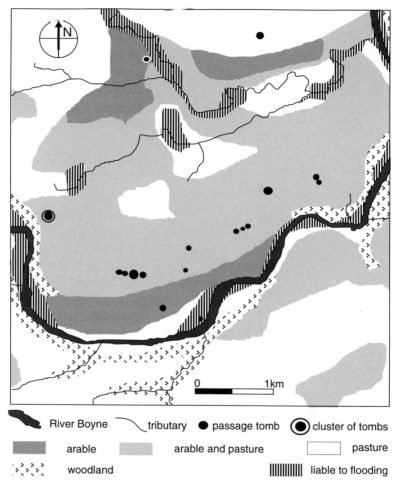

Fig. 4:2—Reconstruction of the likely pattern of potential Neolithic land use in the vicinity of the Boyne Valley passage tomb cemetery (after Cooney 1991).

obvious example is the Boyne Valley in Co. Meath, where continued agricultural utilisation has removed any surface traces of earlier prehistoric boundary organisation in an area that was a major focus of Neolithic activity. The environmental evidence from the excavations at Knowth (Eogan 1984) and Newgrange (O'Kelly 1982) can be used to suggest that the pattern of land use in the Boyne Valley was likely to have had some complexity, with pastoral and arable activity taking place close together (Fig. 4:2). It seems likely that there would have been fixed boundaries between areas or fields in different use (Cooney 1991, 132).

The very extensive Céide field system in north-west Mayo (Caulfield 1978; 1983; 1988) appears to have been designed for a largely pastoral economy, hence the large rectangular (grassland) fields. This system appears from its size and the regularity of the field walls, in both structure and orientation, to have been undertaken as a single large-scale programme of clearance and enclosure. Given what we now know of the nature of Neolithic agriculture, it can be argued that we should see the organisation of the landscape around settlements into fields as likely to have been the rule rather than the exception. It is to be expected that the Neolithic landscape would have evolved over a lengthy period with regional and local diversity and major forest clearance and land enclosure concentrated in the core areas of settlement. In some cases clearance and land organisation may have been small-scale and piecemeal. In a mixed farming strategy, or at least one with greater emphasis on cereal production than is evident at Céide, a greater variety in field size is probable, with the possibility of smaller cereal plots, involving greater investment of time and labour, being located closer to the farmsteads. At Lough Gur small fields or garden plots occur within the settlement on the Knockadoon peninsula (Grogan 1989; Grogan and Eogan 1987, 486; Ó Ríordáin 1954, 385–6, 435–8). It is possible to envisage that an increasingly ordered landscape developed in major settlement areas during the Neolithic. Initial clearings would have given way to larger areas enclosed within field fences and walls as the landscape came increasingly under human management, although in some areas forest regeneration was allowed to take place. Thus, as the farmland was organised, it is probable that tillage was located in the vicinity of the habitations, with grazing areas, whether open or enclosed, at a further remove. Within the farmland, hedgerows (Groenman-van Waateringe 1981, 288) as well as stone walls and earthen banks and ditches were developed. In the Boyne Valley the evidence suggests significant areas of trees, particularly hardwoods such as elm and oak, surviving as uncleared stands (Groenman-van Waateringe 1984). A range and variety of high-quality timber would have been available as a resource for house-building, the construction of outbuildings, workshops and fences, and a wide range of other potential uses (e.g. A. O'Sullivan 1990). Wooden trackways were being laid down in wetland to provide a link between dryland areas (B. Raftery 1990, 11). All of this evidence supports the view of the Neolithic landscape as a mosaic put forward by Mitchell (1976, 104–5), but it also indicates that the settlement and farming aspect of the landscape was on a more permanent basis than has previously been suggested.

Neolithic settlement
The study of 'settlement' in the Neolithic has all too often concentrated on a very narrow definition of this term and has involved the study of the habitation sites of the period rather than an assessment of the nature and distribution of human groups within the landscape, the interaction within and between these groups and the relationship between society and the environment. The small number of known domestic sites has been seen as a major restriction to the development of settlement studies. On the other hand, the recognition that the habitations, although of considerable importance, form only one component in the overall settlement pattern has enabled major advances to be made in the assessment of human dispersal in the landscape and the nature and extent of resource exploitation during the Neolithic. As discussed below, the development of more complex settlement models has also provided a more comprehensive framework for further advances, particularly in the area of prospecting for habitation sites through the recognition of major trends in the location of habitations and their spatial relationship with other settlement components.

    Two principal levels of information are therefore available for analysis. Firstly, there are the basic components of habitation, the houses and other structures with the associated domestic material lost or discarded during their occupation. These provide information on the layout and ordering of the settlement, which may have consisted of a single household or multiple household units,

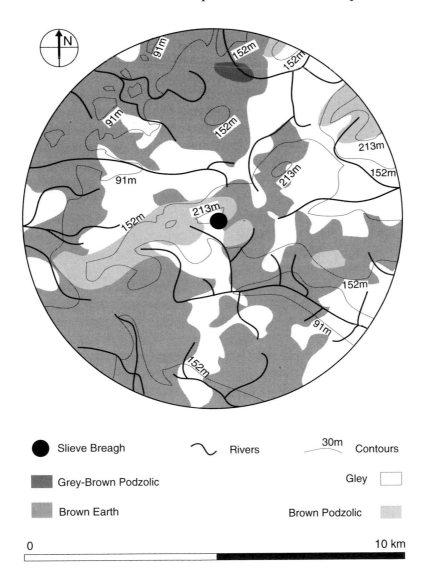

Fig. 4:3—Territory within 5km of the two Neolithic houses at Slieve Breagh, Co. Meath, showing topography and modern soils.

cient for between five and ten individuals. This evidence is, in itself, a strong indication that the family formed the basic social unit. The size range of the houses does show a wide variation but this need not be in direct relationship to the size of the occupying family; other factors, such as social status and function, may also have played a part. Houses of both circular or oval and rectangular form occur. Eogan (1991, 108) has suggested that at Knowth rectangular houses are earlier than circular ones, but at both Knowth and Lough Gur it can be argued on the grounds of their spatial complementarity and similarities in material culture that circular and rectangular houses were in use at the same time. From this it does not appear that there was any kind of chronological sequence or switch from rectangular to circular shape. The largest houses are invariably rectangular, with floor areas of between 35 and 55 square metres. There is only a slight overlap in size with the smaller circular or oval houses (see Fig. 4:6), which range in area from around 20 to 35 square metres. While it is tempting to suggest different social functions, the evidence from all of the excavated examples indicates that both types played a predominantly domestic role. There is certainly a considerable architectural and structural variety even between houses of the same basic shape, from the plank-built rectangular houses at Ballynagilly (ApSimon 1969a), Ballyglass (Ó Nualláin 1972) and Tankardstown (Grogan 1988a) to the heavily insulated post structures which are a feature, in both circular and rectangular form, of the Lough Gur settlement (Ó Ríordáin 1954; Grogan and Eogan 1987). Wood was the main building material and only occasionally, as in the damp-proof course at several Lough Gur houses, was stone utilised. Where the wood has been identified it appears that the main structural timbers were of oak. The lifespan of the houses may have been up to a human generation (*c.* 20–25 years) and it seems likely that houses may have been replaced or relocated close to existing structures, given the careful locational preferences favoured by people for their settlement sites.

A basic range of features, including a fireplace and storage or refuse pits, occur within the houses. Other furnishings, such as sleeping platforms and storage cupboards, have been discovered

in stone in the Orkney Islands (Clarke and Sharples 1985), and it
can be extrapolated that versions of these structures in more per-
ishable materials were used in other parts of Britain and in
Ireland. Other storage and waste disposal facilities are represented
by exterior pits and post-holes in the vicinity of several houses.
Smaller ancillary buildings, representing stores, barns or workshops, have been noted at some sites such as Knowth (Eogan
1984, 233) and Lough Gur (Grogan and Eogan 1987, 468–71).
The tripartite internal division of the Ballyglass house and one of
the Tankardstown (Gowen and Tarbett 1988) houses suggests the
incorporation of some of these functions within the structure of
the house itself. The incomplete remains at Ballynagilly may also
represent the central compartment of such a house. A broad
comparison has been made between the Ballyglass house and
those on Linearbandkeramik sites in central and western Europe,
where it has been suggested that the central living compartment
is flanked by a byre and a second-storey granary over an entrance
lobby (Grogan 1980; but see Whittle 1985, 81–2, 219). Detailed
study has yet to demonstrate the validity of this hypothesis but
the subdivision of the tripartite houses implies a functional division. It is clear that organisation of activity was not confined to
the interior of the house but that the definition of domestic space
extended to a larger area. This can be seen for example in the
spatial relationship between structures on site, and even in something as apparently prosaic to the modern eye as the placement of
rubbish pits. On sites where more than one house appears to
have been occupied contemporaneously the houses are in a dispersed, rather than nucleated, pattern within the settlement area.

Enclosed settlements

The majority of houses were not enclosed, although given the
restricted nature of several excavations this can only be accepted
as a general statement. Exceptions have been noted at Lough
Gur, where several enclosed habitations date to the Late
Neolithic (Grogan and Eogan 1987, 468–71). At Knowth the
large rectangular house was cut by one of two concentric palisades (Eogan 1984, 223). The extensive hilltop settlement at
Donegore, Co. Antrim (Mallory and Hartwell 1984), and part of

the summit at Lyles Hill (Gibson and Simpson 1987; 1989) a few miles to the south were enclosed within double, but not necessarily contemporary, palisades. Both sites are in a similar location overlooking the Six Mile Water river. In the case of Donegore the palisades accompanied interrupted or causewayed ditches and banks, forming a causewayed enclosure of the type well known in southern Britain (Mercer 1990) and on the Continent but previously unknown in Ireland. The Lough Gur enclosures — low earthen banks retained by orthostatic walls — may have had a purely social function and we should bear in mind that the presence of any kind of enclosure may have been most significant in creating and defining a perceptual barrier. But the Knockadoon peninsula itself could have served a defensive role, and similarly the palisades at Knowth and the two Antrim sites may have been genuinely defensive. Certainly in Britain there is evidence for defensive ramparts as well as for offence. For example, at Carn Brea in Cornwall (Mercer 1981, 66–9) there are large numbers of arrowheads, both outside and within the defended settlement. This should warn us against an image of a pacifist Neolithic society. That arrows were used as weapons in Ireland is shown by the tip of a flint or chert arrowhead found embedded in the hip bone of an adult male in the Poulnabrone portal tomb, Co. Clare (Lynch 1988, 106).

Diversity in settlement: the use of short-term, specialised sites

While the sites dealt with above can all be considered as permanent habitations, there are a number of sites that have produced structures and/or domestic debris in a context which suggests short-term activity. Hut sites on Knocknarea at Carrowmore, Co. Sligo, were defined by rather than contained within low earthen banks into which the tips of stakes supporting a lightweight structure were driven (Bengtsson and Bergh 1984). The presence of large numbers of finished artifacts, especially hollow scrapers, suggests that there was a particular activity associated with the structures. A multi-component settlement pattern where some activities of the community occur at a remove from the main habitation sites is a pattern well known amongst hunter-gatherers, but it was clearly also employed by early farmers. This approach has been applied to the study of Neolithic settlement, for example in Denmark (Jensen 1982, 90–7; Madsen 1982) As yet a typology of site functions is not applicable to the Irish evidence, but it is clear that many sites with a habitation element do not represent permanent domestic occupation and may be associated with a broad range of activities (Woodman 1983, 32). It is possible that in some cases rather than being subsidiary to permanent settlements these sites represent the use of a more flexible settlement pattern which had some degree of mobility. Within the Boyne Valley at sites about 2km apart but in a similar location, at Townleyhall 1 and 2 (see Fig. 4:5) in Co. Louth, there were stake-built structures, possibly heavy tents. At Townleyhall 2 several such structures had been erected, and the evidence of overlapping fireplaces shows that these represent several, perhaps intermittent, periods of occupation (Eogan 1963, 63); a similar episodic use is represented within a small banked enclosure at Townleyhall 1 (Liversage 1960).

The extraction of flint was the main function of the site at Ballygalley Hill, Co. Antrim (Collins 1978). In a similar category can be placed the quarrying activity at Tievebulliagh, Co. Antrim, for the extraction of porcellanite as a raw material for axes and other objects (Mallory 1990). At Goodland, Co. Antrim (Case 1973), the extraction of flint nodules and the primary reduction of these to a portable raw material for tool production elsewhere was accompanied by ritual activity which appears to have been concentrated inside a ditched area and was concerned with the deliberate and repeated placement of portions of the extracted nodules in pits within a matrix of habitation debris including deliberately broken pots. The debris was probably derived from occupation associated with the industrial use of the site rather than material transported from permanent settlements. Goodland is a reminder that the everyday and the sacred would have been interwoven aspects of life. At Scotch Street, Armagh, there is a small circular ditched enclosure (Lynn 1988) with hundreds of small sherds of pottery and other material in the ditch fill. This is open to interpretation as the result of either mundane domestic activity or separate episodes of deliberate deposition.

The nature of the site and spreads of pottery suggests that the latter explanation is more likely.

From the available and admittedly not very plentiful radiocarbon dates, sites used for a specific reason would appear to be predominantly a feature of the Middle and Later Neolithic periods. This suggests that an increased complexity in the settlement pattern was developing during the Neolithic. Part of this development may have been linked to a more extensive use of the landscape, including organised extraction of raw materials servicing large-scale production of stone tools at sites like Tievebulliagh and Brockley on Rathlin Island (Jope 1952; Sheridan 1986, 25–7; Mallory 1990). Other activities that were place-specific may have included herding or hunting camps and the procurement of building materials for major monument construction, such as the quarrying of greywacke for the Boyne Valley passage tombs (Eogan 1986, 111–14). In the human perception of place these activities may have complemented the organisation of agricultural activity as many of them would have taken place outside the ambit of the farmed, humanly structured landscape. In terms of time as well it seems likely that they would have been used at certain times to avail of good weather, seasonal resources, slack times in the agricultural cycle, or whenever may have been deemed the right time.

The development of burial practice in the Irish Neolithic

As we have seen, the settlement evidence suggests that early farming people were tied to the land in a series of territorial networks, the most basic of which was their own home. Very much part of these networks were also the places in which people were buried. Burial and its associated ritual offers not only the chance to pay respect to the deceased but in doing so to re-affirm and/or reposition social bonds within the community and the present community's links with the ancestors and the landscape. In recent years the role that formal burial places may have in expressing a critical link between society and the land has been widely explored (e.g. Renfrew 1976; 1981; Chapman *et al.* 1981; Hodder 1984). This encompasses issues such as the relationship of the formal burial place to critical resources (Chapman and

Randsborg 1981), the social implications of the use of a fixed, permanent burial spot (e.g. Morris 1987), the use of space inside and outside tombs (e.g. Thomas 1988b; 1990), and the relationship between settlement pattern and burial location pattern (e.g. Cooney 1983). Concerning the burials themselves we are increasingly realising that formal burial was often a multi-stage process in which different stages may also have involved a change in location. This may have afforded the living the opportunity to manipulate the dead and transform their meaning for their own ends, such as creating the impression of communal equality by a communal form of burial (Shanks and Tilley 1982, 151). The physical burial evidence gives us the opportunity to look at the people themselves in terms of gender, age at death and some of the diseases they suffered. Bearing in mind the difficulty of deliberate transformation, this information — allied to the presence or absence of grave-goods, the provision of which would of course have been a decision of the living — may enable us to discuss whether there is evidence for achieved social ranking, which is based on an individual's achievements in life, or ascribed social ranking, whereby rank or status is passed from one generation to the next (e.g. Clark and Neeley 1987).

Classically we think of formal burial in the Irish Neolithic in terms of interment in megalithic tombs. Three of the four well-established tomb types — court, portal and passage tombs — as well as the recently recognised megalithic tombs of simple form (Shee-Twohig 1990, 9) belong clearly within the Neolithic, with the fourth type, the wedge tomb, probably dating initially to the Later Neolithic but extending well into the Bronze Age (see discussion in Harbison 1988, 100–2; O'Kelly 1989, 115–22). It has been argued that each of these types has a package of morphological, locational and depositional features which make them distinct (e.g. Evans 1966, fig. 1; de Valera 1979, 100–29; O'Kelly 1981; Ó Nualláin 1989, 101–44). There has been a tendency to treat the development of the tombs in chronological terms (e.g. ApSimon 1985/6) and much discussion has taken place on issues such as the extent of external influence or internal development, whether passage tombs or court tombs represent the first tomb type to be used in the country, the relationship between the court and portal tomb (both of which can be classified as long barrow-type monuments), and the context in which wedge tombs began to be built.

It might be argued, however, that even given the coarse time framework we have and are likely to continue to have for much of the Irish Neolithic, what is much more important is that the use of different tomb types clearly overlapped. Even if a tomb went out of burial use its presence in the landscape would have given it a continued significance and left it open to new interpretations and new meanings (Cooney 1990, 751; Hodder 1989, 70); a clear example would be the art in passage tombs (see Shee-Twohig 1981; R. O'Sullivan 1989). As R. Bradley (1985a, 9) has put it, monuments intended to be permanent dominate the landscape of later generations. It is evident also that only a small proportion of the population ended up after death in a megalithic tomb and that there were other formal modes of burial in the Irish Neolithic, centring around the concept of individual burial. This includes the building of monuments to celebrate one or a very limited number of individuals in Linkardstown tombs, burials on settlement sites and in caves (B. Raftery 1974; Ryan 1981; Herity 1982; Molleson 1985/6; Grogan and Eogan 1987, 471–2; Brindley and Lanting 1989/90; Ó Floinn 1992). This rich array of evidence offers the opportunity to look at the significance of burial and related activity for Neolithic people and the social groups to which they belonged, and to assess the degree to which burial practice and rite are useful in recognising differences in social organisation at different times or in different regions during the Neolithic.

A fundamental assumption central to Irish megalithic tomb studies has been that passage tombs are distinct and different from the other three well-known types of tomb, which are seen to share a similar scale, dispersed distribution and perhaps social patterning (e.g. Cooney 1979; ApSimon 1985/6, 11; Woodman 1992, 304). By contrast, passage tombs are seen as being distinguished by their grouped distribution in cemeteries (Fig. 4:7), their variety of scale and complexity from small, morphologically simple tombs to mega-sites (Fig. 4:8) like those at Dowth, Knowth and Newgrange in the Boyne Valley. Further distinc-

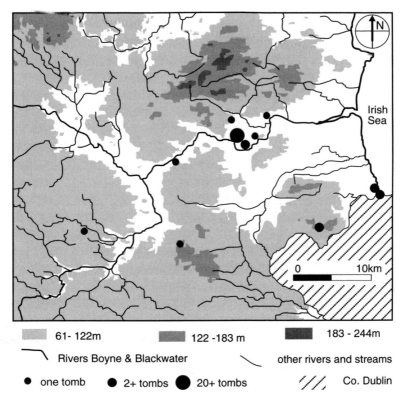

Fig. 4:7—Distribution of passage tombs in the Bend of the Boyne and the wider Boyne Valley area.

tions include a particular set of items deposited with burials, on which motifs are sometimes placed which are also part of the range of designs occurring on the structural stones of some passage tombs. Based on these features, it has been proposed that the passage tombs represent a ranked society in contrast to the more localised, simpler and relatively autonomous social groups represented in and by the other types of tomb.

The emergence of the overtly hierarchical nature of the groups in control of the construction and use of passage tombs has been explained in a number of different ways. Herity (1974, 192–203) suggested that its origins lie in Breton passage tombs and that around 3200 BC Breton settlers established themselves

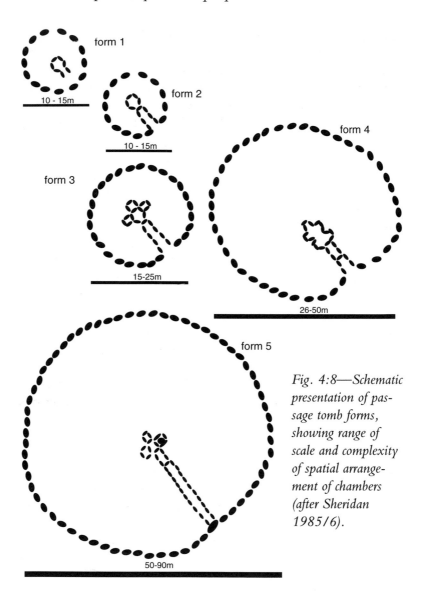

form 1

10 - 15m

form 2

10 - 15m

form 3

15-25m

form 4

26-50m

form 5

Fig. 4:8—Schematic
presentation of pas-
sage tomb forms,
showing range of
scale and complexity
of spatial arrange-
ment of chambers
(after Sheridan
1985/6).

50-90m

in the Boyne Valley, building the large tombs there and spreading westwards to other areas. Darvill (1979, 325–7) saw its background rather in the social groups who were using court tombs. Accepting an earlier date for court tombs and contrasting their distribution with that of the passage tombs, he proposed a social development that took place within Ireland, from a segmentary to a chiefdom-type society. Burenhult (1984, 142–6), on the results of a programme of research and excavation at the Carrowmore passage tomb cemetery, set the beginnings of the passage tomb tradition within a much earlier time context, argued for an indigenous Mesolithic origin and, following O'Kelly (1981, 182), suggested that there was an evolution from simple to more complex forms, reaching a high point in the three large sites in the Boyne Valley. Sheridan (1985/6) has set forward a series of stages in this sequence and suggested that the aggrandisement of passage tombs was integral to the use of the tombs by the living to increase the scale of their power and prestige by increasing the scale of the places where the ancestors resided. It has been pointed out by Sheridan (1985/6, 28–9) and by Bradley and Chapman (1984) that links evident in the large tombs (and the activities associated with them) with the Orkneys, southern Britain, Brittany and Iberia can be better accommodated within a model of 'converging evolution'. What this suggests is that part of the prestige of the social élites in these different areas would have been built around access to and knowledge of exotic items and ideas. Thus contact is likely to have taken place particularly after the development of social élites in each area. Taking this perspective, it is interesting that M. O'Sullivan (1986, 80–1) has commented that the closest links between Breton art and that in the Boyne Valley occur with his plastic style of ornament which post-dates the construction of both Knowth and Newgrange, and that Eogan (1990, 135) places links in Irish passage tombs with Iberia in the context of an established tradition of the construction and use of megalithic tombs there.

We can see, then, that there have been major changes in views on the development of passage tombs in Ireland since the early 1970s. But the fundamental distinction between the passage tombs and other types of tombs has been maintained. It can be argued on a number of grounds, however, that the situation was more complex. Firstly, if we accept that the use of the different tomb types overlapped, and their distributions certainly overlap, it appears that the tomb types should be considered in relation to each other. Rather than viewing each tomb type as representing

a different cultural grouping or as reflecting changing burial practice over time, it may be more appropriate to suggest that when a
tomb was being constructed there may have been a number of
options, so that the design of the tomb is seen as a deliberate
choice. For example, it can be argued that the people who built
court tombs and those who built passage tombs had a cultural
affinity because the same basic range of material occurs on the
settlement sites that can be associated with the two different types
of tomb. In this context the particular architectural configuration
chosen to contain and celebrate the dead can be seen as part of
the mortuary ritual and not simply as a cultural inevitability. The
location of the tombs as well suggests that we need to consider
the different types in relation to each other.

While the passage tombs clearly differ from the other tomb
types in scale and degree of ritual behaviour expressed in the
tomb and its contents, we should see this as only one of a number of developments that occurred during the second half of the
fourth millennium BC. These developments have a regional
basis, suggesting that we are seeing the emergence of distinctive
regional patterns in mortuary practice alongside the continued
use of different tomb types. For example, elaboration may also
have been occurring in the court tombs with the use of transeptal
and other more architecturally complex forms (Fig. 4:9) which
allowed more formal definition of burial chambers, greater
potential for movement, control of space and manipulation of the
deposits within the tomb (Thomas 1990, 173), and the possibility
of only a small élite having access to the tomb, with most people
confined to the outside. Considering the distribution of transeptal
and other complex court tombs such as central court tombs (Fig.
4:10), it is reasonable to suggest that this could be seen as a
regional development in the north-west of Ireland in the area
with the highest density of court tombs (de Valera 1960). The
possibility of recognising other regional patterns is seen in the
concentration of dual court tombs across the south Ulster area.

In other areas there appears to have been a move towards a
more conscious celebration of individuals in death with the construction and use of Linkardstown tombs in south Leinster and
northern Munster. Here the emphasis is very much on single

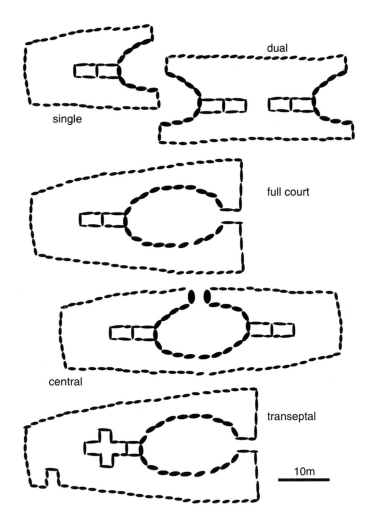

dual

single

full court

central

transeptal

10m

Fig. 4:9—Schematic presentation of court tomb forms, showing variety of arrangement of court, chambers and covering cairn (see de Valera 1960).

inhumed adult males with an accompanying decorated pot, which is the dominant characteristic of the burial record from these sites although the focal burials are sometimes accompanied by others (Herity 1982, 251; Manning 1985, 67–8; Wallace 1977, 5–7). The occurrence of similar forms of pottery in some

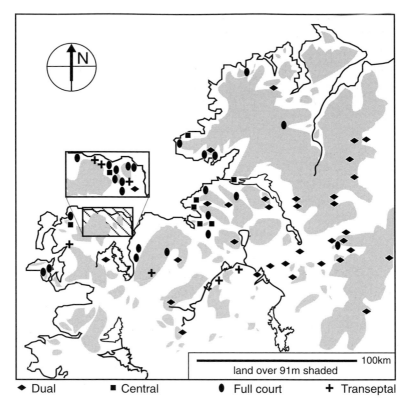

Key:
◆ Dual   ■ Central   ● Full court   + Transeptal

Fig. 4:10 —Distribution of elaborate court tomb forms in the north-west of Ireland (based on information in Ó Nualláin 1989).

court tombs and portal tombs (Herity 1982, 267–80) is a reminder of the contemporaneity of use of different forms of bur- ial monument and rite, and indicates that a material item treated in one community as a personal possession and deliberately placed with an individual, in a purpose-built Linkardstown tomb, might in other communities end up in a burial deposit containing other objects and the remains of several individuals, for example in the court tomb at Annaghmare, Co. Armagh (Waterman 1965, 39–41).

Rather than viewing tomb types individually, then, we should consider them in relation to each other. There was not a simple chronological succession of different tomb types, nor do the tombs indicate different cultural identities. The situation was one where the boundaries between the different tomb types were probably not as clearly defined as we often assume, where developments varied from region to region, and where they reflected differences in the role of the dead in the pattern of regionalised social and economic changes. Of course, underlying the use of monuments for the dead in the Irish Neolithic is the fact that each site is different, not only in the sense of being hand-built but also that they were to be the places of burial and related activity for particular human groups. The history of use of excavated sites shows considerable variation, and in this and other respects we can suggest that there were differences not only between tomb types but also within tombs belonging to the same type.

If we look at the pattern of site location, for example, the concept of placing tombs in close proximity to others is best developed in passage tombs, as in the Boyne Valley and the three other major cemeteries at Loughcrew, Carrowkeel and Carrowmore, but it is not unknown in other megalithic tombs (Cooney 1990) and single passage tombs are also known. The hill/mountaintop location which has been stressed as a characteristic of passage tombs is in its extreme form only a feature, albeit a significant one, of a small minority of them (Cooney 1983, 183–5) and is countered by the occurrence of impressive sites like Heapstown Cairn, Co. Sligo, in low-lying locations. Looking at the general altitudinal location of tombs, the majority occur below 152m (Fig. 4:11). This characteristic is worth a comment in itself as the supposed dominance of upland location of passage and court tombs in distinction to the lowland location of portal tombs and Linkardstown tombs has been a feature of previous discussion and interpretation (e.g. Herity 1982, 289–93). The relationship of tombs to settlement areas may have varied, but interesting contrasts in the relationship seem to occur within as well as between tomb types. Thus we can not only contrast the location of most passage tombs in areas of potentially good agricultural land with a minority occurring on mountaintops but also look at variations in the siting of court tombs. In some areas, as in northwest Mayo (Caulfield 1983), court tombs appear to have been

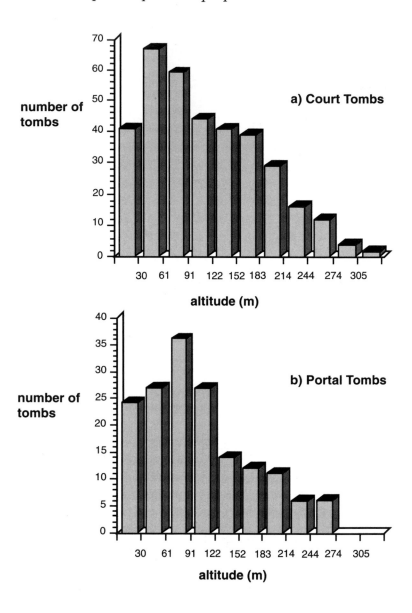

Fig. 4:11—Altitude range of (a) court tombs, (b) portal tombs, (c) passage tombs and (d) Linkardstown tombs and related burials (after Ó Nualláin 1983 (a and b); Cooney 1983 (c)).

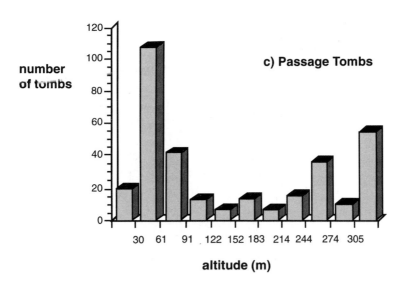

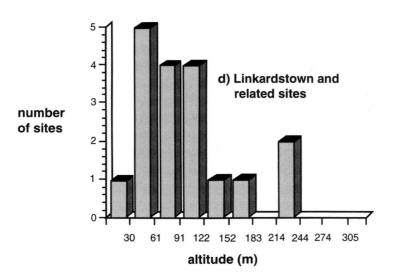

placed in the middle of an organised landscape, while in other
cases they are sited apparently on the margins of settled land or
on the boundary between two different kinds of land, as is the
case in the Carlingford group in Counties Down and Louth
(Evans 1978, 89–96; Cooney 1991, 136).

Another element of the siting of tombs is the issue of whether
different tomb types have distinct patterns of location. Looking at
particular regions, for example north Leinster for portal, passage
and court tombs and south Leinster/north Munster for
Linkardstown tombs (Fig. 4:12), we can recognise differences
between the typical location patterns of the different tomb types.
But the topographical transects used here to illustrate the placing
of tombs in the landscape indicate that these differences are not
absolute: there are overlaps between the different tomb types. As
would be expected there are also regional differences, influenced
by such factors as the nature of the terrain. These variations in
siting reflect variation in the history of tomb use both within as
well as between the different types. What is interesting throughout the megalithic tradition is that the approach and access to the
tombs was clearly influenced by location. There appear to have
been recognised types of locale considered suitable for the placement, construction and use of a tomb. Thus for example there
was the practice of placing a portal tomb on a terrace on a valley
side or hill slope with the entrance facing up the slope (Ó
Nualláin 1983, 86). This would have defined how people
approached and viewed the tomb in the landscape. It is clear that
at least in some instances the construction of a tomb came after
the location had already been identified as a focus of human
activity. Some tombs appear to have been deliberately placed
over a settlement, as at Ballyglass (Ó Nualláin 1972), and some
over deposits that may have been deliberately placed on the site,
e.g. Ballybriest, Co. Derry (Evans 1939), before the structure was
erected. In some cases this pre-tomb activity may have created a
ready-made site suitable for the construction of a monument
(O'Kelly, Lynch *et al.* 1978, 335), but the term 'ready-made'
should not be seen simply as meaning the physical requirement of
an open space: it can be taken to mean that the site was perceived
as a proper one for the location of a tomb. How that decision

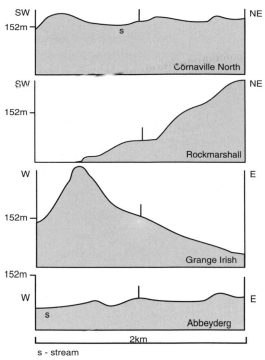

Fig. 4:12a—Topographical transects illustrating the location of court tombs in north Leinster: Cornaville North, Co. Meath; Rockmarshall and Grange Irish, Co. Louth; and Abbeyderg, Co. Longford.

s - stream

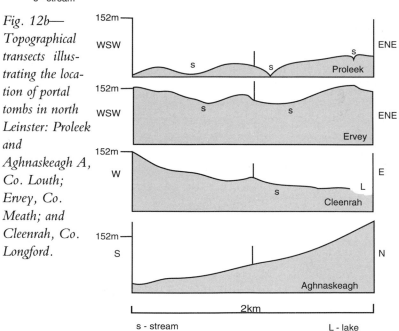

Fig. 12b—Topographical transects illustrating the location of portal tombs in north Leinster: Proleek and Aghnaskeagh A, Co. Louth; Ervey, Co. Meath; and Cleenrah, Co. Longford.

s - stream   L - lake

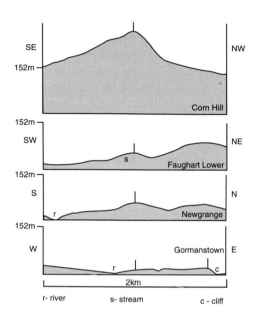

Fig. 4:12c—
Topographical transects
illustrating the location of
passage tombs in north
Leinster: Corn Hill, Co.
Longford; Faughart
Lower, Co. Louth;
Newgrange and
Gormanstown, Co.
Meath.

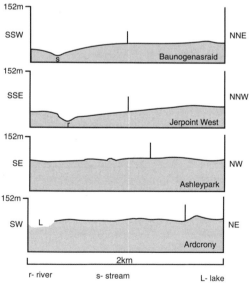

Fig. 4:12d—
Topographical transects
illustrating the location of
Linkardstown tombs:
Baunogenasraid, Co.
Carlow; Jerpoint West,
Co. Kilkenny;
Ashleypark and
Ardcrony, Co.
Tipperary.

was reached we cannot obviously reconstruct in any detail, but it is significant that the first formal activity connected with tomb construction was in some cases what appears to be a foundation deposit, literally making the site sacred. For instance, at the Fourknocks I passage tomb under the floor of the passage was a deliberately placed deposit of the inhumed remains of a small child set in a pocket of cremated bone of an adult (Hartnett 1957, 205).

This brings us to what could be regarded as the central aspect of the tombs, the deposition and elaborate treatment of human remains. The placement of mortuary deposits in the tombs appears in some cases to have been a single operation, as in the court tomb at Tully, Co. Fermanagh (Waterman 1978), and the tomb was subsequently blocked up. This would certainly appear to have been the practice in Linkardstown tombs and probably in some of the portal tombs. In other instances it seems that the tomb was kept open, as at the passage tomb Knowth 16 (Eogan 1984, 109–32, 308–12) and the court tomb at Ballyalton, Co. Down (Davies and Evans 1934), perhaps over several hundred years. The mortuary deposit is in some cases only the partial remains of one individual; in other cases it is a collective deposit of the remains of several individuals, and there may be a number of these in a tomb. In some cases the human bones are placed as a 'pure' deposit, while in other tombs they are mixed with artifactual material and charcoal.

There is evidence for the use of both cremation and inhumation, although the former is apparently more common in passage and court tombs (Eogan 1986, 135–9; Herity 1987a, 111–21). The problem of the poor preservation of inhumed bone in acid soils has of course to be faced up to, and the contrasting good preservation on calcium-rich soils, as at Poulnabrone portal tomb on the Burren in Co. Clare (Lynch 1988), is a reminder that a significant part of the burial record has disappeared from some of the excavated sites. Nevertheless it is clear that rather than seeking to identify cremation or inhumation as entirely separate burial rites we should recognise that they were in use contemporaneously. Individual unburnt bones, particularly skulls and long bones, were sometimes placed with a cremated burial deposit. As

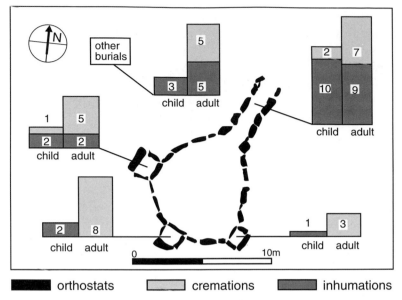

Fig. 4:13—Location and interpretation of burial evidence by age and rite at Fourknocks I, Co. Meath, passage tomb (after Cooney 1992).

well as being used to distinguish different body parts, the burial rite varied with the age of the deceased. It appears that cremation in some communities may have been largely restricted to adults, with the children and adolescents being inhumed. Burial deposits also varied within tombs, with children sometimes placed in different locations to adults (Cooney 1992). At Fourknocks I passage tomb (Hartnett 1957), for example, the burial deposits show a preponderance of cremated adults in the burial chambers, with inhumed remains of children being an important element in the deposition of bone in the passage of the tomb (Fig. 4:13). In the passage also there was the deliberate placement of unburnt adult human skulls.

The evidence underlying all these variations comes from what is a very restricted number of burials and from excavations stretching back to the 1930s, so there is variation in the degree of detail of recording from different sites. Looking at the burial figures from the court, portal and passage tombs and formal individ-

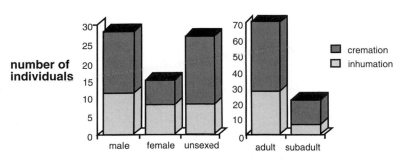

number of individuals

a) Court Tombs

Fig. 4:14—Burial evidence shown by rite and gender (for adults) and general age groups in deposits in Irish megalithic tombs (court, portal and passage tombs) and from Linkardstown tombs and related sites.

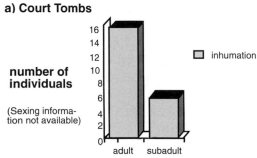

number of individuals

(Sexing information not available)

b) Portal Tombs

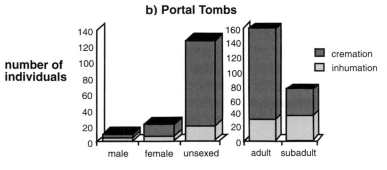

number of individuals

c) Passage Tombs

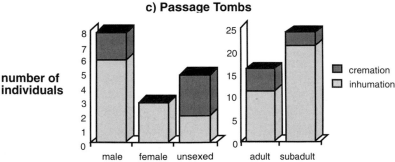

number of individuals

d) Neolithic Individual Burials

ual burials (Fig. 4:14), we have treated the data in three ways: the total number of people represented, the proportions of adults and children, and within the adult burial population the number of males and females present. In total from published sources there are about 400 individuals known from excavated sites. Overall the record is dominated by adult burials (68%), with child/adolescent burials accounting for only 32% of the total. This is not the proportion one would expect if the deceased population in the tombs was representative of the entire living population where there would have been a high infant mortality rate (Weiss 1973; Hassan 1981). The individual burials include both the Linkardstown tombs, dominated by adult male inhumations, and individual burials at sites like Lough Gur, where child inhumations were prominent (Grogan and Eogan 1987, 471–2). The only clear gender pattern to emerge is the dominance of adult males in individual burials; in the megalithic tombs the large proportion of adults whose sex could not be determined from the bone remains makes interpretation very difficult. Deposits in passage tombs account for over 50% of the burials. The degree of restriction of access to formal burial reflected in these figures can be indicated, admittedly at a very generalised level, by estimates of the possible level of population by Burgess (1980, 170), who suggested a figure of about 150,000–200,000 for Ireland at about 3000 BC.

Trying to make an overall interpretation of this material is very difficult given the evidence for both chronological and spatial variations and the different histories of use of sites. The presence of collective burial deposits suggesting prior treatment before placement in the tomb, the deliberate disturbance of deposits to accommodate new burials, the possibility of the circulation of bones of ancestors by the living (Barrett 1988, 31), and accidental disturbance by burrowing animals bring additional problems. Our perspective suggests that there are a number of major trends in the material indicating the importance of formal burial for our understanding of Neolithic societies in Ireland. At one extreme we have individual burial. This may involve the deposition of a complete individual with grave-goods, as in the Linkardstown tombs, or it may be represented by a token deposit of inhumed or cremated bone, as in some of the court tombs. There is evidence too that an individual burial was sometimes deliberately placed as the first deposit in a tomb, in a special context, as at the Mound of the Hostages at Tara, where a pile of cremated bone representing one individual was placed with 15 beads and a mushroom-headed bone pin in a Carrowkeel pot outside the passage wall (Eogan 1986, 140). Far more common is evidence for multiple burial, either disarticulated inhumed remains or cremation deposits containing the remains of a number of people. The latter can be placed in the tomb either as cremated bone on its own or as part of what may have been the pyre material. Interestingly these collective deposits, which might be looked upon as a transformation of individuals into both a communal entity and the ancestors, are sometimes accompanied by what appear to be personal possessions, particularly leaf-shaped arrowheads, hollow scrapers, round scrapers and plano-convex knives in court tombs, and a set of what could be called special items in passage tombs — stone balls, bone and antler pins and pendants. The complex role that artifacts played in the ceremonies surrounding mortuary practices is indicated by the nature of the latter objects, by the varying pattern of use of Carrowkeel pottery in passage tombs (Eogan 1986, 140), and by the placement of pots from a range of ceramic styles with the court tomb deposits (Herity 1982, 361–4; 1987a, 148–55). There is a relative exclusion of children from formal burial, perhaps tying in with a concept of communal burial as children would not be seen as full members of that community. The occurrence of child burials with grave-goods at Lough Gur (Grogan and Eogan 1987, 471) indicates, however, that particular children may have been seen by the living as having some kind of status, perhaps suggesting a pattern of ascribed ranking.

The social context of material culture and place

We have seen above that structures and artifacts played an active role in mortuary practice. While it may be more difficult to interpret, it is clear that the same can be said about material culture in an everyday context. If we take the example of the most commonly recognised Neolithic artifact — the stone axe (Grogan and Cooney 1990) — the purely functional aspect of most examples is not in question, but it is also clear that they were utilised in other roles. Axes were made from both locally available and more exotic materials and it seems likely that the latter would have been perceived as possessing an enhanced value. That the axe had a symbolic role is indicated by the presence of a small number of imported jadeite axes which were clearly not intended for functional use. If we look at the varying contexts in which the axes occur it appears that deliberate deposition was common (e.g. Cooney 1989, 148–9). This is likely to have been the case with wetland finds, deposits in megalithic tombs and hoards. Indeed, a wider pattern of deliberate placement of material appears to be a more significant feature of this period than has previously been recognised, since this aspect of the evidence has been seen predominantly in the context of domestic use and 'stray' finds have usually been treated as the result of accidental loss. The expression of a special role for material such as flint artifacts and pottery is illustrated by examples such as the Carrowkeel vessels deposited in the bogs at Bracklin, Co. Westmeath, and Lisalea, Co. Monaghan, the latter associated with two stone axes (Herity 1974, 158–9), and the occurrence of flint hoards (Flanagan 1966; Woodman 1967; Eogan 1984, 24–6). The occurrence of specific items of material culture across a wide range of contexts is of considerable importance to the archaeologist and may also express the significance that they had for Neolithic people.

In a related sense the domestic space that people inhabited was not just a passive background. As in the tombs, the space in and around settlements was a structured setting for activity. This can be seen at the detailed level of the form of the house, where the contemporary occurrence of both rectangular and circular forms suggests a varied expression of domestic space. In other studies this has been seen as linked to differing social patterning at the level of the family (e.g. Ehrenberg 1989, 160–1). In a long-term perspective it appears, however, that the rectangular form becomes redundant during the Early Bronze Age and the circular house becomes dominant throughout later Irish prehistory and into the Early Christian period (Lynn 1978). While the size of the houses indicates the family as the basic identifiable unit it is clear that social identity was based on a larger group. Small clusters or hamlets may represent social groups based on close cooperation and kinship, and the form of settlement may reflect this social cohesion. Enclosed sites such as Donegore or Knowth reflect a similar or greater level of cooperative and communal activity. In other cases cooperation and links between dispersed farmsteads may have been expressed in the construction and use of a megalithic tomb, or the organisation of the farmed landscape into field systems. It is important to realise that such projects would have been an essential expression of group cohesion and identity. The ceremonial behaviour surrounding their construction and subsequent use provided opportunities to maintain or to legitimate changes in the social structure.

In the later Neolithic it is clear that this kind of cooperative and communal activity took place at a larger scale in some areas, while in other cases the pattern is one of continuing local social identity. The classic examples of the former are the mega-megaliths which form the focal points of the four major passage tomb cemeteries and the large-scale coaxial field systems at Céide. This could be viewed as reflecting an evolution of social complexity over time (e.g. Darvill 1979; Sheridan 1985/6; Renfrew 1973), but it should be clear from the above discussion that the pattern of social development varied from area to area and cannot be seen as representing a simple unilineal sequence. One might expect that a strong attachment to long-existing local identity would have carried on, seen, for example, in the continuation of pottery production and use at a small-scale, localised level (Sheridan 1991, 322).

A unifying trend that is apparent across a range of burial contexts is a move over time towards the use and deposition of more overtly 'special ' objects. This would appear to indicate an increasing emphasis on the individual and personal possessions. These objects may have also acted as media for the display of power and prestige. It may well be that this concern with ranking among the living was at work even when communal cremation was reaching a peak in the Boyne Valley passage tomb cemetery. In the eastern tomb under the main mound at Knowth a decorated flint macehead of Maesmawr type (Eogan and Richardson 1982; Simpson 1988, 29) was deposited at the entrance to the right-hand recess and it was covered by a layer of shale and five successive cremated bone deposits. This is a symbol of power *par excellence*, probably originating in Scotland, and its deposition with collective burial deposits may indicate the contemporary dialectic between an ideology based on the veneration of the dead and the growing power of certain individuals or a restricted minority of the population group who may have been responsible for the organisation of the elaborate external and internal ceremonies connected with the use of the tombs and who had access to non-local prestige items. In the southern part of the country the development of emphasis on the individual in death is overtly expressed in the form and contents of the Linkardstown tombs. The complexity of behaviour behind mortuary and related practice is seen in the deposition of ornate pots, similar to those in Linkardstown tombs, in some court and portal tombs but here not associated with individual burial. We should remember, of course, that it is the living who are the active participants in funerary and ancestor ritual: it is their actions which structure and change ideas about how mortuary practice should be carried out (Barrett 1990, 182–3). It is clear that by the end of the Neolithic the dominant trend was for the recognition of the role of ranked individuals both in life and in death. While multiple burial continues, the focus in formal burials is increasingly on the individual. The ancestors have become part of a more remote, less relevant past. It is the achievements and social place of the living that are increasingly celebrated in death.

5   THE FINAL NEOLITHIC: CONTINUITY IN A CHANGING SOCIAL CONTEXT

Changing approaches to and perceptions of the period

The Final Neolithic (*c*. 2800–2300 BC) has been the subject of considerable discussion in Britain and on the Continent (Harrison 1980; Burgess and Shennan 1976; Burgess 1980, 62–78; R. Bradley 1984, chapters 3 and 4), but the Irish evidence, which has increased dramatically as a result of major excavations in the Boyne Valley in particular (Sweetman 1976; 1985; 1987; O'Kelly, Cleary *et al* 1983; Eogan 1984), has received relatively little attention. This is despite the important changes in approach to and perception of the period, especially with regard to the role of Beaker pottery and other prestigious material such as the earliest metal objects, in the socio-economic organisation of communities at a local, regional and inter-regional level. The background to these developments in Ireland is a broadening in the extent and density of settlement coupled with the emergence of new and complex ritual practices. It is clear that areas, such as the south-west, which may have been relatively less exploited in earlier periods became important foci, and in some regions it is possible to trace an expansion of settlement and associated developments in ritual.

This stage is characterised by changes in burial practice. The megalithic tradition, with the exception of a new type — the wedge tomb — gradually diminishes to become just one of several components in the ritual repertoire. Apart from notable exceptions, such as the major habitation core at Lough Gur, there are few archaeologically recognisable occupation sites, and the increasingly diverse material assemblage is therefore without many good contexts. Nevertheless, it is apparent that large-scale public monuments provided focal points for communal ritual, much as the megalithic tombs had done in the preceding period. Burial also appears to have been a component, albeit minor, of these monuments, but the funerary practice is generally removed from the monumental ambit and there is an increasing diversification in the burial form. One of the major questions to be asked of the available data, particularly the new evidence from critical areas like the Boyne Valley and Lough Gur, is the explanation of the clear shift in ritual and funerary practice and the introduction of exotic items, such as Beaker and associated ceramics as well as the earliest copper artifacts, into the material repertoire of the period. Do these changes reflect an influx of new peoples into the island, as has been the view generally proposed (e.g. Eogan 1991, 117), or were dramatic internal changes occurring in Irish Neolithic societies, stimulated by contact with foreign developments (Waddell 1978, 125–6)? The approach taken here is based on a re-evaluation of the evidence within the framework of models of development in prehistoric societies. We examine the evidence from the perspective of the changes discernible within Late Neolithic society which could have brought about the alterations identified in the archaeological record. In other words, were there internal dynamics within society which necessitated change, and to what extent could the stresses between individual and community identified in the previous chapter have been accommodated within the existing socio-economic structure? The survival of long-standing burial traditions well into this period and the continued success of important settlement foci suggest that the changes occurred at differing rates and that side by side with alterations there was continuity in material culture and other aspects of society.

Settlement

The overall evidence for the Final Neolithic shows two generalised but nevertheless important trends. The first is an increase in the number of areas with evidence for settlement and

site	axes	flint	pottery	beaker	beads
open					
A	1, 4 broken	80	100	1	
B	3, 8 broken	22	650	300	4
C	15, 60 broken	310	14500	?	39
D	5, 70 broken	270	4000		41
enclosed					
J	4, 57 broken	226	1032	114	9
K	13, 35 broken	346	2610	704	42
I	8, 5 broken	96	2587	311	51
10	10, 102 broken	773	2369	600	38

Fig. 5:1—Comparison of occurrence of Beaker pottery and other material on sites at Knockadoon, Lough Gur, Co. Limerick (after Grogan and Eogan 1987).

this is indicated, for example, by the distribution of wedge tombs in the west and south where there was comparatively less visible evidence for activity earlier in the Neolithic. At the same time some regions, such as the north-west, display a lessening of settlement indicators, perhaps suggesting a reduction in the level of population density. The second is a greater expansion of settlement, probably representing a growing population, within existing settlement zones. This is shown by infill within areas that had already been occupied for a long period.

At Lough Gur there appears to have been a continuity in both settlement distribution and population groups with evidence for an increasingly hierarchical social order (Grogan and Eogan 1987, 470–1). Social differentiation is indicated by the ongoing construction and occupation of the enclosed habitations, discussed in Chapter 4, within a largely open settlement arrangement. The expansion of the settlement pattern within the local landscape beyond the environs of Lough Gur itself suggests an increase in population (Grogan 1989). There is a continued use of Neolithic ceramics, both plain and decorated, and an overall indication of economic and technological stability. However, the presence of Beaker and associated pottery may indicate the acquisition of exotic material by an emerging social élite. This view is supported by the recurring correlation between the occurrence of large quantities of Beaker and the presence of personal ornaments and non-local material on the enclosed sites which had already emerged as distinctive in the preceding stages of the Neolithic. One can contrast in particular the overall spread of pottery across both the open and enclosed sites with the greater concentration of Beaker on the enclosed sites (Fig. 5:1).

In the Boyne Valley, another of the core areas in the preceding period, the focal points of Knowth and Newgrange continued as centres of activity, albeit of a largely non-funerary nature. The overall evidence indicates stability in both population and economy (Cooney 1991, 134–5; but see van Wijngaarden-Bakker 1986, 101, for a contrary view), but there was a marked change in the function of these sites towards a domestic and, at Newgrange at least, a changed ritual role. The apparently dramatic shift in ritual practice away from emphasis on communal burial is difficult to unravel but must have been related to specific changes within the social system. There was certainly a complexity of ideas and behaviour involved which also appear to have changed during the period. Underlying all the changes there was a continuity of place, suggesting that there was a desire to incorporate many of the existing monuments, perhaps as the basis of legitimation of the new social order. This is specifically indicated by the encirclement of tombs, such as Sites A and Z at Newgrange, within new large open-air enclosures (Stout 1991, 261; Sweetman 1985, fig. 2), and ultimately by the encircling of Newgrange itself by the Great Stone Circle, by the deliberate placement of settlement around the perimeter of the two great passage tomb mounds of Knowth and Newgrange, and by the Beaker burial in the passage of one of the satellite tombs at Knowth (Site 15) (Eogan 1984, 308–12). There is also an element of deliberate damage to earlier monuments. The most significant example of this conspicuous destruction may be the spreading of the quartz mound revetment in front of the main tomb at Newgrange. O'Kelly (1982, 73) saw this as the result of natural causes but it may have been brought about by deliberate human action aimed at closing off the tomb following intensive activity around the southern perimeter of the site. Simpson (1988, 35) has drawn attention to the relevance of events in the Orkney Islands to what was happening in the Boyne Valley at this time, including the deliberate slighting of megalithic tombs, suggesting that there was an interchange of ideas, material culture and practice between people in the two areas. This appears to have been at the level of those in control of ceremonial and ritual action and again reflects a continuity from a pattern established during the construction of passage tombs in the Boyne Valley. The range of behaviour that we see in the Boyne Valley during the Final Neolithic suggests that during this period the past was being actively reconstructed to produce new meanings for a changing present (e.g. Vestergaard 1987, 63).

At Knowth domestic activity occurred at three locations around the base of the main mound while a fourth area produced a mixed assemblage including some food vessel and coarse Middle Bronze Age pottery (Eogan 1984, 245–308), but no definite structures could be recognised there. The difficulties of interpreting the evidence at Newgrange are discussed in the excavation report (O'Kelly 1983, 53), but it is probable that there were a substantial number of houses there (Fig. 5:2). Our reconstruction of the outlines of these houses is based on the location and spacing of the fourteen rectangular hearths and three

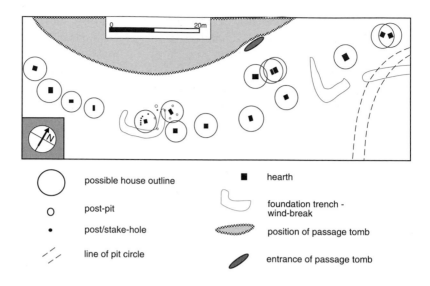

◯	possible house outline	◼	hearth
○	post-pit		foundation trench - wind-break
•	post/stake-hole		position of passage tomb
⁄⁄⁄	line of pit circle		entrance of passage tomb

*Fig. 5:2—House clusters within the Beaker settlement at Newgrange,
Co. Meath (based on information in O'Kelly 1983).*

fireplaces and other features set along the southern perimeter of
the main mound. On contemporary sites in Britain this type of
rectangular hearth was set centrally within a circular or oval
house (e.g. Britnell 1982; Clarke and Sharples 1985). Based on
this assumption four distinct clusters of houses can be identified
within the Beaker settlement at Newgrange, with two more
isolated houses further to the north; these latter two structures are
not shown in Figure 5:2. Each of the clusters had up to four,
probably circular or oval, houses 5–6m in diameter. One example
had an inner setting of posts, probably roof supports, immediately
around the hearth, while another house had an internal arc of
posts/stakes (O'Kelly 1983, fig. 10, pl. 7). The overlapping of
some hearths and the close proximity of others indicates the
replacement of houses and the possibility of more than one phase
of occupation on the site. Although O'Kelly (1983, 23–4)
suggested the presence of a rectangular house in the eastern part
of the area shown in Figure 5:2, the 'foundation trench' on
which this view was based may have formed a wind-break or

partial enclosure to the south and west of the house cluster defined by three hearths. It is possible that the house clusters represent family groups within the settlement.

Sweetman (1985, 208–9, 214–16) has demonstrated that this linear settlement arrangement is later than the activity centred on the pit circle to the east. There were two small areas of habitation within this pit circle; at the southern edge of the circle there seems to have been a house or hut with a diameter of *c.* 6m. This had been rebuilt or remodelled on at least one occasion (Sweetman 1985, 203, fig. 3). A hut also stood within the enclosure at Monknewtown, Co. Meath (Sweetman 1976, 36–8, fig. 7), but it is possible that the use of these structures was associated with the ritual use of the enclosures (Sweetman 1985, 214) rather than representing houses used on a daily basis. Just to the west of the area shown in Figure 5:2 there was a substantial wooden building which had been burnt (O'Kelly 1983, 35). Further to the north-west, on the ridge between Newgrange and the two smaller passage tombs to the west of it, Sweetman (1987) excavated part of a structure which also appears to have had a non-domestic function.

Ritual diversity

Two major contrasting developments, both of them with clear antecedents in the earlier Neolithic, are evident. In some areas there is a separation between public ritual and formal burial, with the latter dominated by individual interment. Large monuments, sometimes with a minor funerary aspect, became the focal point for communally orientated endeavour and ceremony. But this activity was directed by people who must have had status and authority: this was expressed in the construction of large open-air enclosures, their physical presence and location and the control of what went on within them (e.g. Clarke *et al.* 1985, 43–5). The enhanced social role of élite groups or individuals was also expressed through the provision of a person-centred, rather than communally orientated, burial context and this is emphasised by the frequent provision of a purpose-built grave. At the same time over much of the western and south-western part of Ireland megalithic tombs of a new variety — the wedge tomb —

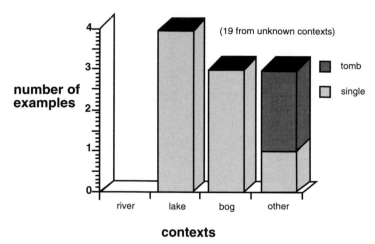

Fig. 5:3—Context of discovery of maceheads of the Early Series (after Simpson 1988; 1989a).

continued the dual funerary/public ritual function of the earlier megaliths, as well as demonstrating the regional strength of collective burial. There was not a complete separation of the two traditions; wedge tombs do occur in areas otherwise dominated by single burials and some of the new single-burial sites were used for successive deposits, which may also have been the case in some megalithic tombs. So the two traditions of mortuary practice were not mutually exclusive even if they do represent contrasting expressions of social organisation and ritual activity.

Another context for offerings, other than burials, is indicated by the pattern of deposition of status objects such as stone maceheads, some of which at least were imported from Britain (Simpson 1988; 1989a). Out of the eleven maceheads of Simpson's Early Series that can be seen as belonging to this period or slightly earlier and with known circumstances of discovery, the majority are from lakes and bogs, with one example from each of the two major passage tombs at Knowth and another from Lough Gur (Fig. 5:3). Early metal objects, even those that may appear to be tools, because of their rarity and innovative nature were probably also treated as status objects. The evidence from the early copper axes (the Lough Ravel and

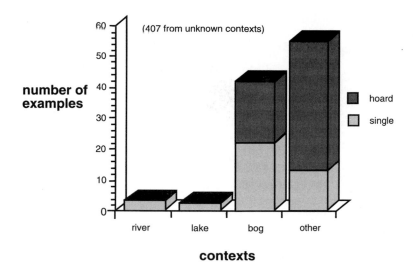

Fig. 5:4—Contexts of early copper axes (Lough Ravel, Ballybeg types and ingots) (based on information in Harbison 1969a with additions).

Balleybeg types) and ingots (Fig. 5:4), bearing in mind the very large number of uncontexted objects and the occurrence of a significant number on dry land, also shows a trend of deposition in wetland, particularly in what is present-day bog. Occurrence in hoards, on both wet and dryland sites, is also a feature of these early axes (Harbison 1968), and this may also suggest an increasing amount of formal, ceremonial activity being carried out in non-funerary contexts. Whatever about the actual areas from which the knowledge of copper-working was derived, probably from Atlantic Europe and/or the Middle Rhineland, it appears that the manufacture, circulation and deposition of flat axes and other early metal objects (e.g. copper tanged daggers, awls and possibly halberds) was a phenomenon contemporary with the emergence of other exotic items such as Beaker pottery (Sheridan 1983, 15). Rather than assuming that they represent the presence of new individuals or groups on the island it seems more likely that they are part of a package of material culture centring on Beaker pottery which spread along networks of contact established between social élites in different areas. It should not be surprising that some of this material ended up being deposited in very particular circumstances, an act which may have furthered the social place and standing of the individuals carrying out the deposition.

Megalithic tombs and individual burial

While monuments such as passage and court tombs were no longer being constructed, they continued to be used on occasion for burial and may have served as local focal points for funerary ritual. In some areas, such as the Boyne Valley, tombs remained significant features of landscape which were sometimes incorporated into new open-air enclosures. Similarly, activity during this period is attested at a few court tombs, such as Audleystown, Co. Down (Collins 1954, 25–7). Although the small number of excavated wedge tombs and the paucity of finds from most of them precludes any definitive assessment of their background, they show structural similarities with court, passage and Linkardstown tombs (de Valera 1960, 70; Waddell 1978, 124). These similarities and the presence of material of a Neolithic character indicate their affinities within the Irish megalithic tradition and are more convincing than postulated relationships with external forms (such as the Breton *allées couvertes*; de Valera and Ó Nualláin 1961, 115; ApSimon 1985/6, 11).

These affinities include the occasional use of circular cairns as at Baurnadomeeny, Co. Tipperary (O'Kelly 1960), and oval examples as at Carrickavantry, Co. Waterford (Ó Nualláin and Walsh 1986, 26), and the presence of stone settings within the cairn, for example at Island, Co. Cork (O'Kelly 1958), and Ballyedmonduff, Co. Dublin (Ó Ríordáin and de Valera 1952). The small passage tombs at Carrickalong and Harristown in Co. Waterford had markedly undifferentiated passages and settings, in the form of buttressing along the sides of the chamber, in the manner of wedge tombs. Indeed, the primary burials within both of these tombs were of Final Neolithic/Early Bronze Age rather than Neolithic character (Powell 1941; J. Hawkes 1941). Wedge tombs were located in a range of different locations in the

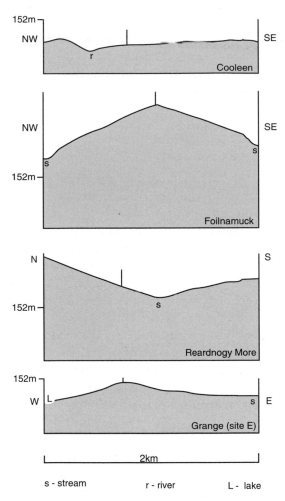

*Fig. 5.5
Topographical
transects showing the
location of a selection
of wedge tombs in
County Tipperary:
Cooleen,
Foilnamuck,
Reardnogy More,
Grange (site E).*

landscape, as can be seen in the examples from Tipperary shown in Figure 5:5. As one might expect, in different kinds of terrain distinct patterns of location can be identified, as on the karst upland of the Burren in Co. Clare where there is a major concentration of these sites on the areas of limestone pavement. It is also relevant to note the frequent location of wedge tombs close to tombs of other types and the occurrence of groups of wedge tombs in close proximity, as at Parknabinnia on the Burren, which should be treated as cemeteries (Cooney 1990, 750).

Wedge tomb deposits include Neolithic pottery and Beaker, both of which occur for example at Lough Gur (Ó Ríordáin and Ó h-Icheadha 1955), while several tombs have no grave assemblages. While the use of wedge tombs for communal burial also demonstrates a continuity with Neolithic burial customs there is an increase in the incidence of inhumation compared with the earlier cremation-dominated traditions in Court and Passage Tombs (Fig. 5:6; compare with Fig. 4:14). A similar complexity of burial practice to that in other megalithic tombs is suggested, for instance, by the apparent separate placement of the skull from the other bones of an adult female at Labbacallee, Co. Cork (Leask and Price 1936).

In some of the formal individual burials there is the retention of a megalithic component as, for example, at the rock shelter at Rockbarton ('Caherguillamore'), Co. Limerick (Hunt 1967), and Rath, Co. Wicklow (Prendergast 1959). These sites display affinities with the earlier Linkardstown tomb tradition in the accompaniment of individual corpses by elaborate decorated vessels. The use of cists, including megalithic examples contained in round cairns, occurs at Moneen, Co. Cork (O'Kelly 1952), Longstone Rath, Co. Kildare (Macalister *et al.* 1913; Grogan 1983/4, 307–8), and Ballynagallagh, Co. Limerick (Cleary and Jones 1980), where a pit cremation was primary to the cist

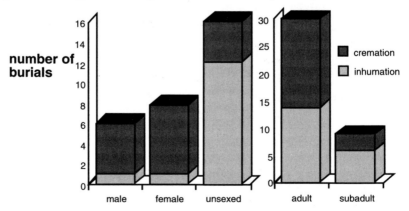

Fig. 5:6—Burial evidence shown by rite and gender (for adults) and general age groups in deposits in wedge tombs.

inhumation. Other aspects of this diverse range of burial forms occur in the pre-cairn deposit at Moneen, as it includes pieces of a human skull and an apparently complete insular Final Neolithic vessel (O'Kelly 1952; Brindley *et al* 1987/8, 13). Domestic debris, which included Beaker and bowls, saddle querns and an axe-hammer, came from the multiple cist cairn over this deposit and may have been derived from a pre-tomb habitation, part of which was sealed under the site. The ring-ditch at Site 1, Dundrum Sandhills, Co. Down (Collins 1952, 5–14), and the probable ring-ditch burials at Rathjordan (Ó Ríordáin 1947, 4; 1948, 30–1) and Cahercorney, Co. Limerick (MacDermott 1949), also indicate the provision of covering or enclosing features for individual burials. Cremation, occurring at Dundrum Sandhills, is also present at the Baurnadomeeny wedge tomb (O'Kelly 1960). Here several burials occurred in pits and small elaborate cists under and around the cairn, which are similar to those at Millin Bay (Collins and Waterman 1955) and within the Monknewtown enclosure, Co. Meath (Sweetman 1976), where one of the burials consisted of a cremation in a Carrowkeel pot.

In contrast to their importance in Britain and on the Continent (e.g. see Mercer 1977; Thomas 1991, 128–38), where individual burials accompanied by Beaker pottery are very much a feature of the use of this ceramic type, identifiably Beaker-associated burials are extremely scarce in Ireland. The plain vessel accompanied by a cremation in the partly collapsed passage of Site 15 at Knowth (Eogan 1984, 308–12, fig. 117) is one of the few definite examples. The paucity of funerary associations for Beaker in Final Neolithic society is also a characteristic of the groove-decorated pottery or Grooved Ware which has recently been identified as a ceramic type at sites in the Boyne Valley and the Lough Gur region of Counties Limerick and Tipperary (Cleary 1983, 63, 88–91, fig. 36; Grogan 1989). At Knowth, for instance, the domestic Beaker assemblage at concentration D (Eogan 1984, 286–304) has also produced Grooved Ware (G. Eogan and H. Roche, pers. comm.). But at this site also part of a human skull was associated with a Grooved Ware vessel in one of the satellite passage tombs, Site 18, while at another, Site 6, a fragmentary vessel may have been associated with a cremation

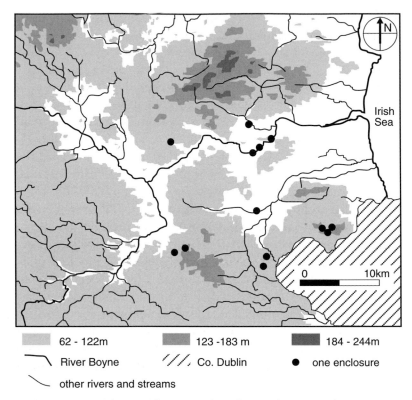

Fig. 5:7—Distribution of ceremonial earthen enclosures in the Boyne Valley area (after Stout 1991).

deposited in the right-hand recess (Eogan 1984, 312–13, fig. 118). This type of pottery has the same bucket shape and decoration as British Grooved Ware and its presence indicates that, as in Britain, a number of distinct pottery styles were in use contemporaneously but perhaps with a different status and role (see R. Bradley 1984, 49–53, 70–3; Thomas 1991, 79–102).

Defining ceremonial space: embanked enclosures
These large enclosures are concentrated in County Meath, within and on the edge of the Boyne Valley and in the Fourknocks area (Fig. 5:7; Stout 1991), but small clusters of related sites occur in other areas, such as Counties Louth and Down (Buckley and

Sweetman 1991, 70–3; Hartwell 1991), the Boyle Valley, Co. Roscommon (T. Condit, pers. comm.), and Limerick, where the Grange Stone Circle (Ó Ríordáin 1951), Circle O (Grogan and Eogan 1987, 496–7) and Ballynamona are located in the Lough Gur area. There are a small number of other sites, such as Dún Ruadh, Co. Tyrone (O. Davies 1936). Smaller embanked stone circles in Counties Cork and Kerry (Ó Nualláin 1975; 1978; 1984a; 1984b; Grogan 1989, 89–92) may be part of a related tradition. The sites are characterised by an enclosing bank of earth and/or large stones and normally have a single, sometimes monumental, entrance. The material for the bank is often supplied by scarping the interior of the site around the perimeter of the bank itself, but internal ditches occur at Circle O, Lough Gur, and Dún Ruadh.

Only six of the above sites have been excavated, but in three cases — Monknewtown (Sweetman 1976), the pit circle at Newgrange (Sweetman 1985) and the Grange Stone Circle — Beaker pottery forms the major part of the assemblages. Grooved Ware occurred at Grange and Monknewtown, and while not found within the pit circle, Grooved Ware occurred in other Beaker contexts at Newgrange (Cleary 1983). The apparent presence of food vessel pottery in the structural make-up of the Grange site suggests that this monument, in its final form at least, was not completed until the Early Bronze Age. Features of the enclosures in the Boyne area and elsewhere can be compared with those of the 'henge' tradition in Britain (Harding and Lee 1987; Wainwright 1989) where there is a similar tendency for the enclosures to be built in groups within established settlement areas.

The continuity implied by the location of these monuments within areas of established Neolithic activity, and particularly in core areas like the Boyne Valley and Lough Gur, is further supported by the evidence for habitation, survival of Neolithic elements in the material assemblage and a strong similarity in the subsistence strategy. In terms of the actual siting of the monuments (Fig. 5:8) there is a pattern in that they tend to be placed where they can be looked into from higher ground in the vicinity. It could be argued that this concern with making the

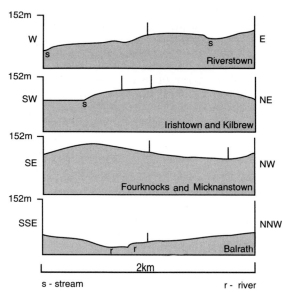

Fig. 5:8—
Topographical
transects showing the
location of a
selection of
ceremonial earthen
enclosures in
County Meath:
Riverstown;
Irishtown and
Kilbrew;
Fourknocks and
Micknanstown;
Balrath.

activities within the enclosures visible but only from a distance is compatible with the use of the sites being controlled. As in the megalithic tombs, it is likely that restrictions were put on those allowed access to the interior even though the interior of the enclosures was in the open air. It is probable that the construction and use of the enclosures represent an ongoing attempt to maintain the internal balance of social power but within a wider inter-regional context. In such a scenario the social élite pursue new ritual mechanisms in an attempt to preserve their dominance within the local communities by adopting more widespread trends through their existing contacts with areas such as the Orkneys, north Wales and southern England (e.g. R. Bradley 1984, 61–7). The adoption of fashions like enclosure-building, Beaker and groove-decorated ceramics and the increasing popularity of artifacts such as barbed-and-tanged and transverse arrowheads, wrist-bracers and perhaps copper items such as flat axes, tanged daggers and awls occurs within an Irish dimension where these new status symbols are incorporated within a continuing Neolithic tradition. In this sense the absence of 'Beaker burials' is not surprising, while the increase in individual burials in a wide variety of forms can be read as representing the ongoing development of individual status recognition within society and the separation of formal burial from other ceremonial activity controlled by the living.

As we have noted, burial is an occasional element in enclosures, whether in a formal context at Monknewtown or informally as at Grange where isolated human bone deposits occurred (Ó Ríordáin 1951, 67–8). The presence of token animal cremations in elaborate pits defining the Newgrange pit circle (Sweetman 1985, 213–14) cautions against viewing the human deposits at the other sites as more than an aspect of a complex burial ritual and against viewing the faunal assemblage from Newgrange and other sites simply in economic terms (compare van Wijngaarden-Bakker 1986 and Mount 1992). The high proportion of pig bones from the Beaker site at Newgrange may relate to the ceremonies and feasting connected with the use of the pit circle and other sites, as has been suggested to have been the case at major henge sites in Wessex in southern Britain (Richards and Thomas 1984, 204–14). Habitation and industrial activity also occurred within the Newgrange site and indicate that enclosures may individually have had a range of functions but they were primarily used for formal, ceremonial, repetitive — i.e. ritual — activity. That the monuments seen on the ground today may be only the latest in a number of phases of construction and use is indicated by the presence of ditches within the embanked enclosures at Ballynahatty, Co. Down (Hartwell 1991, 14), and Micknanstown and Balrath, Co. Meath (Holloway in Stout 1991, 280). Furthermore, the recognition of a pit circle close to the Ballynahatty enclosure (Hartwell 1991, 14–15) suggests that the complexity of activity evident in the Boyne Valley was paralleled elsewhere.

Contacts between regional core areas
We can see the embanked enclosures as one indication of the links between major areas of importance within Ireland and between similar areas in Ireland and Britain. One might expect that the reality of these links would also be expressed in the presence of similar artifacts in different core areas (R. Bradley

1982a, 35). In terms of new ceramic styles the Grooved Ware mostly comes from domestic contexts in association with Beaker, with the single exception of the occupation site on Geróid (Garret) Island in Lough Gur (Liversage 1958), where it occurred with Neolithic pottery. Several Beaker assemblages contain no Grooved Ware so the relationship between these two exotic ceramics is not constant. In the Boyne Valley the presence of Grooved Ware mirrors the relationship between this pottery and the passage tomb complex in the Orkney Islands (R. Bradley 1984, 58–69). Further evidence for interaction between these two important regions is provided not only by the maceheads from the eastern tomb and western tomb under the main mound at Knowth but also by three further Orkney-type maceheads from the Boyne Valley. There are several others from the northern part of the country. In addition to the maceheads themselves, miniature copies, usually of pottery, were deposited in the passage tombs as personal items accompanying the burials; at Knowth East miniatures of both Orkney and Thames pestle-type maceheads came from the chamber, while Newgrange and Carrowkeel K produced only Orcadian types (Simpson 1988, 33).

This type of inter-regional exchange, whether of artifacts, monuments or ideas, also seems to characterise the relationship between the Boyne Valley and the Lough Gur area where, despite the absence of a strong megalithic tradition, similar social developments appear to have been occurring against a background of influence of ideas and items associated with passage tombs. In this regard it is of note that the Beaker/Grooved Ware assemblage at Longstone, Co. Tipperary (P. Danaher, pers. comm.), succeeded an occupation horizon containing several Carrowkeel vessels. Also there are two definite passage tombs, Deerpark (Duntryleague), Co. Limerick, and Shrough, Co. Tipperary, on the periphery of the Lough Gur core (Herity 1974; de Valera and Ó Nualláin 1982; Grogan 1989). The wider dimension of inter-regional exchange is indicated by the cushion macehead of probable Orkney origin from Lough Gur Site C and the Orkney pestle type from the lake itself (Simpson 1988, 28, 31–5).

Major trends in the Final Neolithic

We would view the Final Neolithic as characterised by two major trends. The first is the alteration of social organisation towards a greater emphasis on the individual, and in particular the role of a small number of powerful individuals. This was a feature already perceptible in the later Neolithic in relation to the changing role of burial. Now it is seen also in the increase in the number and range of special or prestige objects. These items are rarely deposited in graves and contrast with the quantity of high-status burials in, for example, southern Britain which were accompanied by Beakers, wrist-bracers, awls, daggers and occasionally gold, jet or amber (Thomas 1991, 128–42). Thus we can observe that while close contacts with Britain are indicated by the Beaker pottery and the associated 'package' of prestige goods, the use of these items is sufficiently different in Ireland to confirm an indigenous background for the similar social developments here. It is also a reminder of the active role of material culture in that the use of these prestige items was adapted to fit into the changing social context developing in different areas within Ireland.

The second major trend is wider evidence of settlement in the landscape. This appears to be based on population continuity and expansion, a point which is underlined by the persistence of major activity in, for example, the Boyne Valley and the Lough Gur region. Indeed, we have seen that the new elements in the material culture are concentrated in those areas but with a wider distribution especially in the northern part of the country. The expansion of the settlement pattern into parts of the west and south-west is, perhaps, too easily exaggerated in view of the absence in some regions of high-visibility Neolithic markers, such as megalithic tombs. However, the emergence in those areas of the wedge tombs, clearly continuing the megalithic tradition, indicates an intensification of activity. In the south-west the distribution of flat axes of local copper (e.g. Flanagan 1979) also suggests social differentiation based on access or lack of access to new technology and artifacts, but the ongoing use of communal burial monuments indicates that the communal identity was still a dominant feature of society. The contrast between this pattern and the regional cross-links displayed by the core areas with their exotic imports and imitations is a striking one. While regional differentiation becomes more marked in the Early Bronze Age, the variation in social systems and in the prestige aspect of material culture is considerably less evident by then.

6 THE EARLY BRONZE AGE: INTEGRATING DIVERSE PATTERNS OF BEHAVIOUR

Pulling the evidence together

The problems in the study of the Bronze Age of Ireland have been set out on numerous occasions. In brief they can be stated as follows: for the Early Bronze Age there is a range of evidence encompassing burial and ceremonial sites with associated well-known ceramic traditions and metalwork, but there are few connections between the various sectors of the evidence. For the Late Bronze Age the abundance of metal objects has been set against the relative absence of other forms of archaeological evidence. Our understanding of the transition from the Early to the Late Bronze Age, that is the Middle Bronze Age, is to say the least unsatisfactory. It has to be said that many of these problems may be a result of the way in which archaeologists have approached the study of this period. Thus, for example, with increasingly extensive programmes of excavation it is becoming clear that Bronze Age settlements are not as elusive as we had assumed in the past.

Looking specifically at the Early Bronze Age (2300–1700 BC), the study of the period has traditionally followed the boundaries of the major sets of evidence present; thus we have a good understanding of the burial evidence on the one hand and of the metal artifacts on the other (e.g. ApSimon 1969b). The limited degree of overlap between these data sets, as indicated by the rarity of the occurrence of metal artifacts with burials, has led to a situation where discussion of the period has tended to be

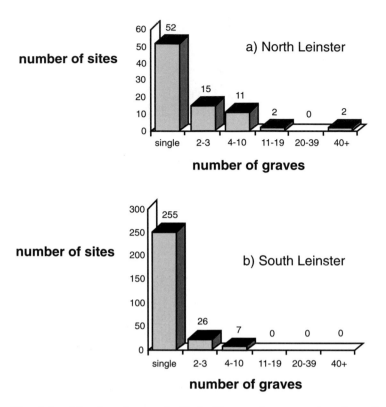

Fig. 6:1—Number of graves in Early Bronze Age cemeteries. Overall
Irish figures (Waddell 1990a) d), compared with those from
north Leinster (Cooney 1987) a), south Leinster (after Mount
1989) b), and Munster c) (Grogan 1989).

approached from either a metalwork (e.g. Harbison 1969a;
1969b) or a burial/ceramic angle (e.g. Waddell 1990a). Yet it is
clear that this separation seen in the evidence is not a feature sent
to try the archaeologist's patience and capabilities of cross-
typological matching but is rather a direct result of human
behaviour in the Early Bronze Age. For whatever reason, people
deliberately chose to deposit metal objects particularly in wet or
watery places, mostly singly but occasionally as hoards. In some
places deposition took place over prolonged periods of time, so
there were places formally recognised as suitable locales for

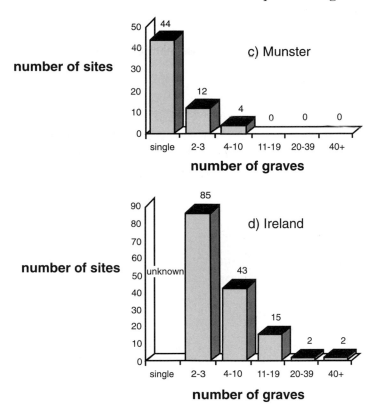

deposition. Formal burial generally took place in a cist or in a pit, either with no surface indication or with a visible marker of some kind. These markers suggest links of various kinds with a number of what could be termed ceremonial monuments. While isolated examples do occur, formal burial was very often in small cemeteries (Fig. 6:1), suggesting that in many areas the scale of social integration and identity was quite local, with large cemeteries very much the exception. The deposition of material dating to this period indicates that some megalithic tombs were still in use.

Interpretation of the Early Bronze Age has been dominated by a typological and chronological approach where variation in the pottery or metal type or in the burial practice has been seen as representing change over time. This narrow view ignores people's complex use of material culture and the possibilities of social meaning in the data. In a situation where much of the evidence consists of high-quality artifacts it is possible that what we see over time is the decrease in the exclusivity of certain forms as they become more widely adopted and new forms taking their place which, because of their cachet of restricted availability, symbolise the superior position of the people who possess them (Miller 1982, 89; R. Bradley 1984, 71–2). Different types of funerary ceramics and mortuary rite may have signified social distinctions (e.g. Mount 1991). As time went on, these meanings may have changed and new forms have been adopted, but the older forms would also have remained in use. Indeed, very often social change is legitimated by being presented as having a reference to and continuity with the past (Bloch 1977; Sahlins 1987, 49–54). It is only by appreciating the complex meaning of the evidence that we are likely to reach an understanding of Bronze Age society. For the archaeologist this evidence may appear to be fragmented; for the people who created it, it all formed part of a patterned but seamless web. It is with this perspective in mind that we should approach the period. Thus the much-discussed paucity of settlement sites has to be considered in the context of the burials, ceremonial monuments and metal objects which show widespread patterns of distribution. These have relevance in analysing the general patterns of settlement distribution.

The pattern of settlement
At the level of domestic organisation the settlement evidence resembles that of the Neolithic, even if the number of sites on which we can base a reconstruction is less than for the preceding period (Harbison 1988, 110; O'Kelly 1989, 217–23). The house sizes suggest that the residential unit was a single nuclear family. Interestingly, houses of both rectangular, as at Site F at Lough Gur (Ó Ríordáin 1954, 415ff), and circular design are known. At Carrigillihy, Co. Cork, recent radiocarbon dating has confirmed the Bronze Age date of the site (O'Kelly 1989, 219–22). Here an oval drystone and timber house was built within an enclosure about 24m in maximum diameter. A square house was later superimposed on the ruins of the earlier oval house (O'Kelly 1951). The settlement sites encompass houses and ancillary

buildings, in some cases set in contemporary fields. At both Belderrig (Caulfield 1988) and Carrownaglogh (Herity 1981) a round house was set within a cultivated area defined by stone walls, preserved under a cover of blanket bog. At Belderrig the Neolithic fields which had become at least partially bog-covered were reclaimed around the end of this period and the fences altered and extended, in one stretch by oak posts. In looking at the wider question of the organisation and spread of settlement these latter sites are a reminder that the changing nature of the landscape and climate must be taken into consideration.

It is indeed somewhat ironic that our best evidence for the human organisation of the landscape in the Early Bronze Age comes from areas that were to become marginal to settlement as they became peat-covered. Evidence from sites like Belderrig, Carrownaglogh and Cashelkeelty (Lynch 1981) has to be assessed as to whether we are looking at sites that were even at the time on land of peripheral importance or whether they may reflect mainstream Bronze Age settlement, both in their form and location. It is striking that the dates from these sites all fall around 1700–1450 BC; while this may be coincidental it is possible that they represent expressions of settlement expansion. In all cases the field evidence suggests small-scale, gradual intake, unlike the organised landscape created earlier at Céide or in a broadly contemporary context on Dartmoor, Devon (Fleming 1988). This can be taken to suggest that both the decision to enclose land and the working of the land itself were undertaken at a local level, possibly involving relatively small communities.

It is agreed that the Irish landscape underwent fundamental change during the Bronze Age. Blanket bog growth became accentuated after 2500 BC, soil deterioration was also common and Edwards (1985, 207) has commented that by the early second millennium BC forest cover had effectively disappeared from the greater part of the country. The causes of these changes appear primarily to have been climatic deterioration and human activity. While for people living at the time this may have resembled a gradually increasing 'wethouse effect' there are also indications that there were particular times when conditions became markedly worse, for example when there were volcanic dust veils

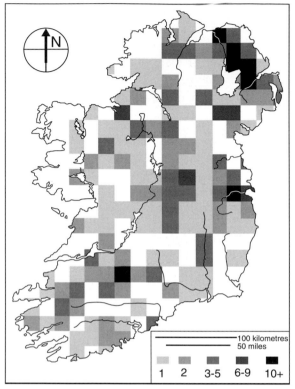

Fig. 6:2a—
Density
distribution (in
20km² blocks) of
Early Bronze
Age flat axes
(based on
information in
Harbison
1969b).

100 kilometres
50 miles

1   2   3-5   6-9   10+

(Baillie and Munro 1988), and these events might have had an influence on the pattern of settlement. Under the conditions outlined above one would expect settlement to have contracted from wetter, upland areas to drier, more fertile and lower-lying areas. To some extent the archaeological evidence backs up this contention but examples to the contrary can also be cited. The situation is made more difficult in that population levels, while fluctuating, were probably increasing and that agricultural methods had become more diversified compared to the Neolithic so that a greater range of land could be used for agriculture. It is clear as well that one is looking at a period of relatively rapid social change which would also have influenced the form and location of settlement.

With this complex interaction of factors in mind, at a broad island-wide level it can be observed that the distribution of Early

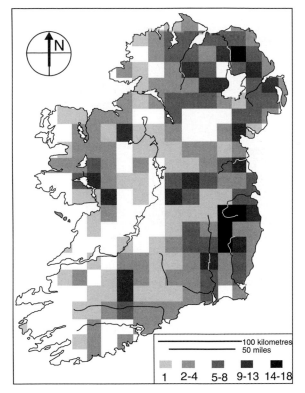

Fig. 6:2b— Density distribution (in 20km² blocks) of Early Bronze Age burials (based on information in Waddell 1990a and Kilfeather 1991).

Bronze Age burials and artifacts indicates that most of the country was occupied. The distribution of flat copper and bronze axes (Fig. 6:2a), for example, indicates significant activity in areas that had an apparently lower profile during the Neolithic, such as the north midlands. The cist and pit burials (Fig. 6:2b), whose location has often been taken as a surrogate for where settlement might have been, are both widely distributed but also show clustering, particularly in the north-east and south-east of the country. The burials tend to be concentrated in low-lying areas and this may represent, in some regions, a greater preference for a lower-lying location relative to Neolithic distribution patterns (Woodman 1985b, 268). The metal artifacts similarly are low-lying in distribution, but a significant number come from 'wet' locations such as bogs, rivers and lakes. This pattern can be seen in the admittedly small percentage of flat axes for which the

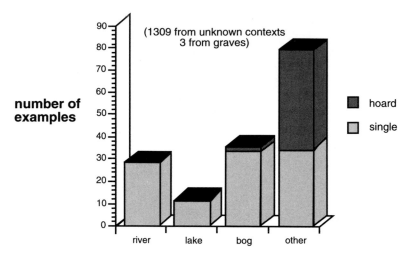

Fig. 6:3—Context of discovery of flat axes (based on information in Harbison 1969b with additions).

details of context are known (Fig. 6:3). Approximately half of them come from wet contexts and this, allied to the occurrence of axes in hoards, reminds us that patterns of deposition and distribution of metalwork cannot always be related to the proximity of settlement. *Fulachta fiadh,* mounds of burnt stone (with associated troughs and other features) accumulated as a result of the use of hot stone cooking techniques, by their nature occur in zones close to water sources and their distribution offers insight into what may have been a specialised or seasonal but nevertheless integrated aspect of the settlement pattern. While this type of site was in use for a very long period of time, systematic radiocarbon dating shows a predominance of second-millennium BC dates for their use (Brindley *et al.* 1989/90, 28). Their numbers, at a surviving minimum of 4,000, certainly back up the suggestion of the increasing spread and density of settlement (Buckley 1990, 9).

We can appreciate the complexity of the settlement picture by looking in more detail at areas where there is evidence available to integrate the different distribution patterns. In the area south of Limerick there has been a survey of the prehistoric evidence

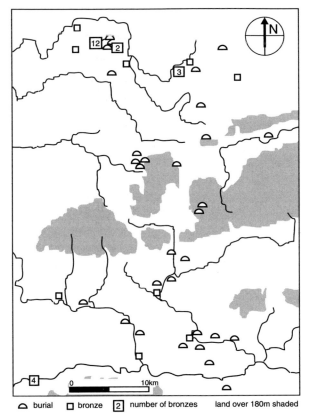

Fig. 6:4—
Distribution
pattern of
Early Bronze
Age burials
and bronze
artifacts in
south Limerick
and north
Cork.

△ burial   ☐ bronze   ② number of bronzes   land over 180m shaded

(Grogan 1989) and arising from the Limerick gas pipeline a study of a cross-section of the region (Gowen 1988). Here there is a notable shift away from the settlement focus at Lough Gur after the Neolithic. There are barrow complexes and *fulachta fiadh* in the lower parts of the river valleys to the south. The bronzes were concentrated at Lough Gur; some of the objects were apparently deposited in the lake itself. This, along with the construction and use of the Grange stone circle and other stone circles, suggests that Lough Gur had become a focus for ceremonial activity rather than settlement. There was a shift in the settlement focus to the south. Activity was concentrated in the river valleys, with the main burial sites along the valley floors (Fig. 6:4) and the habitation sites probably on higher ground

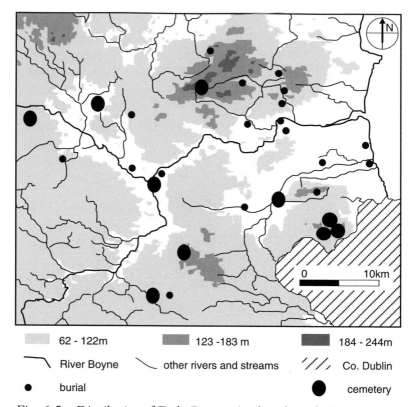

62 - 122m   123 -183 m   184 - 244m

River Boyne   other rivers and streams   Co. Dublin

burial   cemetery

*Fig. 6:5—Distribution of Early Bronze Age burials in the Boyne
Valley area.*

along the valley-side ridges. There is also a shift in the nature of
activity in the Boyne Valley alongside continuity in some areas in
the broader north Leinster region. Most notably there is restricted
evidence for Early Bronze Age burial in what had been the core
area during the Neolithic, the Bend of the Boyne, and there is
also an absence of settlement evidence. The burials now occur in
areas to the east, north and west which may previously have been
more peripheral (Fig. 6:5; compare Figs 4:7 and 5:7).
Interestingly these include both upland and lowland locations. In
the light of the probable continued fertility of the core area in the
Boyne Valley the lack of archaeological evidence for settlement is
puzzling and may be the result of the very low visibility of

settlement data. But it would appear that in this period certain activities, which would be expected to dominate the archaeological record if they were present, including burial and deliberate deposition, were largely and perhaps formally excluded from the Bend of the Boyne. On the other hand, at Fourknocks and Tara there is continuity in the sense of place and activity as in both cases passage tomb mounds were used as cemeteries during the Early Bronze Age.

Putting this evidence into perspective is difficult given the paucity of direct evidence and the lack of secure dating. It does seem that there was a widespread break with the pattern established in the Final Neolithic. Increased utilisation of both lower-lying ground along river valleys and uplands in some areas suggests a different economic strategy, perhaps fuelled by increasing population, deteriorating conditions in some areas already settled, and a wider-ranging farming system underlain by aspects of the 'secondary products revolution' (Sherratt 1981; Champion *et al.* 1984, 156–62, 205–9). At the end of the period the location of settlement and fields in areas that even in contemporary conditions would have been marginal suggests an expansion of settlement. An interesting aspect of the Early Bronze Age evidence is that while the pattern of settlement is problematic to interpret, it does appear to be based on a communal level of organisation. It is, however, accompanied by a growing emphasis on the individual in burial and on the production of items for personal consumption. It is through their treatment in death and their possessions in life that we can best approach an understanding of how people were incorporated into social entities.

The complexity of the burial evidence

A very generalised chronological succession of burial forms can be seen in Ireland. Beginning with crouched inhumation in well-structured cists, there is a change to cremation and a gradual replacement of the cist as the concept of an accompanying pottery vessel is overtaken by that of inverting a vessel over the burial. Alongside this succession must be set the clear evidence that both cremation and inhumation, cists and pits and a variety of funerary ceramics were in use contemporaneously, both in cemetery sites and apparently isolated burials (Grogan 1988b, 156). Distinct regional differences are also clearly present in the burial record. It has to be emphasised, however, that it is the chronological pattern that has dominated most previous discussions of the burials. The contrasts set out here have been pushed into a one-dimensional framework in which variations are explained as change over time. For example, variation in burial rite has been seen in terms of the waxing and waning in popularity of either cremation or inhumation (Harbison 1988, 106). There has been much discussion of the origins of innovation in the burial rite, but the social implications of the burial record have been treated in a simplistic way. The dominance of single burial on the one hand has been regarded as indicating a more egalitarian society compared to the Neolithic, while on the other the placement of bronze daggers and stone battle-axes in some burials has been taken to suggest that people were more warlike and under territorial and social pressures. These views have to be very seriously questioned when the context of the evidence is examined. In many aspects of the burials it is the contemporaneity of different practices that gives the most insights into society, not the background chronological sequence. It also has to be borne in mind that the meaning of different practices for the people involved could have altered both over time and in different parts of the country.

With regard to the type of grave used, on cemetery sites one finds the contemporary use of both cists and pits. At Cloghskelt, Co. Down, the 23 graves ranged from regular cists to partially encisted graves to pits (Flanagan 1976, 7). The general dominance of cists in the archaeological record must be seen in the context of the accidental discovery of many sites, particularly through ploughing or quarrying. In the case of accidental discovery the chances of recognition of cists are much higher than for pits or partially cisted burials (e.g. Barclay 1982). This should also make us cautious about the perceived dominance of single graves, the small size of most cemeteries (see Fig. 6:1) and the representation of pit burials in the archaeological record. Thus of 85 Early Bronze Age burial sites known from north

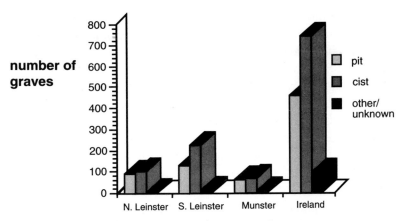

Fig. 6:6—Regional variation in Early Bronze Age grave types. Comparison of patterns in north Leinster, south Leinster (Mount 1990) and north Munster.

Leinster 52 consisted of a single grave, and only ten of those 52 were pit graves (Cooney 1987). The likelihood that some at least of what are apparently single graves formed part of a cemetery is demonstrated by instances of further burials coming to light in the vicinity of an initial find, as is the case at Killeenaghmountain, Co. Waterford, where three separate discoveries were made close to each other (Rynne 1970; Ryan 1975; Ryan, pers. comm.). At the same time it is clear that alongside the countrywide pattern outlined by Waddell (1990a) regional differences occur in both grave type and the relationship between single graves and cemeteries (Fig. 6:6). North Leinster can be contrasted with the other two regions in that it has a greater range of cemetery size (see Fig. 6:1), including the two exceptionally large cemeteries at Knockast, Co. Westmeath (Hencken and Movius 1934), and Tara (de Paor 1957), each with over 40 burials. These are the two largest Bronze Age cemeteries in the country, followed by Cloghskelt in Co. Down, mentioned above, which contains 23 graves.

Looking at the contents of the graves it is clear that a majority of graves contained the remains of only one individual. However, multiple, either collective or successive, burial occurred in well

over 25% and possibly up to 40% of the graves where such details
are recorded (Mount 1991; see discussion and numbers given in
Ryan 1980b; Sheehan 1985; Doody 1987a, 17). The cremation
deposit of five individuals under a vase urn in a cist at Knockroe,
Co. Tyrone, represents a collective deposition (Williams and
Wilkinson 1988). In contrast, at the Carrig, Co. Wicklow,
cemetery (Grogan 1990) one of the cists contained five successive
cremated interments, some of which in turn were multiple
burials. The cremation deposition of five individuals in the cist at
Ballyveelish North, Co. Tipperary, was viewed by the excavator
(Doody 1987a, 17–18) as a single episode but is alternatively
open to interpretation as being a successive deposit. The concept
of the cemetery consisting of two or three or more graves
(Flanagan 1976, 9; Waddell 1970, 99; 1981, 166) shows that
people had both formally defined places of burial and the practice
of successive burial in the same location. We also appear to be
seeing the reuse of individual graves or graves containing single
collective deposits, i.e. the individual grave became a 'cemetery'.

Within the population represented in the burial record it is
clear, as in the Neolithic, that children are under-represented.
From a situation where in the living population they would have
been in the majority, and where there would have been a high
level of infant mortality (e.g. Burgess 1980, 161–2), they are in a
minority in the burial population (Fig. 6:7). This has been
demonstrated in detail in southern Leinster (Mount 1991, 22) and
north Munster (Grogan 1989). It is possible that in most cases
children did not receive formal burial unless their death
coincided with that of an adult, more specifically a relation.
Existing graves, perhaps for the exclusive use of individual
families, may on occasion have been opened to take the remains
of children. From this it would appear that children were not
normally regarded as full members of society. There are
exceptional cases, such as the eight-year-old child buried with a
bowl food vessel in a cist in the mound of Fourknocks I
(Hartnett 1957, 254), where it is clear that social status was
ascribed to non-adults. The prominence of child burials within
the Bronze Age cemetery at Fourknocks I is unusual, and it may
reflect a tradition of child burial here as the latest Neolithic

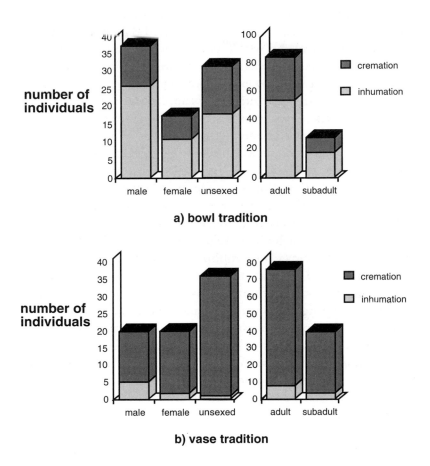

Fig. 6:7—Early Bronze Age burial evidence. Comparison of burial rite, gender (adults only) and general age groups associated with the bowl (a) and vase (b) traditions.

burials in the passage of the tomb have a higher than average proportion of children (Cooney 1992, 133–5).

In southern Leinster there are indications that males are over-represented in the burial record (Mount 1991, 24), although elsewhere there are suggestions of similar proportions of males and females. It is clear that the burial record does not reflect the pattern of burial of the whole population. We are looking at a selective burial record, where formal burial was restricted to an élite section of the living population and where, depending at least on the recognisable axes of less age and gender, individuals were treated differently. Neither can the burial rite itself be seen as reflecting either a unitary set of practices or something that simply changed over time. Different burial rites and different burial practices can be seen to have been in use at the same time on individual sites. For example, at Sonna Demesne, Co. Westmeath, a small cemetery of three graves consisted of a short rectangular cist containing the cremated remains of a child accompanied by a bowl, flanked by two pit graves, both containing headless (adult?) inhumations (Waddell 1990a, 154). At Fourknocks II, Co. Meath, there were two instances of a cist containing a crouched adult inhumation being underlain by the cremated remains of another adult (Hartnett 1971, 66–8). General differences in burial rite can be recognised that show change over time, such as the marked decrease in the use of inhumation when the burial is accompanied by pottery of the vase food vessel tradition compared to burials accompanied by bowl food vessels (see Fig. 6:7), some of which are earlier than vases, and the ubiquity of cremation when the burial is covered by urns in the vase tradition (vase and encrusted) or by collared urns. But this is happening side by side with a complex array of mortuary practices being utilised by people at any one time.

Two other dimensions of burial practice further stress the complexity of the record. Firstly there is the question of visibility in the Bronze Age landscape. Waddell (1990a, table 5) noted that the ratio of flat cemeteries to those covered by a cairn or mound is something in the order of 3:2. The mound was either purpose-built or involved the reuse of an existing monument. Single graves are also in some cases covered by a mound, cairn or barrow, and there appears to be an increasing emphasis on the visible expression of discrete, individual graves as the Bronze Age develops. Secondly, in the reuse of existing sites there is clearly a deliberate link being established with the past. This link may involve the

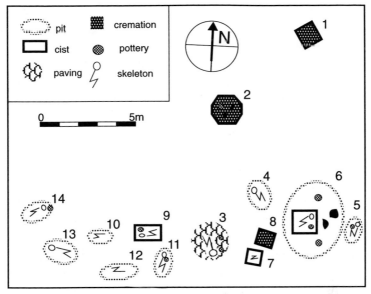

Fig. 6:8—Schematic presentation of the Early Bronze Age flat cemetery at Keenoge, Co. Meath (after Waddell 1990a).

active disturbance of the existing burial deposits and structures, as in the case of the passage tomb at Tara (de Paor 1957) and the wedge tomb at Kilmashogue, Co. Dublin (Kilbride-Jones 1954), or conscious respect of them, as in the case of the portal tomb at Aghnaskeagh, Co. Louth (Evans 1935; Brindley 1988).

What are we to make of the meaning of this tremendous diversity in burial practice? As a first step we can accept that the burial patterning is the result of deliberate social activity and, whatever about the difficulties of detailed interpretation, that it reflects something of the nature of contemporary society and the place in it of the individuals who were accorded some degree of formal burial. There are distinct patterns of differentiation within the burial record. We can examine this by concentrating on just one dimension of the evidence — the non-ceramic grave-goods (see Kilfeather 1991). Firstly, these are relatively uncommon. However, neither their character nor occurrence is random. At the Keenoge cemetery in Co. Meath (Fig. 6:8) eight of the fourteen burials had grave-goods, and of those eight only three (burials 3, 9 and 13) had non-ceramic grave-goods (Waddell 1990a, 126–7). At the large Knockast cemetery in Co. Westmeath (Hencken and Movius 1934) only fifteen of the 43 burials had associated finds and in turn only five out of the fifteen had non-ceramic grave-goods. Where non-ceramic grave-goods occur with a single burial, as opposed to a cemetery, the special nature of the burial is often shown by its being covered by a visible mound or cairn. There are strong indications of gender differentiation in the non-ceramic grave items, with a dominance of such male-associated items as metal daggers, knives/razors and flint plano-convex knives (e.g. Harbison 1968; Kavanagh 1976, 324–9).

The placement of such objects with an individual in the grave can be taken to denote that the mourners are actively representing and defining the dead person, and themselves, as having some social status (see Barrett 1990, 184). As we have seen above, social status can be described as being either earned or achieved or ascribed. The burial evidence suggests that, regardless of the means by which it was attained, visible social status seems to have resided particularly with adult males. In this respect we can argue that there may not have been a strict separation of ascribed and achieved status as the ability to earn status may have been largely limited to adult males. Ascribed status suggests a more formal degree of social ranking and the transfer of power within the same family or kinship group from one generation to the next. That this type of status obtained in at least some parts of Early Bronze Age Ireland is indicated by the only inhumed burial of the Bronze Age cemetery phase at the Mound of the Hostages, Tara, where the crouched inhumation of a 14–15-year-old youth was associated with a bronze dagger, a corroded bronze object and a necklace of faience, bronze and jet beads (Ó Ríordáin 1955). It seems very unlikely that this person was accorded status on account of any personal achievement but rather that his elaborate burial reflected the social standing of his family.

Rather than simply imposing a chronological strait-jacket on the wide array of burial evidence it is much more meaningful to examine it in terms of the contrasts it presents: the regional preferences, changing trends over time, inhumation versus cremation, single interment or multiple burial, cist versus pit, the presence or absence of grave-goods. It was through a deliberate choice from a range of variables that people would have ascribed social significance to the particular burial customs that were in use. To take just one example in the funerary ceramics, pottery belonging to the vase tradition does extend longer in terms of its use over time than bowls. But to adopt a chronological view would be to miss out on the considerable time overlap in the use of these two different types of ceramics and the very interesting regional variability in their use (Fig. 6:9). It seems clear that the use of bowls was more popular in the Leinster area, and that, while vases were more popular in other parts of the country, the relative dominance of vases is most marked in Munster. There may also have been changes in emphasis in what was the focal point of mortuary ritual over time. It is in this context that we should see the decrease in the use of cists over time in tandem with the increasing provision of a covering urn over cremations. A useful perspective to take is to see the evidence in terms of two trends: firstly, to think in terms of the burial record as indicating a society based on family or kin relationships which would have formed the context for social ranking and, secondly, a complementary trend, but one which may have been contradictory at times, of emphasis on adult males, suggesting that in some social groups gender differentiation was an important element in the display of power and prestige. One of the ways in which social standing would have been recognised by both the haves and the have-nots was through the possession of material items of restricted supply and circulation and therefore held in high regard and in considerable demand, in what has been referred to as a prestige goods economy (e.g. R. Bradley 1984, 46–7). The act of placing an object with the owner in the grave or the bestowal of an object on the deceased would have concurred with the role of these prestige goods and would also have taken them out of circulation. In this sense we can link the burials with other strategies of deliberate deposition and the removal from circulation of status items, particularly metalwork.

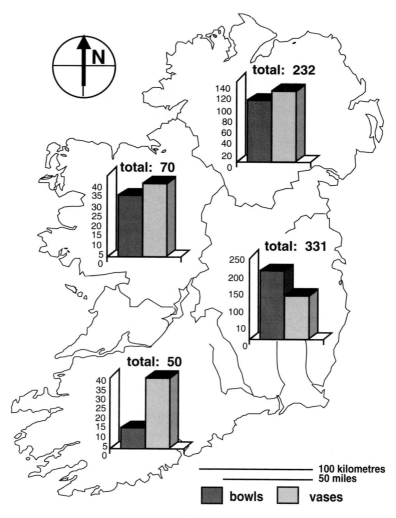

Fig. 6:9—Comparison by province of the occurrence of (burials associated with) the bowl and vase traditions.

Metalwork in the landscape

In the study of metalwork discussion has concentrated primarily on the production and typological classification of different types of artifacts. But the comment made by Eogan (1983, 1) in relation to hoards can be applied to metal artifacts in general: 'it should be remembered that they are social documents; they must, accordingly, be considered in relation to their contemporary cultural context'. It must be said, however, that metalworking is one of those aspects of the archaeological evidence that have been treated in a very cut-and-dried manner. The occurrence of much of the metalwork in isolation from other material, the clear presence of technical advances and typological developments have all contributed to a tradition of study emphasising individual artifact types (e.g. Harbison 1969a; 1969b) and studies of metallurgy and the production of the objects (Flanagan 1979; 1982). While this is of course necessary and laudable, it does not address the central issue of how and why the metalwork entered the archaeological record. A separation has been made between single, 'stray' finds and hoards — two or more artifacts deposited together. In turn, hoards have often been divided into separate categories, either 'ritual' (social) or 'utilitarian' (economic) (see Eogan 1983, 3–12; R. Bradley 1990, 4–14). The utilitarian deposits have been looked on as either founders' hoards — worn-out objects or scrap collected for their metal value — or traders' or merchants' hoards, composed of new artifacts, on their way to the consumer. The ritual deposits have suffered from lack of careful definition or discussion of the nature of the ritual which might have provided a context for their deposition (but see R. Bradley 1990, 28–42). In general they are seen to consist of high-quality objects deposited in such a manner or location that casual loss or temporary storage are unlikely explanations of their occurrence. So in effect they are defined with reference to what are taken to be the 'normal' (economic) deposits. Very often the distinction has been made on the basis of location — that is, utilitarian hoards are in places (dry land) where the objects could be recovered, while ritual hoards are in locations (bogs, rivers, lakes) where recovery would be difficult if not impossible.

Underlying this scheme separating out strands in the context of the metalwork is a lack of consideration of the linking factors between single and multiple deposits or between economic and social reasons for hoards. Firstly, it is worth considering that for much of the Bronze Age and for the majority of Bronze Age people possession of metal artifacts would have been relatively restricted — hence, for example, the rare occurrence of metal objects on settlement sites. Secondly, the same types of artifacts may turn up in totally different kinds of contexts, both as single finds or in hoards either of a 'utilitarian' or 'ritual' nature. Thirdly, the full array of this evidence is as a result of human activity. Gregory's (1982) distinction between objects acting either as gifts or commodities depending on the social distance between the people exchanging them is a very relevant reminder that the same object may change its character. Thus within a social group an object may be exchanged as a gift with attached social ties, while when it is exchanged between strangers it serves more often as an economic commodity (see discussion in R. Bradley 1985b). Applying some of these ideas to the Irish context, attention can be focused on the copper and bronze axes which are the most numerous metal artifact type from this period. Harbison (1969b) gave a figure of 1,950 axes known up to the late 1960s when all his various typological classes were combined together. These of course are only the axes that have survived to become part of the archaeological record, but as Flanagan (1979; 1982) has shown, looking at the maximum production potential figures through the Early Bronze Age, axes would still have been uncommon items (Flanagan 1979, 158–60). Even allowing for the melting down of old objects and other loss factors, at times relatively small numbers of axes may have been produced and been in circulation. In that situation it seems unlikely that axes would have been accidentaly lost and much more likely that deliberate deposition, for whatever range of reasons, would have been the major factor in their removal from circulation.

The overall pattern of the discovery contexts of axes in Ireland has already been shown (see Fig. 6:3) and this can be amplified by looking at the patterns in two regions, north Leinster and Munster (Fig. 6:10). Here the wetland contexts have been emphasised as deposition in bogs, rivers and lakes forms the most coherent pattern in the data, with bogs being the dominant wetland context. Axes were deposited in dry ground also, and in that context the most striking feature is the more frequent occurrence of hoards in Munster compared to north Leinster.

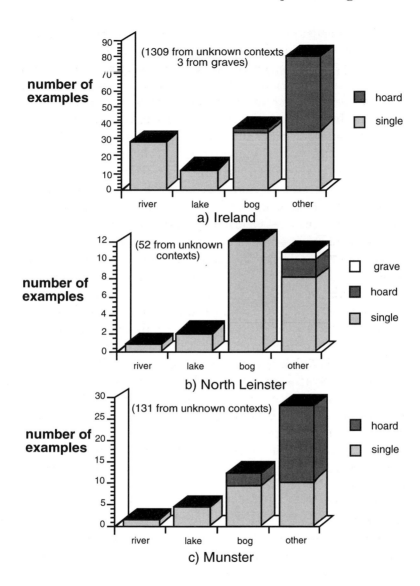

Fig. 6:10—Contexts of discovery of Bronze Age flat axes. Overall figures from (a) Ireland (based on Harbison 1969b with additions) compared with those from (b) north Leinster and (c) Munster.

This is a reminder of the regional differences one might expect in depositional behaviour. Focusing on the north Leinster figures, the 'other' category includes the axe from Newgrange associated with a putative metalworker's area (O'Kelly and Shell 1979; O'Kelly 1983, 16) and three axes attributed to towns which may originally have been found in the rivers Boyne and Shannon. Two copper ingots formed part of a hoard at Growtown, Co. Meath. The one axe from a burial context is from Jordanstown, Co. Meath, and was apparently found with an extended inhumation. This is a very unusual context for a flat axe but there are a couple of other examples, such as the axe found with a burial in a cist at Knockinelder, Co. Down (Ó Floinn 1979). So the separation of axes from burial contexts is not absolute but in general terms it is very striking, particularly when put in contrast to metal daggers, which are frequently found accompanying burials (Harbison 1968).

Deposition took artifacts out of circulation, but the movement of objects during their use may also give important information about the role of material culture during the Early Bronze Age and the nature of contact and exchange between communities and individuals. Continuing with axes as the focus of discussion, Flanagan (1979, 148–58) has drawn attention to the complex movement of the axes before they were deposited. By identifying axes apparently made in the same mould and tracing their distribution (Fig. 6:11), including products of surviving stone moulds, he has shown that axes were moved a considerable distance from their production point. This clearly reflects the nature of the organisation of metalworking and exchange. Centres of production need not reflect the settlement pattern; indeed, the coastal distribution of the moulds (Flanagan 1979, 157) suggests a production emphasis in these areas, a pattern seen elsewhere in Europe (R. Bradley 1985b, 698). Bradley also drew attention to the fact that metalwork in Ireland was accumulated in coastal areas in the form of hoards (see Harbison 1968, 40). As Flanagan (1979, figs 9 and 10) has shown, some of the axes in these hoard deposits originated over a very wide area. It is possible to argue that we see in these coastal areas the treatment of metal objects as commodities to be produced and exchanged

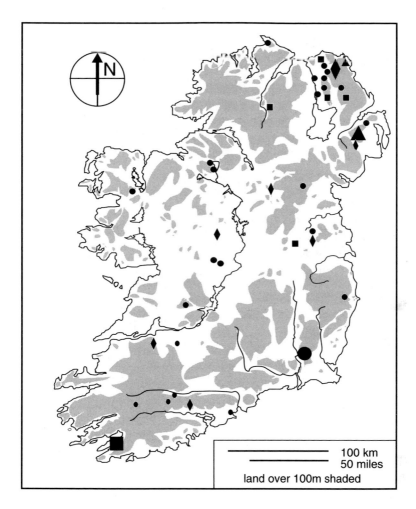

●	Ballyglisheen - mould	•	Ballyglisheen - product
■	Doonour - mould	▪	Doonour - product
◆	Lough Guile - mould	◆	Lough Guile - product
▲	Ballynahinch - mould	▲	Ballynahinch - product

*Fig. 6:11—Distribution of identifiable flat axe products from actual
matrices in relation to the location of the parent stone mould
(after Flanagan 1979).*

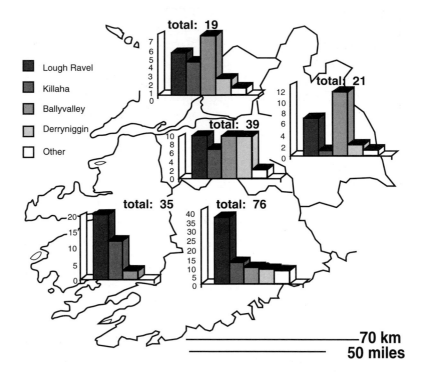

Fig. 6:12—Relative occurrence by county of Early and Middle Bronze Age flat axe types in Munster (based on Harbison 1969b with additions).

over wide areas, while in other parts of the country possession of metal objects as items of status (Clarke *et al.* 1985, 101–3) was the key to their circulation. Support for the thesis that production may have been concentrated in areas adjacent to the coast comes from the observation that the only sources of known metal production in the Bronze Age are in the south-west of the country, particularly at Mount Gabriel, Co. Cork (W. F. O'Brien 1990).

The extensive mining of surface copper beds at Mount Gabriel took place particularly during the period 1700 –1500 BC during the latest stages of the Early Bronze Age and into the Middle

Bronze Age. In his detailed study of this complex W. F. O'Brien (1990) suggests that this indicates increased metal production at a period broadly contemporary with the use of Harbison's (1969b) Ballyvalley and Derryniggin axes. Looking at the distribution of the different types of Early Bronze Age axes in Munster (Fig. 6:12), it is significant that there appears to be a shift over time towards a greater number of axes occurring in the northern part of the province during the later stages of the period. This would appear to support O'Brien's thesis (1990, 288–9) that control over ore supplies and the distribution of metalwork would have placed groups in the south-west in a pivotal position in regional exchange systems. It is the emergence of local élites there with a position of regional prominence that O'Brien sees reflected in the appearance of the stone circle complex of monuments. Individuals and élite groups in other areas, such as north Munster, may have expressed their position, status and prestige through the possession and deposition of portable items, which in some cases at least are likely to have been produced outside the region of circulation and deposition.

We have made this argument above particularly in relation to axes but it is perhaps most clearly expressed in the sheet-gold lunulae and sun-discs (Taylor 1970; 1980). These are personal items, sharing the same geometrical decoration found on the contemporary ceramics and some of the Ballyvalley axes and more occasionally on Derryniggin axes. The precious nature of the raw material, the personal decorative nature of these objects and their deliberate deposition singly or in pairs all indicate the increasing importance of differentiation within society and the growth of authority vested in symbols of personal power. What is particularly interesting is that gold objects are all apparently eventually taken out of circulation and we can see different uses of material culture, some certainly conveying an expression of power and prestige, during the Middle Bronze Age.

7 LATER SECOND-MILLENNIUM BC DEVELOPMENTS: RECOGNISING THE MIDDLE BRONZE AGE

Moving beyond the metalwork

The period after 1700 BC heralds a number of important changes, of which the most widely recognised is in metalworking and especially in the technology of bronze production. Until recently it has been difficult to identify other elements of the Middle Bronze Age (c. 1700–1200 BC) in the archaeological record (e.g. Herity and Eogan 1977, 164–6; but see Burgess 1974, 167–9) and there are strong elements of continuity from the Early Bronze Age, for example in relation to mortuary practices, especially the use of cordoned urns (Brindley 1980). A much more comprehensive view of the period is now emerging in Ireland and the wide array of evidence is amenable to social assessment, as well as to the identification of external contacts on a basis other than just that of the metal artifacts. Only a small number of domestic sites can definitely be assigned to this period but of note is the fact that three of them were enclosed. The site at Carrigillihy has already been discussed. On the shore of Cullyhanna Lough, Co. Armagh, a roughly circular stockade of upright posts 16.7m in diameter enclosed two structures (Hodges 1958). One of these was an oval post-built house (6.5m by 5.3m) with internal timber supports for the roof. The second was represented by a semicircle of posts with a maximum diameter of 4.6m; this was apparently open on the eastern side and may have been a shelter or workshop. The site was dated by dendrochronology to c. 1526 BC (Mallory and McNeill 1991,

108). A possible domestic site at Raheen, Co. Limerick (Gowen 1988, 84–94), was apparently enclosed within a double ditch. Within the enclosure were a hearth and a pit. Material recovered included sherds of at least twelve coarse vessels of the type found in nearby burial sites, part of the mould for a palstave axe, and fragments of cattle, pig and sheep/goat bones. The settlement at Downpatrick with two circular houses had an assemblage dominated by cordoned urn pottery (Pollock and Waterman 1964). While the nature of the activity at *fulachta fiadh* is well understood, their place in the settlement pattern is less clear. The dating evidence indicates a concentration of sites in this period (Brindley and Lanting 1989/90). In south Limerick they can be shown to be part of an integrated system including domestic and burial sites, and this may prove to be the case elsewhere. Very large numbers are known especially from County Cork (Power 1990) where they occur in the same areas as the various elements of the stone circle complex, with which they also overlap chronologically. Whether the use of the sites as cooking places was primarily part of the domestic or the ritual landscape is uncertain, but the Limerick evidence at least shows that they were located within the main settlement zone. The *fulachta fiadh* in Kilkenny (Condit 1990) have a complementary distribution to both ring-ditches and other Bronze Age monumental sites.

Bronze-manufacturing centres such as that at Site D, Lough Gur, are too rare to determine whether they represent the standard form of production site. Site D consisted of a small hut and yielded part of a composite stone and clay mould for casting a palstave, while fragments of clay moulds for the production of socket-looped spearheads and a clay crucible were also found (Ó Ríordáin 1954, 400–3), as well as a bronze knife blade possibly related to razor-type objects. As discussed in the last chapter, extensive research on the copper mines of west Cork has shown that large-scale extraction was occurring at this stage in the Bronze Age (W. F. O'Brien 1990). The Mount Gabriel mines appear to have been a major element in the production and exchange mechanisms of south-west Munster. However, it is clear that they also impacted on areas further north, especially on the region around Lough Gur (Grogan 1989). The expansion of

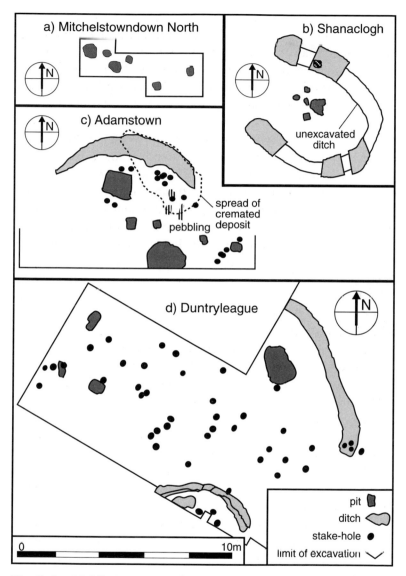

Fig. 7:1—Middle Bronze Age burial sites at Mitchelstowndown North, Shanaclogh, Adamstown and Duntryleague,Co. Limerick (after Gowen 1988).

settlement in the region around Mount Gabriel is indicated by the large number of monuments of the stone circle complex (e.g. Ó Nualláin 1984a; 1984b; 1988) which have a wide range of ritual, including funerary, aspects. The gradual shift northward in the distributions of broadly successive Bronze Age axe types has already been noted, and although axes, such as those of Ballyvalley type (Harbison 1969b), are found within the Mount Gabriel region, the known mines — and possibly others of this period — appear to have acted as suppliers for areas of major consumption further to the north. The restricted range and types of artifacts typical of this period in Ireland — the major examples being razors, dirks and rapiers, palstaves, wing-flanged axes and socket-looped spearheads—and the relatively small overall numbers of objects known suggest that access to these items was still restricted. That these objects served as items of conspicuous consumption is indicated by the fact that many of them were formally deposited in specific locations in the landscape.

The burial record

A complex array of elements occur within the burial tradition of the period (Fig. 7:1). This includes isolated pit cremations, enclosed and unenclosed pit cemeteries, barrows, ring-ditches and mounds as well as the use of earlier megalithic tombs. There is a contrast between the evident continuity of some Early Bronze Age customs and burial sites and the alterations in treatment of the body and the form and number of grave-goods. There is a gradual disappearance of the prestigious cinerary urns of the developed Early Bronze Age, and although the cordoned urn — in all cases containing cremations — is the characteristic funerary vessel of the early part of the period, it is then superseded by coarse, flat-bottomed pottery which was already in use in domestic and funerary contexts. Dates from Altanagh, Co. Tyrone (Williams 1986, 71–2), and Carrig (Grogan 1990) show the continuation of cordoned urns up to and beyond 1450 BC, i.e. well into the Middle Bronze Age. The change-over which occurred at this time also involved the abandonment of other high-status burial offerings and the widespread adoption of token cremation burial accompanied by the coarse pottery as complete vessels or sherds (see discussion in Grogan 1988b, 152–6).

Continuity is attested at three important cemeteries which demonstrate the ongoing use of places with an already long history of burial. At Cush, Co. Limerick, there is a funerary complex dating from the Early Bronze Age to the Iron Age (Fig. 7:2); three of the sites here have burials dating to the Middle Bronze Age. At Cush 3 the flat cemetery produced a burial in an inverted cordoned urn and another was in an inverted coarse vessel, while coarse sherds may have come from a burial disturbed by the later ringfort (Ó Ríordáin 1940). The site also produced two unaccompanied cremations. To the west a flat cemetery contained two cordoned urn burials, one of which was

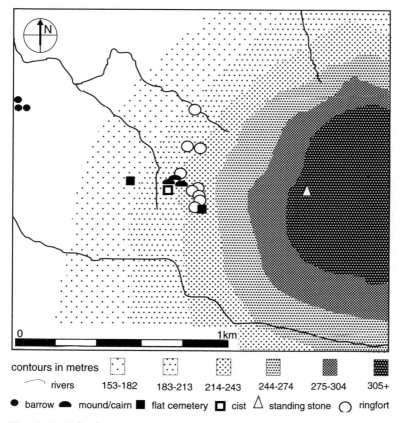

Fig. 7:2—The funerary complex at Cush, Co. Limerick.

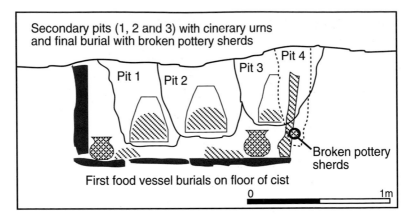

Fig. 7:3—Burial sequence in Grave D, Carrig, Co. Wicklow (after Grogan 1990).

upright (Rynne and O'Sullivan 1967). Both urns contained razors. The cemetery cairn at Knockast, Co. Westmeath (Hencken and Movius 1934), produced three cordoned urns, two of them of unusual form (Kavanagh 1976, 376), including one undecorated vessel. These two pots may indicate interchange between domestic and purely funerary ceramics. Three of the burials at Knockast were accompanied by coarse pottery. Another cemetery with burial continuity stretching back into the Early Bronze Age is at Carrig, Co. Wicklow, overlooking the valley of the River Liffey (Grogan 1990). Here (Fig. 7:3), in a cist used originally for cremations accompanied by vases, two later cordoned urns (in pits 1 and 2 in Fig. 7:3), one containing a razor, were in turn succeeded by a large inverted urn with heavy cord decoration in pit 3. Subsequently a pit (4) dug into the cist fill was used for a token cremation with sherds of coarse pottery. To the north of the site another cremation was partly contained in an inverted coarse pot in a small pit. The remainder of the cremation and part of the pyre were packed around the vessel. The pit was sealed by a large capstone and marked by a standing stone.

A long sequence of burial but lacking an Early Bronze Age element is apparent at the barrow complex of Carrowjames, Co.

Mayo (J. Raftery 1938–9). Tumulus 1 had a central cremation accompanied by a razor, as did the primary burials in Tumuli 2 and 3 which were contained in cordoned urns. All three sites also produced unaccompanied cremations. A coarse vessel lying on its side at Tumulus 4 was interpreted as a pre-barrow burial (J. Raftery 1940–1, 21), but it was on the very outer edge of the surrounding bank and could just as easily post-date the barrow.

At Carrowjames, and also at Cush, there is funerary activity dating to the Iron Age, and at the Carrig cemetery Late Bronze Age burials occur. This demonstrates a further element of continuity in the location of burial. The long-term persistence of burial traditions, such as token cremation, coarse pottery and barrows or ring-ditches, is dealt with at a later stage but it is worth noting that these elements first make their appearance in the Middle Bronze Age. This marks the waning of an earlier tradition of highly ornate funerary ceramics being used in a mortuary practice which involved the interment of most if not all of the burnt or unburnt remains of individuals and that had its roots back in the Neolithic.

In County Limerick several excavations have drawn attention to the concentration of burial and other activity along the river valleys of the Morningstar, Camoge and Mahore to the south of Lough Gur. The results of excavations indicate the nature and variability of formal mortuary practice in this region during the Middle Bronze Age. Although many of the sites had been truncated by later agricultural activity it is evident that ring-ditches and, to a lesser extent, barrows formed the principal markers of formal burials (Fig. 7:1). These have produced extensive evidence for the deposition of token cremations, occasionally accompanied by coarse vessels (usually upright) or sherds. Other sites include enclosed and unenclosed pit cemeteries and isolated pit burials (Gowen 1988; Grogan 1988b). Several of these sites have been radiocarbon-dated to the period between 1500 and 1300 BC; the persistence of this burial rite is indicated by the date of 1000 BC from a pit burial at Raheenamadra (Grogan 1989). Only one site, Adamstown (see Fig. 7:1c), contained evidence of inhumation: an adult male mandible was found in a large rectangular pit which also

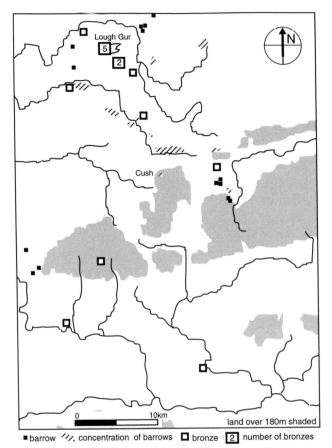

Fig. 7:4—
Distribution
of barrows
and Middle
Bronze Age
bronze
artifacts in
south County
Limerick and
north County
Cork.

■ barrow ⁒⁒. concentration of barrows ☐ bronze ☐2 number of bronzes

contained burnt and unburnt animal bones. Stake-holes alongside the pit suggest that it may have been within some form of cover or structure (Gowen 1988, 94–8). Many of the sites had evidence of other activity represented by pits, post- and stake-holes and occasional fireplaces; the small ring-ditch at Duntryleague 9 was apparently contained within a large enclosure defined by a ditch (Gowen 1988, 72–8; see Fig. 7:1d).

Over 400 barrows or ring-ditches have been identified in the area between Lough Gur in the north and the Ballyhoura Mountains in north Cork to the south (Grogan 1989); many of these occur within sometimes extensive cemeteries (Figs 7:4 and 7:5). Although the use of some sites in the Neolithic and Early

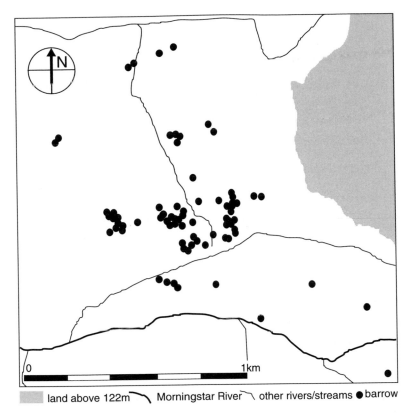

land above 122m ⌐⌐ Morningstar River ⌐⌐ other rivers/streams ● barrow

Fig. 7:5—The barrow cemetery at Mitchelstowndown North, Co. Limerick.

Bronze Age is well attested, the vast majority of those excavated have produced convincing Middle Bronze Age burial. The average diameter of the sites is 10m, with 70% falling between 6m and 10m. Major clusters are represented at Mitchelstown-down North (58 sites, Fig. 7:5), Ballynamona/Lissard (41), Elton (27) and Tankardstown (20), but many smaller cemeteries also occur. The sites are concentrated along the flood-plains of the rivers on poor soils. They are often located opposite each other on either side of the rivers or tributaries and would appear to represent a strong element of territoriality (Grogan 1989). The distribution pattern suggests that the cemeteries occur on the periphery of small territories stretching back off the valley floor.

Fulachta fiadh, which are otherwise rare in Limerick, also occur within the clusters, as did the settlement site at Raheen. While the evidence from the extensive complex of activity in Limerick is as yet unparalleled in Ireland, close comparisons can be made with areas of Britain (e.g. along the Great Ouse Valley, Buckinghamshire: Green 1974).

It would appear from the Limerick evidence that we should think in terms of people having a localised sense of identity which may have been expressed both in the use and the location of cemeteries. The cemeteries do not appear to have had formal boundaries, but on the other hand there is very careful definition and bounding of space within individual sites. We argue that the focus of settlement would have been at a higher location in these river valleys, but the site at Raheen suggests that there may not have been a total separation of the cemeteries from the everyday, domestic landscape. However, if the cemeteries can be regarded as being in a largely peripheral position in relation to the focus of settlement this could be interpreted literally as a retreat of the ancestors as they are seen as having less power and relevance for the contemporary community (e.g. Hodder 1982, 196). Mortuary practice may have centred on the ceremonies prior to and surrounding burial and on the individuals who were being buried rather than on the long-term presence of the ancestors close to the community. If this interpretation is valid then the distance between settlement and cemetery could have provided the context for the development of more ceremonial funerals.

The ongoing importance of reference to the past is indicated by the use of some Neolithic monuments as a focus for burial and other activity which continued from the Early Bronze Age into this period. At the wedge tomb of Largantea, Co. Derry, cordoned urn sherds were in a secondary position to Beaker and bowls (Kavanagh 1976, 361) while coarse pottery and a razor occurred at a higher level (Herring 1938). At Loughash, Co. Tyrone, cordoned pottery from the chamber, which also contained sherds of Beaker and a vase urn, was associated with a razor, and part of a palstave mould also came from the tomb (Davies 1939). Moulds for socket-looped spearheads came from the wedge tombs at Moylisha, Co. Wicklow (Ó h-Icheadha

1946), and Lough Gur (Ó Ríordáin and Ó h-Icheadha 1955).

The use and construction of stone circles continues into the Middle Bronze Age. Burial appears to have formed an integral component of the range of activities carried on at these sites. Burial, as we have discussed above, may have become in many cases more of a symbolic gesture rather than involving the placement of all the cremated remains in the earth. Token cremations occur at Drombeg (one accompanied by sherds of coarse pottery; Fahy 1959), Bohonagh (Fahy 1961) and Reenascreena South (Fahy 1962). Radiocarbon dates from Cashelkeelty, Co. Kerry, where there was a cremation in a slab-covered pit (O'Kelly 1989, 237) indicate that the circle there was constructed towards the beginning of the Late Bronze Age, and the excavator suggested that the associated stone row dated to 1150 BC (Lynch 1981, 66). The stone rows at Maughanasilly, Co. Cork, and Dromatouk, Co. Kerry, date to around 1500 BC (Lynch 1981, 71, 73). The wider complex of monuments which includes the circles and alignments cannot in its entirety be dated on the basis of this scant evidence, but it is clear that many of the sites date to the Middle Bronze Age. This is also the case with the circles, cairns and alignments of mid-Ulster (e.g. Beaghmore; Pilcher 1969).

Death, display and deposition in the Middle Bronze Age

There are two principal contexts in which we can observe formal, repetitive human behaviour in the Middle Bronze Age. The complexities of the burial record, which is one of these contexts, have been outlined above, and the second such context is the deliberate deposition of metal artifacts. While these are apparently very separate activities a link can be established between them. During this period there appears to have been a movement in the display of social status away from the burials and towards the formal deposition of prestige objects. Apart from razors (see Binchy 1967; Kavanagh 1991), metal objects of this period do not appear to have been considered appropriate as grave-offerings, but they were increasingly placed in special, usually wetland, contexts. The following discussion attempts to explain how and why emphasis in display apparently shifted from

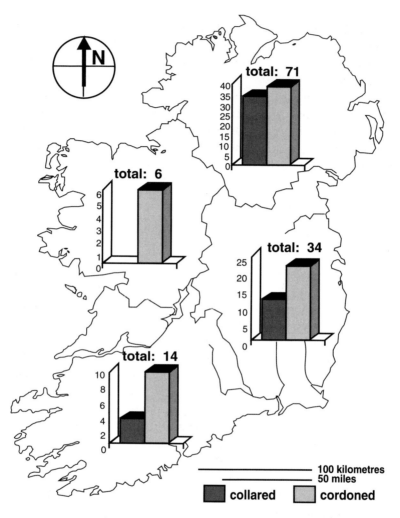

Fig. 7:6—Distribution by province of (burials associated with) collared and cordoned urns (after Kavanagh 1976 and Waddell 1990a with additions).

burial to deposition.

As outlined above, there appear to be two stages in the development of the burial traditions of the period. The first is marked by the extensive adoption of the cordoned urn with its comparative wealth of associated grave-goods, including razors and, less frequently, faience and small accessory vessels. The more restricted use of collared urns may also be a feature, and a comparison of the distribution maps of these urn types suggests an element of regionalisation in the traditions of the period (Fig. 7:6), with collared urns outside Ulster restricted to a limited occurrence in the eastern areas of Leinster and Munster. Indeed, it is also interesting that the use of cordoned urns may indicate regional or more localised preferences, as suggested, for example, by the clustering of the cordoned urns within the province of Leinster in the area of County Louth (see Kavanagh 1976, 368–70). The range and number of grave associations, other than pottery, is wider for the cordoned urns than for any other ceramic form of the Bronze Age, and this would suggest their restriction to an increasingly ostentatious élite. There is a very strong association of razors or razor-knives with cordoned urns; Kavanagh (1991, 83) noted that in the eighteen cases where they were contained within a cinerary urn fourteen of the urns were cordoned, and there is no definite evidence that they were associated with the other urn types. There are eleven related burials which consist of cremations with associated razors and occasional other artifacts. Cremations of both male and female adults and occasionally children are recorded from both collared and cordoned urn burials (Fig. 7:7), but the suggestion that power within this élite resided with adult males is supported by the fact that burials with razors, whether or not contained in cordoned urns, are exclusively those of adult males (Kavanagh 1991, 83), as in the case of the one definite cordoned urn burial in a group of three burials within a ring-ditch at Urbalreagh, Co. Antrim (Waterman 1968).

The second stage in the development of mortuary practice sees a change in the burial customs towards the apparent predominance of unaccompanied cremations, cremations in coarse urns or cremations associated with sherds of coarse pottery, marking an important break with the traditions of the Early Bronze Age. Many of the cremations have been described as consisting of small, minute or token quantities, and this is particularly evident in the case of those burials recently excavated in Limerick (Ó Donnabháin 1988, 192). The comminuted nature

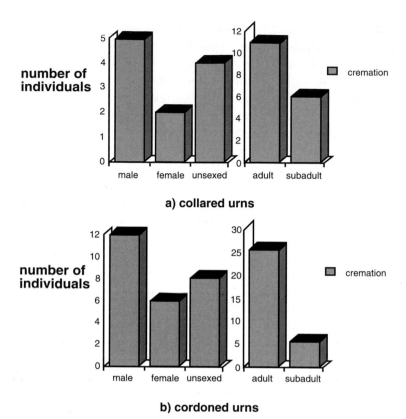

a) collared urns

b) cordoned urns

Fig. 7:7—Collared and cordoned urn burials. Features of rite, gender (adults) and general age groups associated with (a) collared and (b) cordoned urns.

of the bones has been widely observed (e.g. J. Raftery 1938–9; 1940–1). This token and comminuted nature of the cremations as a representation of the individual in burial could be paralleled in the material culture by the common occurrence of pot sherds rather than complete vessels. These characteristics of the burial itself also suggest that other portions of the cremated bone and parts of the pots may have been used at different stages in an extended mortuary ritual where much of the ceremonial emphasis may have been placed on the cremation, funeral and burial rather than on just what was placed in the grave. Apart from the pottery and flint artifacts, grave-goods are rare, a feature contrasting sharply with the cordoned urn burials.

On the other hand, it is clear that the background of these practices was within the cordoned urn burial tradition. While inversion of a cordoned urn over a cremation was the standard practice, the alternative arrangement of placing the cordoned urn in an upright position was also used and is discussed by Waddell (1990a, 14) and Kavanagh (1976, 332). Ten of the 42 cordoned urn vessels whose position in the grave was noted were upright. This custom continued, and of the sixteen complete coarse pots for which information is available six were upright, seven were inverted and three lay on their sides. Furthermore, four cemeteries — Carrig, Cush, Harristown (J. Hawkes 1941) and Knockast — with cremations contained in cordoned urns also produced burials contained in or associated with coarse vessels. At Altanagh the radiocarbon dating of an unaccompanied cremation to this period ties in with the presence of three cordoned urn burials (Williams 1986, 40–3). Cremation dominated the burial rite and the general custom of single burial also persisted. However, as has already been observed, well over 25% of burials in the Early Bronze Age contained multiple remains. With the widespread adoption of coarse urns, collective burial was abandoned and only a single instance of more than one individual in a grave, that of Mitchelstowndown North burial 1 (adult and infant), has been noted. As yet there is no clear evidence to determine the cause of the move away from prestigious urns and other high-status grave-goods. The initial impression is that an alteration occurred in the role of burial as an indicator of social status. If the extensive Limerick barrow complexes are replicated elsewhere, it might seem that there were far more burials in this than in earlier periods, suggesting a widening of access to formal burial in the community, but the emphasis may simply have shifted to other aspects of the funerary ritual.

While there is a possible trend towards greater egalitarianism in the burial tradition of the period, this would be very much at variance with the evidence from other aspects of ritual behaviour. The absence of metal artifacts from graves has been noted as a feature of the post-cinerary urn stage of Middle Bronze Age

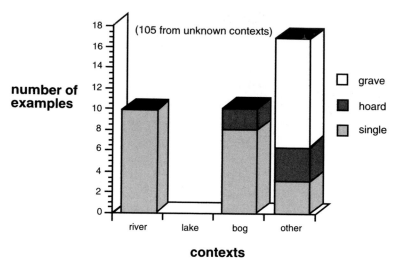

Fig. 7:8—Context of discovery of Early and Middle Bronze Age daggers (after Harbison 1969a).

mortuary practice, but at this time the deposition of objects, in particular bronzes, shows a marked bias towards placement in bogs, rivers and lakes. This custom of offerings (R. Bradley 1990, 37), whether votive or inspired by socially based ritual, is not new to this period but it now assumes sufficient proportions to constitute a characteristic aspect of ceremonial behaviour in the Middle Bronze Age. Taking Harbison's (1969b) axe typology as representing a broad chronological sequence, it would seem that during the course of the Early Bronze Age there was a decline in the deposition of axes in bogs and hoards. However, by the time of the emergence of Harbison's latest type, the Derryniggin axe, a corresponding increase in the use of rivers and lakes is evident and 14% of the axes come from these contexts. Early Bronze Age daggers show an interesting duality of context, with significant numbers deposited in rivers and bogs and the majority of the dryland finds deposited with burials (Fig 7:8). The dirks and rapiers which appear to replace daggers in the Middle Bronze Age show an even more marked association with wet places: 45.7% of the Irish rapiers with details of discovery have been

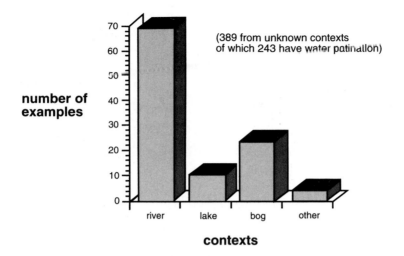

<figure>*Fig. 7:9—Context of discovery of Middle Bronze Age dirks and rapiers (after Burgess and Gerloff 1981).*</figure>

found on wet sites and none are known to have been found with a burial. The pattern of deposition (Fig. 7:9) for the four main types of dirk and rapier (see Burgess and Gerloff 1981) shows the dominance of wetland deposition. This pattern is even more remarkable when only those objects with known circumstances of recovery are taken into consideration. Then the respective percentages for the four rapier types in wetland locations are 26%, 38%, 45% and 51%. Again, if these types represent a broad chronological sequence there is the strong suggestion that the pattern of wetland deposition became more important during the course of the Middle Bronze Age. It is evident from Figure 7:9 that rivers formed the most desirable locations; 68% of all rapiers with known wetland locations are from rivers, compared with 22% from bogs and 10% in lakes. It is also clear that certain specific places of deposition were used frequently, such as Keelogue on the River Shannon with ten rapiers or Lough Gur with three. Although the exact find-spots are all too rarely recorded, some rivers and lakes appear to have been regarded, in this period and in others, as especially auspicious for these deposits. The River Shannon has yielded 31 rapiers (including those from Keelogue), the Bann fourteen, the Barrow eight, while three have come from the Erne and four from Lough Erne. The increased trend of formal deposition in wetlands contrasts with the virtual disappearance of hoards in the Middle Bronze Age. Although all were deposited in bogs only five hoards are known (Eogan 1983, 6). None of these contained rapiers or produced more than three objects. The formal disposal of prestige bronzes was now largely confined to wetland deposition, particularly in the open water of rivers, and appears to have involved deposition of single items. This activity forms a core element in the ritual of the period.

While there may have been a gradual widening of access to metal during the Bronze Age there can be little doubt that most of the objects still represented valuable items not to be lightly discarded. They would not have been accessible to the bulk of society. If, therefore, only the élite could afford to dispose of their possessions in this manner, the apparent egalitarianism of society suggested by the burial record may have been as a result of the separation of the public display of social status and associated ceremonies from the act of burial itself. On the other hand, a wide range of elaborate behaviour may lie behind the simple appearance of the developed burial tradition. The token nature of the burials and grave-goods, the frequent comminution of both, may in itself indicate a complex series of stages within the burial ritual, while the effort required to provide covering mounds or barrows or the encircling features of ring-ditches also belies the apparent poverty of the graves suggested by the absence of high-status offerings. The use of barrows and ring-ditches shows a continuing concern with marking places of burial in the landscape. Looking at the British evidence Barrett (1990, 186) has suggested that what was happening in this context was the extension of the funerary practice to include a wider audience and a greater range of activity which would give witness to the status of the deceased. Barrett and Needham (1988, 133) see the switch in Britain from the deposition of daggers in graves to deposition in rivers as part of a more extensive process of votive deposition connected with the funerary ritual.

The changes in the burial ritual do not necessarily provide evidence for an alteration in the fabric of society but they do argue for a dramatic shift in the patterns of ceremonial behaviour in the period. The Limerick evidence shows the emergence of a complex landscape organisation, with extensive cemeteries, domestic sites and *fulachta fiadh* forming an integrated pattern. The number and range of Middle Bronze Age sites and the degree to which they cluster indicate the possibility of at least localised population expansion during the period. The cemeteries appear to cluster on the edge of territories which may have been more formalised and more consciously defined than in earlier times. The contrast with Kilkenny has already been noted, although in this area the cemeteries are also peripheral and, as with Limerick, the combined distributions of Middle Bronze Age elements suggest territorial divisions based on the river systems. If the rivers had this importance in everyday life it is not surprising that they appear to have been increasingly drawn into ceremonial activity and to have symbolised a different world. Rivers, together with lakes and bogs, are the principal contexts for the conspicuous disposal of wealth in the Middle Bronze Age.

The deterioration of the climate of north-western Europe has been widely accepted even if the detailed evidence is not always indisputably supportive (Burgess 1980, 237, 239; Coles and Harding 1979, 459, 475–6). Higher levels of rainfall and lower summer temperatures seem to have brought about a gradual but marked disimprovement during the Middle Bronze Age. More dramatic deterioration may have followed major volcanic eruptions in the periods around 1628 BC (Baillie and Munro 1988) and the Hekla 3 eruption in Iceland in 1159 BC (Baillie 1989). It has been suggested that the latter event was largely responsible for the collapse of the social and economic systems that had been developing through the earlier Bronze Age and that Late Bronze Age developments were a reaction to it (Burgess 1989, 325; Woodman 1992, 310). We have suggested here that human activity and settlement were spread across the landscape in a complex manner. In this context it seems very unlikely that the end of the Middle Bronze Age can be sought simply in environmental change. It is interesting, furthermore, that Baillie

(1991, 240) has observed that none of the modern volcanic dust-veil events have given rise to the supposedly dire consequences of prehistoric examples. So if these climatic changes had an effect the consequences were neither necessarily dramatic nor direct and would be difficult to separate from other developments within Irish society. They may have influenced a shift in the economic basis of society which in turn may have been one of a number of factors influencing the structure of the power balance both within and between individual communities. It might be these changes in turn that are reflected by the burial evidence, with élites moving the affirmation of their social status away from the traditional burial context by incorporating burial into a wider range of funerary ceremonies and a more public display of their wealth and standing through the deposition of valuable offerings. At a broader level these social changes may also have been aimed at and have resulted in a greater degree of communal cohesion and may have been based on a more defined sense of territory, as reflected, for instance, in the distribution of the cemeteries in the Limerick area belonging to the later part of the period.

8 LATE BRONZE AGE SETTLEMENT AND SOCIETY: SOCIAL COMPLEXITY AND REGIONAL DIVERSITY

New aspects of the Late Bronze Age

Traditionally this period has been seen as very much biased towards one category of evidence, the metalwork, and offering little else for the archaeologist to work with. As we have seen in the previous chapter, this material on its own can potentially give a lot of information and help us to pose questions about the nature of human behaviour and society as well as to shed light on the available technology. Interestingly, this period may have been the first in which bronze objects came widely into use. There is clear evidence for continuity in, and indeed increased concentration on, the deliberate destruction or removal from circulation through deposition of high-quality artifacts. What makes the Late Bronze Age (1200–600 BC) different also when compared to earlier periods is the much greater visibility in the surviving archaeological record of the practice of depositing hoards. Within this period it is possible to recognise through the metalwork an early phase (Bishopsland, 1200–1000 BC) and a later phase (Dowris, from 900 BC on) separated by an apparent gap in the record into which little material fits (known as the Roscommon phase). This is of course purely an archaeological construct and it is worth bearing in mind that our use of prehistoric metal objects to determine the chronology of what are, compared to the date ranges used in earlier periods, tight dating brackets may be an unjustifiable assumption. While the

Late Bronze Age is still dominated by the undoubtedly impressive amount of metal artifacts, our perception of the period is increasingly being altered as a result of additions to the archaeological database over the last twenty years. For example, in the sphere of settlement, while the absolute number of known sites is still small there is a variety in the evidence which clearly suggests social differentiation. This backs up the picture offered by the metalwork (e.g. Eogan 1964; 1974; 1983) of a period during which social organisation became more complex and regional divisions may have become more apparent.

The treatment of the dead

The burial record is fairly sparse and indicates that it is not a sphere where social differences can easily be deciphered. For these reasons it has been treated in a rather cursory fashion in previous discussions of the period. Yet it has an important role from a number of different perspectives. It both continues the trends that emerged in the Middle Bronze Age and forms the background to the burial tradition of the Iron Age (B. Raftery 1981; B. O'Brien 1990). The scarcity of burials that can be definitely dated to the Late Bronze Age must be seen in the context of formal, datable burial practices becoming less visible. In previous periods, as we have seen, only a section of the population merited such treatment. What happened in the Late Bronze Age is that burial rites continued, as in the Middle Bronze Age, to be largely undifferentiated but also that formal burial sites, at least at first glance, appear to have become less common. It is not that people were not buried, but our inability to identify significant numbers suggests that in most cases, regardless of status, people were buried in a simple manner. It is, after all, the absence of accompanying objects that leads to our difficulty in recognising Late Bronze Age burials. Regarding individuals of some social standing, the trend that began in the Middle Bronze Age of placing emphasis on the rites and practices surrounding their funeral, as opposed to their actual mode and place of burial, appears to have continued. Instead of objects being placed formally with the deceased they may have been put in a different context by the living to achieve the same goals of demonstrating the status of those individuals who controlled wealth (e.g. Eogan 1964, 285; R. Bradley 1990, 102–3). It seems very plausible when we consider the archaeological record to suggest that now, even more clearly than in the Middle Bronze Age, it is in the sphere of life rather than death that differences in social standing were expressed.

The known formal burials are predominantly cremations, often representing only a token burial deposit, which were placed either in a coarse upright pot or directly into a small pit. In some cases burials were accompanied only by sherds of similarly coarse pottery. Most known burials were placed within or associated with a circular ring-ditch or barrow. It would appear that in some instances burials took place near the cremation pyre and that the remains of the fire were incorporated into the burial rite, although it is possible that the mixing of charcoal and cremated bone may result from another set of ceremonies. Examples of burials that have been seen as belonging to this period, because of their associations and/or radiocarbon dates, include Rathgall, Co. Wicklow (B. Raftery 1973), Mullaghmore barrow A (Mogey *et al.* 1956) and Ballybeen (Mallory 1984a) in Co. Down, Altanagh, Co. Tyrone (Williams 1986), Carrig, Co. Wicklow (Grogan 1990), and Carnkenny in Co. Tyrone (Lynn 1973–4).

At Rathgall, within a hillfort and associated with an extensive area of Late Bronze Age settlement, was a shallow, ditched enclosure (a ring-ditch) enclosing an area 16m in diameter (Fig. 8:1). At the centre of this area there was an unaccompanied cremation deposit of a young adult in a stone-lined pit which had been dug through fire-reddened soil, possibly the location of the pyre. There were a large number of stake-holes clustered around it in a U-shaped setting open to the east. A second pit towards the northern edge of the stake-holes held the cremated remains of a child and a third, to the south-east, between the stake-holes and the ditch, contained the cremated remains of an adult and child in an coarse, upright pot. Dense black organic material with flecks of burnt bone was packed around the vessel; this may have come from the cremation pyre. Significantly, one of the other pits close to this latter burial contained a fragment of a leaf-shaped sword of bronze, an incomplete socketed bronze

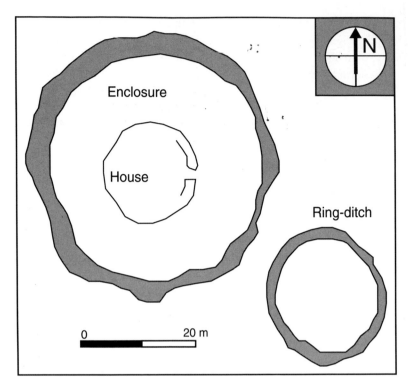

Fig. 8:1—Schematic plan of the house, enclosure and ring-ditch complex at Rathgall, Co. Wicklow (after B. Raftery 1987).

spearhead and a chisel, found together in the upper fill (B. Raftery 1973, 294). What is particularly interesting here is the complexity of human behaviour seen in the rites associated with burial rather than in the burials themselves. Also, the hoard of metal objects was deliberately placed within the enclosure but separated from the burial deposits. This gives an important link between burial and metalwork hoard evidence which we shall return to below.

An interesting aspect of mortuary practice is the evidence for the deliberate placement of burials, or more frequently just a human skull, in a wetland context (see Burgess 1976). For example, Waddell (1984) has shown that the bronze dagger/knife found driven through the upper part of a skull in the bank of a stream flowing out of Drumman More Lake, Co. Armagh, is of socketed form (see Wilde 1861, 465). It would fit into Hodges's (1956) Kells type, dating to the Dowris phase. This is an early nineteenth-century find and a near-contemporary report suggests that the skull was part of a complete inhumation. While it is difficult to assess the degree of formality of burial in this case, it does point to the possibility of deliberate human burial in wet places and/or human sacrifice. The placement of three human skulls under the floor level of the lakeshore Late Bronze Age settlement at Ballinderry, Co. Offaly (Hencken 1942, 17), should also be considered as clearly deliberate (see Fig. 8:6). These belonged to one probable adult female and two probable adult males. The latter two skulls had been cut after death; all that was buried of one was a rectangular fragment, and the frontal bone — the facial region — had been severed from the other. This suggests that a particular significance was attached to the unburnt human skull at this time. In this context it is relevant to recall that the only evidence for inhumation burial in the Middle Bronze Age is the jaw of an adult male from Adamstown, Co. Limerick, and that there is a tradition stretching back to the Neolithic of the unburnt human skull being treated and deposited in special ways and places (e.g. Hartnett 1957; Hartwell 1991). Another example of this deliberate deposition of part of a skull comes from the King's Stables — a purpose-dug, embanked pool close to and contemporary with Haughey's Fort in the Navan complex, Co. Armagh (Lynn 1977; Mallory and Warner 1988). Again it appears that this skull was cut after the individual, probably a young adult male, had died. In this case it was the facial part of the skull that had been deposited and it seemed likely that it had been previously deposited in another context (Delaney in Lynn 1977, 59–61). Two other possible examples of the same phenomenon are the skull, probably of an adult female, found a metre below the crannog at Lagore (Mitchell 1940, 29–30; Hencken 1950, 199) and the skull found in open water mud to the west of the Late Bronze Age occupation at Moynagh Lough, Co. Meath (J. Bradley, pers. comm.). In both cases the lower mandible was absent.

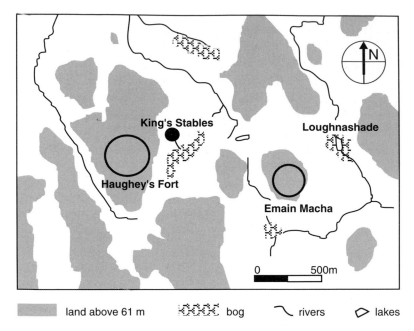

Fig. 8:2—The Navan complex, Co. Armagh, showing the spatial relationship of Haughey's Fort and the King's Stables, Emain Macha and Loughnashade.

A similar ritual treatment of skulls has been demonstrated for southern Britain by the discovery of numerous examples with Bronze Age and Iron Age metalwork in the River Thames and the recent dating of several of these skulls to the Late Bronze Age (Bradley and Gordon 1988). These skulls showed a bias towards adult males, as indeed is also indicated in the admittedly limited Irish evidence. The Ballinderry skull burials also raise interesting questions about the use of wet places. In the first instance it is clear that there is significant evidence for settlement in this kind of location during the Late Bronze Age. At the same time it is clear that throughout the period there was a continuity of the long-established pattern of using rivers, lakes and bogs as places for special deposits.

Reading the settlement and social landscape

Looking at the settlement record, the Dowris phase in particular up to very recently has been seen as dominated by lakeside settlement. But perhaps the most significant recent addition to our knowledge of the Late Bronze Age is the recognition of more dryland sites in different types of location and apparently of differing function and status. These include the large circular houses at Rathgall (B. Raftery 1976a; Fig. 8:1) and Emain Macha, Co. Armagh (Lynn 1986, but see also Lynn 1991a), the hillfort at Haughey's Fort in the Navan complex, about a kilometre north-west of the Emain Macha site (Mallory 1988; 1991a), the enclosure at Ballyveelish (Doody 1987b) and the hut cluster at Curraghatoor, both in Co. Tipperary (Doody 1987c; 1988; 1989; 1990; 1991). These sites are important in providing a more balanced database for the discussion of settlement problems in the Late Bronze Age.

It is helpful to use the evidence from Emain Macha and Haughey's Fort as a context for the broader assessment of these settlements. These sites are close to each other and within the same Navan site complex (Fig. 8:2). At Emain Macha, the clearest aspect of the Late Bronze Age activity is that within the enclosure at Site B around 800 BC a circular ditch was dug enclosing an area some 45m in diameter (Fig. 8:3). Inside the line of the ditch, at a distance of 4–5m, was a ring of pits which may originally have held posts. Between the eighth century BC and 100 BC a sequence of circular houses, 12–13m in diameter, were built within the enclosure, accompanied by larger, circular pens or paddocks 18–20m across (Lynn 1986). At Site A, about 40m to the south-east, three concentric slots, dug in the same sequence as those at Site B (Lynn 1986, 14), enclosed an area between 16.6m and 20.3m in diameter and are dated to 380–100 BC (Warner *et al.* 1990, 47; Fig. 8:4).

The relationship of these sequences of activity at Sites A and B with the bank and internal ditch that form the Emain Macha enclosure is not clear. The enclosure certainly appears to have been constructed by the Late Bronze Age (Weir 1987) and it could be earlier (Simpson 1989b; Mallory and McNeill 1991, 118). Excavation and survey at Haughey's Fort have shown it to

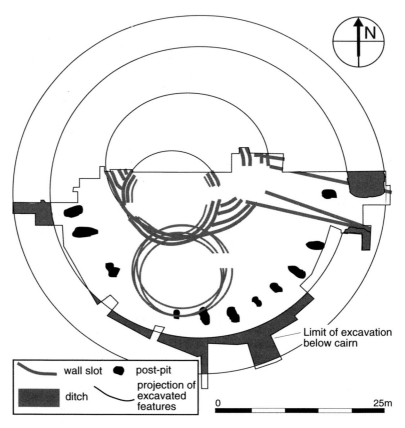

wall slot   ● post-pit

ditch   projection of excavated features

Limit of excavation below cairn

0   25m

Fig. 8:3—Plan of the ring-slot structures and enclosure at Site B, Emain Macha, Co. Armagh (after Lynn 1986).

be of triple bank and ditch form, enclosing an area of some eight hectares. Dates from the inner ditch and the interior of the site indicate that construction and occupation began between 1170 and 990 BC with the main period of use during the Late Bronze Age, although there is evidence for earlier and later use of the site. The evidence revealed by the ongoing excavation shows most notably the presence of a series of large, deep pits in the interior. The contents of these pits indicate that their final function was for the disposal of food debris and other domestic material. Most of the pits fall to the east of and within an area

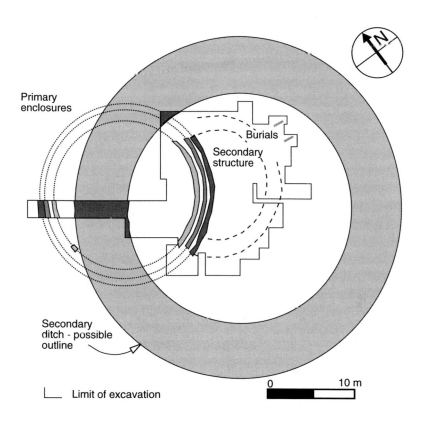

Fig. 8:4—Plan of ring-slot complex and other features at Site A, Emain Macha, Co. Armagh (after Lynn 1986).

bounded by 'stockade' fences defined by three alignments of post- and stake-holes (Mallory 1988; 1991a; 1991b).

Both Emain Macha and Haughey's Fort appear to represent the activities of people with high social rank. The reasons for saying this are that a considerable amount of effort went into the construction of the sites and they show evidence of lavish consumption, feasting and special types of artifacts (R. Bradley 1984, 25–31; Warner 1988). At Haughey's Fort evidence supporting this suggestion is the goldworking on the site, the presence of small gold ornaments (Mallory 1991a, 26) and the

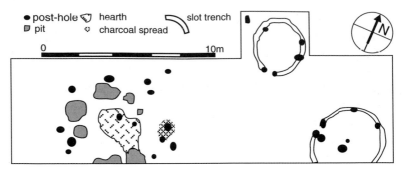

Fig. 8:5—Plan of part of the settlement at Curraghatoor, Co. Tipperary (after Doody 1987c).

unusually large size of some of the domesticated animals (McCormick 1991, 31). The faunal remains at Haughey's Fort are dominated by cattle. By contrast, Emain Macha has a dominance of pig in the faunal remains, a pattern associated with feasting as the pig is primarily a meat animal. In the early Irish historical literature pork was stated to be the most suitable meat at royal feasts (e.g. Lucas 1960). The most extraordinary feature of the faunal remains was the presence of the skull of a Barbary ape which, as Lynn (1986, 16) put it, underlines the prestige of the occupants. This is suggested also by the shale armlets and glass beads from the site.

Rathgall also has features that suggest that we should regard it as a high-status site. Here the ditched burial enclosure and large circular house mentioned above (Fig. 8:1) formed part of a settlement spread that also included a rectangular timber structure that may have been a metalworking workshop with several hundred fragments of clay moulds for casting objects such as swords and spearheads. The scale of metalworking here appears to be much greater than at any of the other sites (e.g. Herity and Eogan 1977, 170, 191–3) where there is evidence for this activity. Prestige items included a couple of small gold objects and glass beads (B. Raftery 1976a; 1987). While no definite association can be made between this settlement and the hillfort defences within which it occurs, it can be argued that, as at Haughey's Fort and Clogher in Co. Tyrone (Mallory and

McNeill 1991, 124), the hillfort may well be contemporary with the Late Bronze Age settlement.

Ballyveelish and Curraghatoor (Fig. 8:5), on the other hand, could be termed lower-order settlements. They were both found as part of the Cork – Dublin gas pipeline archaeological project (Cleary *et al.* 1987) and there was no visible surface indication of either site. They are dated to the Late Bronze Age by secure radiocarbon dates (see O'Kelly 1989, 348–9) and artifactual evidence. At Ballyveelish there was a roughly rectangular enclosure with an entrance to the east. Curraghatoor has so far produced evidence for up to eight small circular houses and other structures and fence lines, possibly at one stage within an enclosure. Both sites produced cereal remains and Ballyveelish produced a faunal assemblage dominated by cattle which McCormick (1987, 28) suggested did not show the development of dairying. Interestingly, although the structural remains at both sites and the faunal evidence at Ballyveelish can be interpreted as reflecting the lifestyle of ordinary people in contrast to the higher-status sites discussed above, they share with them the use of the same type of coarse, bucket-shaped pottery with either a flat, rounded or bevelled rim and a limited number of vessel forms. Pottery seems to have become a much more bland item of material culture as we do not find the range of forms and the decoration seen in the Neolithic and Early Bronze Age, but it does show a direct continuity with the Middle Bronze Age. It seems likely that the emphasis had shifted away from ceramics as a medium for the display of information. Indeed, the prevalence of large vessel forms on Late Bronze Age sites and the use of the same type of ceramics in burial practice suggest that the pottery may have had a limited functional range.

These sites join a small number of known Late Bronze Age settlements which were mostly in lakeside locations, such as Ballinderry (Fig. 8:6) (e.g. see discussion in Herity and Eogan 1977, 187–93). There have been a few additional lakeshore sites found more recently — at Moynagh Lough, Co. Meath, like Ballinderry 2 under a later crannog (J. Bradley, 1982/3; 1984; 1985/6; 1991), at Island McHugh, Co. Tyrone (Ivens *et al.* 1986), and Clonfinlough, Co. Offaly (Moloney 1991). Bearing in

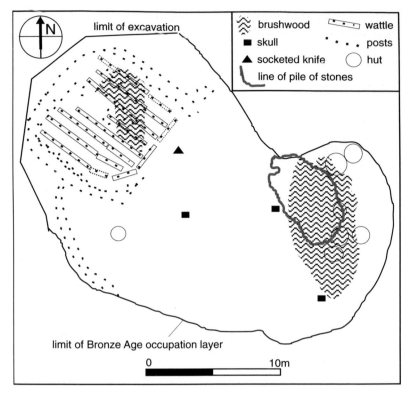

Fig. 8:6—Plan of the Late Bronze Age levels at Ballinderry 2, Co. Offaly (after Hencken 1942).

mind the number of the lakeshore type of site it is unclear whether they represent a significant concentration of sites around lakes, as Woodman (1985b, 271) has suggested, or alternatively just one element in a broader settlement pattern. It is also worth remembering in the context of the dryland sites that lakeshore sites may be much more visible in the archaeological record when landscape disturbance occurs. Their location and structure might suggest a seasonal and/or short-term use; on the other hand, the presence of pottery and saddle querns, for example, suggests an element of stability in the settlement activities. The use of piles to define areas not only has to do with stabilising wet ground but also suggests a concern with bounding space that we have also seen on the dryland sites. There is evidence for a range of activities: domestic and metalworking at Lough Eskragh, Co. Tyrone (Collins and Seaby 1960; Williams 1978), and ceremonial, as seen in the deposition of the three human skulls at Ballinderry 2 and the wooden box containing a hoard of bronze and other objects at the edge of the area occupied at Rathinaun, Lough Gara, Co. Sligo (Eogan 1983, 151–2).

Continued use of upland areas is indicated by field walls. Pollen evidence for this period also indicates an expansion of the farmed landscape (e.g. Mitchell 1986, 137–44), and the evidence for long-term clearance suggests that this was on an organised, permanent basis and of a mixed character, with perhaps an emphasis on cattle. Radiocarbon dating suggests that an impressive field wall system on Valencia Island, Co. Kerry, belongs to the final phase of the Bronze Age, and Mitchell (1989, 97–9) has commented that it may indicate organisation of the landscape for the control of stock.

It is clear that organisation of the landscape involved a concern not only with agriculture but also with the identification and continued recognition of special places where formal deposition of special items took place. This also provides us with a way of linking different zones in the landscape. Wet places —lakes, rivers and bogs— were peripheral from an agricultural perspective but they were used for settlement and had a central significance as places where much of the metalwork that we know from this period was deposited. What is becoming clear is that other artifacts were also deposited in these wet contexts. A striking example is the anthropomorphic wooden figure from a bog in Ralaghan, Co.Cavan (Mahr 1930), which until very recently had been regarded as Iron Age in date (e.g. B. Raftery 1983, 265–6). Recent reassessment of this and other anthropomorphic figures and a programme of radiocarbon dating (B. Coles 1990) have shown that this wooden figure is of Late Bronze Age date (another from Lagore was dated to the beginning of the Early Bronze Age). The radiocarbon dating indicates that it was made sometime around 1096–906 BC (B. Coles 1990, 326–7). A rapier is known to have been found in the same bog at Ralaghan (Burgess and Gerloff 1981, 25). The

Ralaghan figure had been deliberately damaged prior to deposition. Its gender is uncertain or deliberately ambiguous; the hole in the pubic area may have been for the insertion of a separate phallus or it may represent a vagina. An association with ritual having a fertility element is probable, but whether its use as an offering was necessarily part of the ceremony is of course uncertain. Its presence in a wetland context at least shows that such sites were the appropriate resting places of items other than bronze and that rituals other than the making of conspicuous offerings were also practised.

The pattern of metalwork deposition is discussed more fully below, but in considering the landscape it is important to note that, like the deposition activity itself, there may have been a formality and intentionality attached to the places chosen for deposition. We can see this most clearly in the case of the King's Stables in the Navan complex. This is a deliberately created embanked pool into which were thrown items such as animal bones, clay moulds for swords, and part of a human skull (Lynn 1977). It is sited below and about 200m from and to the north-east of the contemporary Haughey's Fort (Mallory 1991a, 10). Below and to the north-east of Emain Macha at a distance of about 200m lies Loughnashade, in which four bronze horns of Iron Age type were found in the late eighteenth century (Warner 1986, 6). Human skulls and other bones were found near the horns. It is tempting to suggest that we are seeing here at Haughey's Fort–King's Stables and Emain Macha–Loughnashade a replication of a specific relationship and axis of activity between an important high-status settlement site and a place of formal deposition (see Figs 8:2 and 8:7). Indeed, it may be the case that a similar relationship was established elsewhere, as the very large assemblage of Late Bronze Age gold ornaments from Mooghaun North, Co. Clare (Armstrong 1917), lies about 750m north-east of the large trivallate hillfort of Mooghaun. It appears that the find-spot of the hoard was originally under the waters or at the edge of a lake which has been reduced in size (Figs 8:7 and 8:8). While at Loughnashade and Mooghaun deposition was made in an existing lake, it would seem that the construction of the King's Stables represents a deliberate attempt to create a small

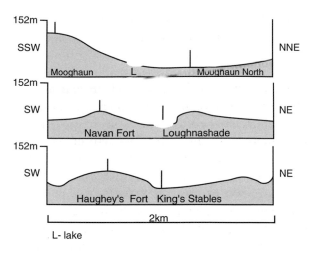

*Fig. 8:7—
Topographical transects
showing the locational
relationship between
hillforts and places of
formal deposition:
Mooghaun and
Mooghaun North,
Co. Clare; Emain
Macha (Navan Fort)
and Loughnashade,
Co. Armagh;
Haughey's Fort and
the King's Stables,
Co. Armagh.*

*Fig. 8:8—The
Mooghaun area, Co.
Clare, showing the
location of the hillfort and
the probable find-spot of
the Mooghaun North
(Great Clare) Late
Bronze Age gold hoard
(after Cooney and
Grogan 1991).*

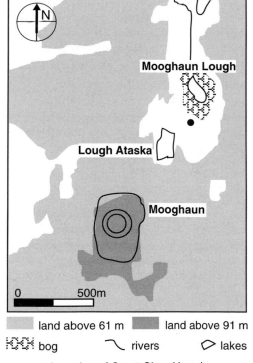

lake or pool specifically to hold deposited material. Instead of building monumental works for the dead or the provision of formal cemetery areas, the most visible ceremonial activity in the Late Bronze Age was the insertion of special items into the natural order, and at the King's Stables this process was taken further by the creation of a new but permanent landscape feature.

Monumental activity was now concentrated on the provision of enclosures around high-status settlements. These enclosures were at least in some cases clearly defensive, as at the fortified settlement at Clogher, Co. Tyrone (Mallory and McNeill 1991, 124). Site complexes that were to take on a central role in Iron Age/Early Christian archaeology, history and mythology were already important at this time. We have suggested above that there is a relationship between different elements within these complexes reflecting the patterning of ceremonial behaviour on them. We can see this complementarity in other aspects of the evidence, such as the faunal assemblages in the Navan complex (Lynn 1977; McCormick 1988b; 1991). At the high-status settlement of Emain Macha itself the faunal assemblage is dominated by pigs, perhaps reflecting the remains of feasting. At Haughey's Fort cattle formed the main meat supply, and in the ceremonial pool at the King's Stables dog and deer bones/joints, as well as a human skull, appear to have been deliberately deposited. These sites suggest that animals were not treated simply as an economic resource but that in specific contexts they also had a clear social role. Thus the complex use of material culture which would be readily acknowledged to be evident in the character and contexts of the metal artifacts can also be seen in other, perhaps apparently more mundane, aspects of life. Of course all of these elements would have been linked for the people who were actually generating and using this material culture. It is with this perception that we should approach an understanding of the role and importance of bronze artifacts.

The social interpretation of the metalwork evidence

The metalwork which has been at the centre of the study of the Irish Late Bronze Age needs to be embedded in a better understanding of its production and use. In the discussion above

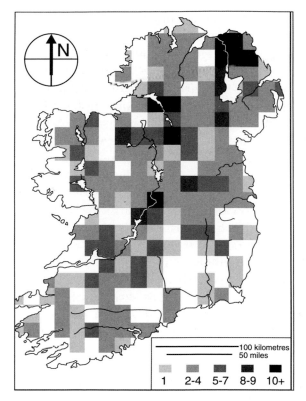

*Fig. 8:9—
Density
distribution (in
20km² blocks) of
Late Bronze Age
metalwork (by
number of
artifacts).*

we have dealt with aspects of the metalwork evidence and have
indicated that it should not be regarded as separate from other
aspects of the archaeological record. The wide distribution of the
metalwork in Ireland (Fig. 8: 9) can be taken as a general
indication of the extent of settlement. The metalwork also
indicates distinct regional groupings (Eogan 1974). Both the
complex technology and the social role of this range of material
culture are indicated by the wide range of tools, ornaments,
weapons and ceremonial objects now in circulation, the frequent
use of gold, the personal nature of the ornaments, and the modes
of deposition of the artifacts, whether as single objects or as
hoards. The concentration of metalwork in the Bann valley in
the north-east, in the valley of the Erne river in the north-west
and in the Shannon river valley in the central to south-western
part of the country seen in Figure 8:9 suggests that deposition

was far from being a random activity across the landscape.

Harbison (1988, 147–8) saw the nature of the development of metal technology and the emergence of new artifact types as being a result of direct contacts between metalworkers in Ireland and those in several parts of Europe. This is a somewhat simplistic view of a situation where there appear to have been full-time smiths. These smiths did not live in a social vacuum; they are unlikely to have been at the top of the social pile and were probably maintained by a social élite who would have provided both patronage and a demand for their products (e.g. Champion *et al.* 1984, 180). In turn, as Waddell (1991, 9) has pointed out, the possession of fine metalwork, the ability to regulate the movement of such objects and the patronage given to the craftworkers who produced them are likely to have been sources of power for élite groups or individuals. There were contacts with Britain and Europe at this time, but they reflect the contacts of the social élites, not simply those of smiths. Metal objects of Irish origin found in Britain and western Europe are, for example, just the most durable result of what were likely to have been a series of interlinking networks involving a range of exchange commodities (Rowlands 1971, 211; 1980).

There is an interesting contrast in the way that hoards and single finds have been treated in the literature. In a period when so much emphasis has been on the study of the metalwork the hoards have been viewed as being of critical importance (e.g. Eogan 1964; 1983). Although numerically far more significant, the single finds have played very much a subsidiary role and relatively little attention has been given to their context and circumstances of discovery. It has been assumed that in many cases they could be treated as stray losses and finds. Here it will be suggested that there is a definite structure and pattern underlying the deposition of the metalwork which can best be appreciated by considering both hoards and single finds.

The hoards offer a particular insight into the use of material culture at this time. Eogan's study (1983) is the first comprehensive treatment and gives a valuable perspective on the nature of the composition and deposition of hoards. It is worth noting that our knowledge of these hoards is, like so many other

	Duration	Number of hoards	Deposition rate
FBA	600 years	50	1 every 12 years
MBA	500 years	5	1 every 100 years
Bishopsland	200 years	25	1 every 8 years
Dowris	400 years	130	1 every 3 years

Fig. 8:10—Estimated rate of hoard deposition within each of the major phases of the Irish Bronze Age (based on information in Eogan 1983).

aspects of the archaeological record, effected by modern activity. Eogan's (1983, 5) discussion of the discovery pattern of hoards showed that the number discovered, for example, in the 1970s — three — was lower than in any decade since the 1810s. This is likely to be a result of the increasing scale and mechanisation of landscape activity rather than an indication that we now have knowledge of most of the Late Bronze Age hoards that were deposited. The pattern of hoard deposition in different phases of the Bronze Age (Fig. 8:10) shows that it is very much a feature of the Dowris phase of the Late Bronze Age, particularly when the length of each of the major phases is taken into account. This kind of calculation does not, of course, deny the possibility that hoard deposition may have taken place over a restricted time period and because of particular social conditions (e.g. R. Bradley 1990, 194–5). In the first phase of the Late Bronze Age (Bishopsland), 25 known hoards may have been deposited. Of these we know the details of discovery of sixteen. Eleven of these (69%) were in dryland sites and five (31%) were in wet places. The majority of the hoards consist of small groups of objects, nearly all personal jewellery in gold, such as neck-rings and bracelets. That an understanding of the pattern of deposition of single finds could offer a valuable complement to that of hoards is indicated by Waddell's (1990b, 13) comment that the hoards of gold ornaments should be considered in conjunction with the continued deposition of rapiers in wet, watery locations — bogs, rivers and lakes (see also R. Bradley 1982b). If we assume a degree of consistency in gender roles which link men with weapons and women with ornaments, the rapiers could be considered in the context of being weapons with strong male associations and the gold ornaments may have been associated with women. This structured set of differences linking landscape, object types and gender might provide a basis for recognising other important differences and deliberate contrasts in the record of this period. It should also be remembered that some of the hoards appear to have been deliberately placed close to important sites, such as the two hoards found near the Rath na Ríogh enclosure at Tara.

It was in the last few hundred years of the Bronze Age, during the Dowris phase, that the majority of the known Bronze Age hoards were placed in the ground. Of the 130 hoards known, the find-places are known for about 89. Fifty-two of these (58%) are in wet locations (Fig. 8:11), predominantly bogs, and 37 (42%) on dry land. There is, then, a clear contrast to the pattern of deposition of the Bishopsland hoards. Again in contrast to the Bishopsland pattern, hoards consisting exclusively of ornaments form only about a fifth of the total. But the majority of the hoards can still be seen in terms of personal possessions, either ornaments or weapons. Other objects found in hoards can be classified as ceremonial, such as the horns, buckets and cauldrons (J. Coles 1963; Gerloff 1986; C.F.C. Hawkes and Smith 1957). Looking at the hoards in terms of the principal artifact types represented (Fig. 8:12), the clearest instance of the popularity of deposition in wetland locations is in the case of the bronze horn hoards, where nine out of the ten known locations are bogs.

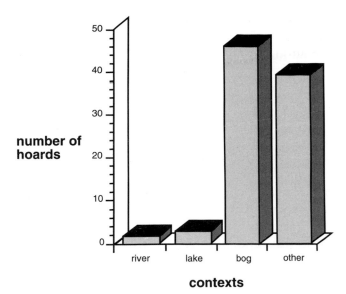

contexts

Fig. 8:11—Context of discovery of Dowris phase hoards (after Eogan 1983).

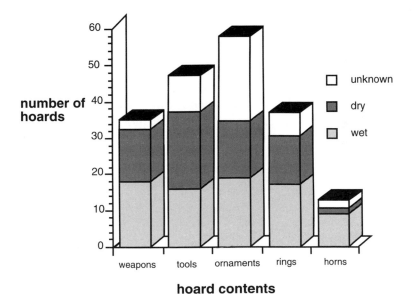

hoard contents

Fig. 8:12—Comparison of the contexts of Dowris phase hoards defined by the principal artifact types represented (after Eogan 1983).

Interestingly, it is only in those hoards containing tools that dryland depositions are more numerous than wetland locations. The horns form the most exclusive hoards in the sense that eleven (85%) out of the thirteen hoards containing horns consist only of two or more horns. Defining exclusivity in this way (Fig. 8:13), ornament and weapon hoards are more exclusive than those containing tools or bronze rings. Three of the four large assemblages — Mooghaun, Dowris, Co. Offaly, and the Bog of Cullen, Co. Tipperary (the find circumstances of the fourth, at Askeaton, Co. Limerick, are unknown) — were found in wet places and are likely to be the result of deposition over a period of time in the same spot. The hoards of the Dowris phase may represent a variety of meanings and human intentions but the deliberate, formal deposition of material would appear to have been the major factor. This could have been the case with even apparently utilitarian items and broken or scrap material which has previously been seen solely in an economic light. R. Bradley (1990, 117–18) has suggested that hoards which contain newly made objects or a range of metalworking residues and are in locations where recovery would be easy could be seen as utilitarian, founder's or scrap hoards. Bearing in mind the difficulty of knowing what were the original total contents of many of the hoards, it appears that relatively few examples of Dowris phase hoards fulfil these criteria.

Looking at non-utilitarian deposition, two particular trends can be suggested: deposition as a type of funerary deposit and as votive offering. The first of these ritual or ceremonial interpretations suggests that the deposition of fine metalwork (both hoards and single finds) may have taken the place of or have become part of funerary ritual as the principal context for the display of conspicuous consumption and destruction. Some of the links have been pointed to above, and here it is worth commenting on the specific example of items of material culture which had previously been placed with burials now being deposited in hoards. At least five boars' tusks, one of the few frequent non-ceramic grave-goods in the Early Bronze Age, were found as part of the hoard of bronzes and amber beads placed in a box at the edge of the Rathinaun lakeside occupation site (Eogan

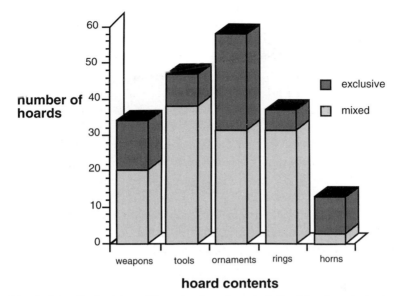

Fig. 8:13—Exclusivity of Dowris phase hoards defined by the principal artifact types represented (after Eogan 1983).

1983, 151–2). Bronze razors, which frequently occurred with cordoned urn burials, turn up in Late Bronze Age hoards at Cromaghs, Co. Antrim, and Booltiaghadine, Co. Clare (Eogan 1983, 53, 65). As in the Early and Middle Bronze Age, the context of the object may have defined its meaning, although there are now a greater range of objects which would seem to have been of a ceremonial nature. It would appear that the Irish evidence combines patterns seen in both western and northern Europe. Richard Bradley (1990, 110–11) has contrasted the prominence of weapon deposits in rivers in western Europe and the transfer of weapons from burial contexts earlier in the Bronze Age to rivers later in this period with the greater role that ornaments and ceremonial objects have in deposits in northern Europe. In Ireland both kinds of deposits occur, and it may well be that we can see the weapons as an expression of 'graveless grave goods' (Eogan 1964, 285) while the ornaments and ceremonial objects may reflect a complementary pattern of votive, non-funerary, deposition. Without wishing to fit the

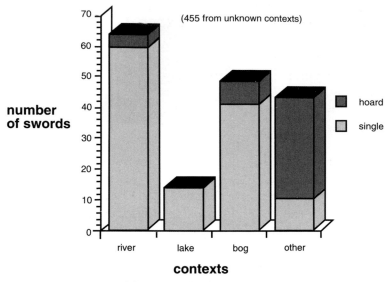

Fig. 8:14—Context of discovery of Late Bronze Age swords (after Eogan 1965).

evidence too rigidly into a particular pattern, it appears that the emphasis on males seen to some extent in Early Bronze Age and to a greater extent in Middle Bronze Age mortuary practice was continued in the Late Bronze Age by the deposition of weapons (or skulls in some cases) which we may argue are likely to be identified with male roles and perhaps with particular individuals.

In the case of both 'funerary' deposits and votive offerings there is no reason why the same purpose might not have been served by the deposition of single items of metalwork rather than a hoard. Indeed, large assemblages such as that at Dowris may represent the continued deposition of individual or small groups of related items in the same spot over a prolonged period of time rather than any single episode (Eogan 1983, 11). Individual types of objects, such as weapons, ornaments and ceremonial objects, may have been of equal significance when deposited on their own. The clearest example of this is the sword (Eogan 1965), introduced during the Late Bronze Age as a replacement for the rapier and dirk. Functionally this has been seen as representing a change from a thrusting to a slashing weapon and part of wider changes in armaments and warfare (e.g. Mallory and McNeill 1991, 131). What may be of equal or greater significance is the continuity in the depositional pattern of these swords with that of the dirks/rapiers (Fig. 8:14; compare with Fig. 7:9). The similarity with the dirk/rapier pattern is very clear, as is the contrast with the hoard pattern (Fig. 8:11) where there is a predominance of bog finds — almost 90% of the hoards with wetland contexts come from bogs. These patterns suggest that different places may have been chosen for different types of depositional activities. This point can be emphasised when it is taken into account that only 34 (26%) of the Dowris phase hoards and none of the Bishopsland hoards contained weapons.

The extent to which the deposition of single weapons such as swords may have been the result of formal, ceremonial and repetitive action is a point of debate. It is clear that concentrations of finds occur in certain lakes, such as Lough Erne, and at specific places along rivers, for example at Keelogue on the Shannon, Toome on the Bann and Portora on the Erne. These places are all at or near fording points, and it is possible that they represent casual losses. Other explanations that have been proposed are that they represent the sites of battles or losses from settlement sites on the banks of the rivers (Eogan 1983, 8; Mallory and McNeill 1991, 139). Bearing in mind the long-term continuity of deposition at these and other places, stretching from the Neolithic to the Iron Age, and the specific, restricted range of objects involved, namely weapons in the Middle and Late Bronze Age when 37% of all contexted swords and 60% of the basal-looped spearheads (Fig. 8:15) come from rivers (O'Carroll 1986), the best explanation would appear to be that there were recognised places where formal, probably public and ceremonial deposition of metalwork took place. Whether the metalwork represented 'graveless grave goods' or votive offerings, prestige, power and position are likely to have accrued to the person or social group who could visibly demonstrate wealth through this public performance. Indeed, it is likely to have provided an arena for competitive destruction, by irretrievable deposition, of fine objects (R. Bradley 1984, 96–106).

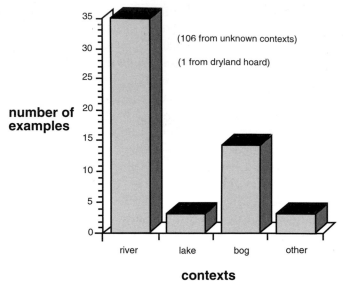

Fig. 8:15—Context of discovery of basal-looped spearheads (after O'Carroll 1986).

Regional styles, regional identity

It is interesting that there is a distinctive clustering of a range of high-quality bronze and gold objects in north Munster, concentrated on either side of the Shannon and its estuary (Fig. 8:16). Along with the presence in this area of the four large assemblages of Dowris phase metalwork, this clearly demonstrates that the area had a special character. A pattern towards concentration of material in northern Munster was detected in the distribution of the earlier metalwork (see Fig. 6:12), with the main production areas lying further to the south. It is still an open question as to whether in the Late Bronze Age this north Munster region became a major production as well as a consumption and deposition zone. As discussed in the last chapter, at the only known production centre in this area, Lough Gur, Sites D and F (Ó Ríordáin 1954, 384–5, 400–1, 415ff; Herity and Eogan 1977, 170), bronze types such as spearheads and palstaves were being produced. In Lough Gur itself high-

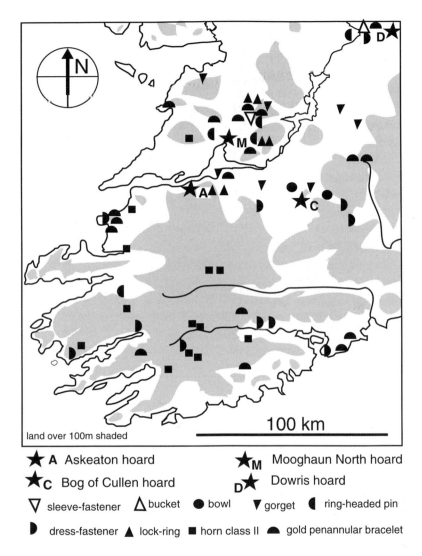

Fig. 8:16—Distribution map of high-quality Late Bronze Age metalwork in the south-west of Ireland (after Eogan 1974).

status objects, such as swords, were deposited. The finding of fragments of clay moulds, possibly for a sword, at Circle K, along with glass beads, has been taken as evidence for bronze-casting (Grogan and Eogan 1987, 385), but the question must be raised

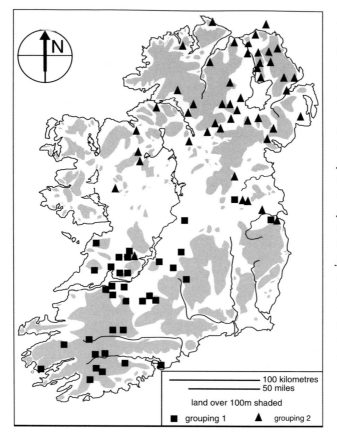

Fig. 8:17—
Distribution
of two groups
of Late
Bronze Age
metalwork.
Grouping 1
consists of
lock-rings,
gorgets, bowls
and Class II
horns;
grouping 2
consists of
sleeve-
fasteners,
striated rings,
buckets,
Class A
cauldrons and
Class I horns
(after Eogan
1974).

as to whether moulds could also have been deliberately deposited and have had a role beyond being the by-products of the manufacture of bronze objects. This possibility is raised by the intentional deposition of moulds for swords in the King's Stables (Lynn 1977, 50–2, 56). This is a reminder of the complex use of material culture where the depositional context of the object may enable it to take on a special role and a meaning that in a dryland context would not normally be considered significant.

Looking at the regional variability in the fine metalwork of the Dowris phase identified by Eogan (1974), interesting patterns can be seen. There is a distinction between types of objects that are found mainly in the south-west, including the north Munster region, and others whose focus of distribution lies in the northern

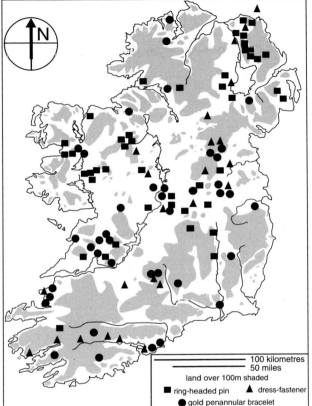

*Fig. 8:18—
Distribution
map of
selected types
of high-
quality Late
Bronze Age
metalwork.*

100 kilometres
50 miles
land over 100m shaded
■ ring-headed pin   ▲ dress-fastener
● gold penannular bracelet

part of Ireland, particularly in the north-east (Fig. 8:17). In a
sense the distinction between these two groups of artifact types is
all the more interesting because of the appearance of some
objects, such as ring-headed pins, dress-fasteners and gold
penannular bracelets (and indeed leaf-shaped bronze swords), in
both the south-west, north-east and elsewhere (Fig. 8:18). This
makes it clear that we can set regional preferences for certain
types of objects against a background of contact between regions
and artifact types and styles that were in use throughout the
country. However, returning to the general density of
distribution of the metalwork (Fig. 8:9), it may be valid to think
of the Shannon as defining a major depositional zone and the
Erne and the Bann other such zones. As Champion pointed out

(1989, 289) with particular reference to the lower reaches of the Shannon in north Munster, similar concentrations of metalwork occur in other river valleys in western Europe, such as the Thames, Seine, Loire and Rhine. In Ireland depositional activities in the three identified zones involved the placing of weapons such as swords in rivers and lakes, ornaments and ceremonial objects in bogs, some of which at the time may still have been open water, and some deposition on dry land. It is in this very specific context of the control of the consumption and deposition of fine metalwork, which certainly only actively involved a small number of leaders or a social élite who had access to wealth, that regional differences can best be identified. For example, what sets the Shannon/north Munster region apart from other areas in Ireland and places it in close comparison with major river valley metalwork concentrations elsewhere in western Europe is the particular clustering of gold objects and the occurrence of the four very large hoards or assemblages.

The question of the strength of regional identity being expressed by the metalwork is difficult to assess, but it is striking that somewhat parallel regional distinctions can be seen in the Iron Age evidence (see below, Chapter 10). More generally, sites and patterns in the archaeological record which in the past have been associated with the Iron Age increasingly appear to have first emerged in the Late Bronze Age. It seems that we have to contemplate a social and cultural linkage stretching from the end of the second millennium BC into the first millennium AD. One of the major problems in Irish prehistory is to understand and explain the nature of that linkage and, more immediately, to examine how the transition from what we describe as the Late Bronze Age to the Iron Age took place and what its implications were for the existing patterns of social organisation and settlement.

9 COLLAPSE, CONTINUITY OR CHANGE — THE TRANSITION FROM THE LATE BRONZE AGE TO THE IRON AGE

Defining a dark age

One of the most enigmatic periods of Irish prehistory is that stretching from the seventh to the third century BC. Effectively there appears to be a major gap in the archaeological record during this time, which has led to its description as a 'dark age'. Yet this is the period when the transition from the Late Bronze Age to the Iron Age took place. A distinctive set of Late Bronze Age evidence and the earliest signs of the use of iron with a European early Iron Age (Hallstatt phase) background before 600 BC is separated from the material of the La Tène phase and the established ironworking that appeared after 300 BC. In between there is at the moment apparently little visible in the archaeological record. It is worth remembering that both the Late Bronze Age and the La Tène evidence has been perceived as being dominated by fine metal objects of bronze and gold. Thus in the context of these kinds of prestige objects the new ferrous technology apparently had little impact. It is the gap between the two sets of fine non-ferrous metalwork that has dominated discussion of the transition from the Late Bronze Age to the Early Iron Age. In turn, as Champion (1971; 1989) and B. Raftery (1976b; 1984) have pointed out, these cultural and chronological terms have also been defined on the basis of this fine metalwork. The conventional dates applied to these periods see the Late Bronze Age ending around 600 BC (e.g. Harbison 1988, 149) and the Early Iron Age starting at around 300 BC (e.g. Warner *et al.* 1990, 46).

The situation is complicated by the introduction of the term 'Celtic'. The beginning of the Iron Age has traditionally been seen as marking the time when Ireland became Celtic and when the Irish language was introduced. On linguistic grounds it has been held that this meant the arrival of new people (Mallory 1984b, 65), coinciding, although deriving from a very different set of evidence, with the mythological view of the background of the Irish Celts (see Champion 1982). On archaeological grounds the evidence can best be read as suggesting continuity with what had gone before, with little sign of external intrusion (e.g. B. Raftery 1989, 120). However, the gap in the archaeological record for the critical transitional period has been seen as indicating a collapse in Late Bronze Age society, with new social and economic patterns emerging in the Early Iron Age (e.g. Scott 1979, 200; 1990, 41–5; Mallory 1984b, 68–9). This collapse has been seen as either the result of or the background to a decisive population intrusion. The nature of the transitional period and the range of explanations that have been put forward necessitate not only the examination of the 600–300 BC period itself but more importantly a wider perspective that investigates its background context (the Late Bronze Age) and its subsequent development (the Early Iron Age).

The introduction of iron and the Late Bronze Age

The archaeological debate about this period has been centred on the question of when iron was introduced and first manufactured in Ireland. In fact the central problem seems to be what happened after the initial introduction of iron technology, which occurred in a Late Bronze Age context. As Champion has recently reiterated (1989, 291–2) on the basis of site stratigraphy, associations between objects and typology, the Irish Late Bronze Age bronze industry producing the range of objects discussed in the last chapter conventionally is not regarded as having continued much beyond 600 BC. There are a number of iron objects that by association or radiocarbon dates can be assigned to the seventh century BC, but the next group of material made from iron belongs to the third or second century BC (Scott 1990). Scott (1979, 194) has also suggested that the transitional phase in between appears to have been a time in which metal became relatively less important. However, there is very little material culture of any kind that can be tied to this period. Both Scott (1979, 195) and Champion (1989, 293) have pointed to the difficulties of the poor preservation of iron and the lack of typological characteristics and associations to suggest that there may be an as yet unrecognised body of transitional period iron artifacts.

In terms of understanding the processes involved in the introduction of this new technology it is important to remember that what we define as early iron objects are effectively dated by reference to the Late Bronze Age, this being a corollary of the usual formulation of using the iron artifacts to date the end of the Bronze Age. For example, the earliest association is said to be that from the enclosure site at Aughinish, Co. Limerick, where a possible horse-bit of iron and a knob-headed copper-alloy pin of early Continental Iron Age (Hallstatt C) derivation were found with a bronze tanged chisel of Dowris type and coarse bucket-shaped pottery with a flat rim (Kelly 1974). At Rathinaun in Co. Sligo the lowest occupation level contained Dowris metalwork and similar coarse flat-rimmed pottery. The next layer up was similar but also contained four iron objects, including a shaft-hole axe, a flesh-hook and a Hallstatt-type swan's-neck pin (J. Raftery 1972, 2–3). Stray finds of looped, socketed spearheads of iron as well as a cauldron of riveted iron sheets from Drumlane, Co. Cavan (B. Raftery 1976b, 191), represent direct imitation in a new medium of classic Late Bronze Age objects.

Both the new iron objects and those bronze objects of Hallstatt context fall primarily into the weapon, ornament or ceremonial category. The best example of the latter is the ornate flesh-hook from Dunaverney, Co. Antrim. In many ways we see a continuity here from the established Late Bronze Age pattern of technological innovation and the presence of new prestige metalwork objects introduced through contacts with Britain and western Europe. It should be emphasised that this seems likely to have been the result of the continued involvement of élite groups in Ireland in exchange networks involving similar groups over wide areas of Europe. Scott (1979, 195–9), although viewing the evidence for the origins of the use of iron in terms of an intrusion into Ireland, noted that there would have been a basic inherited expertise in mining, ore-processing and metallurgy from Late Bronze Age bronze technology. Furthermore, he also commented (Scott 1981, 104) that the linguistic evidence of the later Irish literary sources suggests that words originally connected with the working of bronze were transferred to the technology of iron production. That these metal technologies were in use side by side during the final phase of the Bronze Age in Ireland is clearly indicated by the manufacture in iron of objects previously made in bronze, as discussed above.

In an Irish context the classic examples of bronze objects associated with the early European Iron Age are the local versions of the Continental Gundlingen, Hallstatt C swords (see discussion in Colquhoun and Burgess 1988, 114–16). These are Class 5 in Eogan's (1965, 13–15) typology of Irish Bronze Age swords. Interestingly, Eogan viewed his Class 6 swords as hybrids, incorporating features from the Hallstatt C swords and from the most popular insular sword form in the Irish Late Bronze Age, namely his Class 4 or Ballintober swords. That in some cases at least what was important about these swords was their novel form and appearance rather than the material of which they were made is suggested by the wooden Hallstatt C sword from Cappagh, Co. Kerry (J. Raftery 1960, 24).

As Mallory (1984b, 67) has put it, the evidence for a population intrusion into Ireland at this time rests primarily on these Hallstatt C swords (and scabbard chapes). They have been viewed as supporting an intrusion of adventurers and warriors, their distribution representing a raiding pattern (Burgess 1974, 213; Scott 1979, 199), and as a sign of unsettled times at the end of the Bronze Age. It has been suggested as significant that they do not occur in hoards (Eogan 1965, 21; B. Raftery 1984, 9). However, of the large assemblage from the Bog of Cullen apparently containing a very significant number of swords, detailed descriptions or illustrations of only four swords are known. Two of these appear to be of Class 4, but the others are

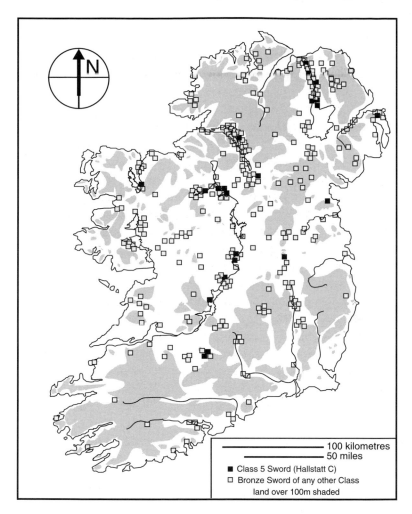

Fig. 9:1—Distribution map of Late Bronze Age and Hallstatt C swords (after Eogan 1965).

clearly of Class 5 — Hallstatt C — type (Eogan 1983, 154–6) and a further four Class 5 swords are probably part of the same deposit (Herity 1969, 9). What is even more important is the fact that the Class 5 swords can be seen as fitting directly into the pattern of sword manufacture, use and deposition stretching back

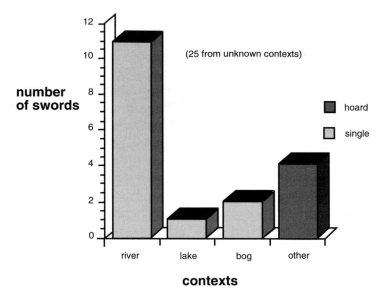

Fig. 9:2—Context of discovery of Hallstatt C swords (after Eogan 1965).

to the rapiers and dirks of the Middle Bronze Age (Champion 1982, 41). Their distribution summarises and parallels that of Late Bronze Age swords in general (Fig. 9:1), and the concentration in the Shannon, Bann and, to a lesser extent, Erne catchments is again reflective of the overall distribution of Dowris phase fine metalwork and long-established zones of settlement rather than relating to access routes to the interior of Ireland. The dominance of river contexts for Late Bronze Age swords is most clearly seen in the figures for the Hallstatt C-type swords (Fig. 9:2; compare with Fig. 8:14). It is clear that the deposition of many of them was a deliberate act, in the same places where other swords and fine metalwork were also placed. Finally, it is not just swords of this type that are generally absent from hoards but all the other types of Late Bronze Age swords as well. In the 130 Dowris phase hoards, swords occur in only nineteen (15%), and in eight of these hoards there are only swords (Eogan 1983, 14). Included in these sword hoards is one consisting of four Hallstatt C-type swords from near Athlone (Eogan 1983, 144–5).

All of these data suggest that the Hallstatt C swords and related material are best seen in the context of a continuing demand and quest by élite social groups in the Late Bronze Age for new items of material culture to use in conspicuous display and deposition to emphasise their power and prestige. At the moment we cannot be specific about exactly how power and prestige were gained, but it seems to have involved the possession and public display of weapons, particularly when they were taken out of circulation by being deposited in wetlands, especially rivers. Champion (1989, 292) has stressed the necessity of considering Ireland as part of a broader western European pattern and it is of interest in this regard that the Hallstatt C bronze swords occur in grave contexts in southern Germany and eastern France but as river finds further west in France, in the east of Britain and in Ireland (Eogan 1965, 14; R. Bradley 1990, 153). In this regard the pattern of deposition in Ireland follows wider Bronze Age trends. It also illustrates that the way in which material culture was used as part of the control and consumption of wealth was not constant but varied from area to area. The manufacture and use of iron became part of this power play in Irish Late Bronze Age society, but it appears to have in no way represented a technological revolution or replacement of the bronze industry. Indeed, that it occurred in the context of existing demands and technology is indicated by the innovative cross-over from bronze to iron in the manufacture of metalwork. The central problem in Ireland is not when the use of iron began but how and when the Late Bronze Age ended.

Crisis or continuity — the end of the Bronze Age

The end of the Irish Bronze Age has recently been presented as a collapse (e.g. Mallory and McNeill 1991, 140). In broader European terms R. Bradley (1990, 150–4) has also written of the end of the period as a collapse of a complex system of networks that linked communities across separate parts of Europe. The reason for this dramatic language is that the Late Bronze Age metalwork seems to come to a rapid end. Hoard deposition is presumed to stop in Ireland apparently by the end of the seventh century BC and does not seem to resume until the last few centuries BC. Again this fits with a broader European pattern of a chronological gap in large-scale production and distribution of metals after the end of the Bronze Age (Collis 1984a, 87–92). It is important to emphasise that the concept of collapse is based primarily on the fine metalwork which we have suggested may have been the basis for status and social ranking in the Late Bronze Age. It is in fact the absence of hoards and artifact associations that suggest a relatively sudden end to long-established social patterns (as well as making the study of the transitional period so difficult). In turn this has been linked to worsening environmental conditions brought about by climatic deterioration and human over-exploitation to postulate an economic collapse which could have underlain and precipitated the demise of the élites who controlled the demand, supply and deposition of the metalwork. The disruption of contacts between different parts of Europe may also have removed access to the flow of innovation and new prestige goods which were the material expression of the power of these élites.

Critical examination of this scenario, however, suggests a more complex picture. For a start, the terms that we have been using here — the Bronze Age, the Iron Age and the transition between them — are at odds with the sense of fundamental continuity that we see in the archaeological record, for example in settlement and burial and everyday material culture such as pottery. This will be explored in the next chapter, but it is important to comment here that deliberate deposition of metalwork after 300 BC takes place very often in the same places and contexts as were used in the Late Bronze Age. The objects have changed but the behaviour is similar. The difficulty of the transitional period is precisely that we have a gap in this kind of behaviour. But does this necessarily imply that single objects, such as swords, may not have continued to be deposited? We have already suggested that the deposition of single items, such as weapons, was an important complement to the hoards. There is simply no way to definitely date the deposition of single objects and no way of saying that such deposition may not have continued beyond the conventional end of the Dowris phase.

The connection between the deposition of hoards and

environmental conditions has been treated in a rather ambiguous fashion. On the one hand, it has been suggested that the emphasis on hoard deposition in the Late Bronze Age may be a human plea to the supernatural order in the light of decreasing soil fertility and increasing wetness (e.g. Coles and Harding 1979, 484). On the other hand, the subsequent supposed absence of hoards has been viewed as a possible indication of this environmental degradation (Mallory 1984b, 68). Both of these views rest on the assumption that environmental changes took place rapidly, and the best evidence for this is firstly the presumed effects of the Hekla III volcanic eruption of 1159 BC (Baillie 1988a; 1989) and secondly whatever environmental events are associated with the apparent gap in oak trees around the middle of the tenth century BC (Baillie 1982, 221, 231). However, unless the impact of these events was very long-lived they have no immediate significance for understanding the dynamics of the end of the Late Bronze Age. Weir's (1987, 41) analysis of the pollen sequence at Loughnashade shows no sign of discontinuity or change in landscape at the end of the Bronze Age. Thus the evidence for climatic deterioration stretches back into the second millennium BC, across much of the period of the Late Bronze Age rather than being in any way associated with the end of the period. Some of the pollen evidence, for example from Redbog, Co. Louth, can be read as showing agricultural expansion during the transitional period. While recognising the danger of over-generalising from the environmental record (Edwards 1985, 211–14), there is certainly nothing to support the concept of a sharp change in climatic conditions during the transitional period.

It has frequently been suggested that the major feature of the 600–300 BC period was an apparent cessation in the deposition of hoards and possibly of all fine metalwork. How can we judge the real impact of this aspect of the archaeological record? It appears that there are at least a few lower-order settlement sites, such as the reused site 26 at Carrowmore (Burenhult 1980, 40-7; 1984, 60), that date to this period and show an essential continuity from the Late Bronze Age to the established Iron Age. Champion (1989, 296–7) has commented that continuity and the absence of distinctive metal artifacts mean that radiocarbon dating is necessary to recognise sites belonging to the transitional period, but this is a period where radiocarbon is unlikely to be able to solve the problem owing to the nature of the calibration curve (Bowman 1990).

The most striking evidence for settlement continuity in fact comes from a high-status site where, if we follow the collapse scenario set out above, we would have expected signs of abandonment or decreasing activity at the end of the Bronze Age. At Site B, Emain Macha, a circular ditched enclosure with an entrance on the eastern side contained a ring of large posts set inside the lip of the ditch (see Fig. 8:3). Material typical of the Late Bronze Age was found, along with flat-rimmed pottery. There were also artifacts of Hallstatt C type, including the chape for a sword scabbard, and a number of small iron objects, including a ring-headed pin of La Tène type (B. Raftery 1983, 153; 1984, 168–70). As we have noted above, a series of circular structures accompanied by larger enclosures were built within the ditched enclosure (Lynn 1986, 16). Along with the artifactual evidence for continuity, radiocarbon and dendrochronological dates indicate that the site was in use between the eighth century and 100 BC. Lynn (1986, 16) commented on the remarkable continuity of structures during this period and on this basis suggested that the transition on the site from Late Bronze Age to Early Iron Age happened without any great upheaval. Subsequently he has suggested, on the basis of a detailed consideration of the radiocarbon dates, that the ditch and associated inner post ring represent the only Late Bronze Age construction (Lynn 1991a, 51). Even accepting this new interpretation of the structural sequence as correct, the placement of the Late Bronze Age and Iron Age structures indicates a remarkable continuity — for example in their focus on the same central point (see Figs 8:3 and 10:1a) — rather than this just being the coincidental use of the same ditched enclosure, as Lynn (1991a, 56) has suggested. It is also relevant to suggest in this context that the figure-of-eight structures could have been primarily ceremonial rather than domestic in nature, as indicated, for example, by the very high levels of pig bones (McCormick 1991, table 2). The use of Site B at Emain Macha involved a consistent, long-term pattern in the placement and nature of ceremonial activity, indicating a sense of cultural continuity and identity across the Late Bronze Age to Iron Age transition (Cooney and Grogan 1991, 37–8). There are no signs of a collapse of the social and economic organisation that lies behind the archaeological evidence. Going on the long-term sequence at Emain Macha it is clear that we should regard the apparent cessation in the practice of hoard deposition at the end of the seventh century as inconsequential to the broader issue of social and settlement continuity.

We have sought here to redefine the problem of the beginning of the Iron Age. There is still the problem of explaining the seeming lack of evidence for the deposition of metalwork in the period 600–300 BC. One possible explanation may be that there was actually disruption of contacts between Ireland and Europe at this time rather than the increased contact that is often assumed. That this disruption happened is suggested, for example, by the paucity of Hallstatt D material in Ireland (B. Raftery 1984, 8; 1991, 31). It may have been part of the broader breakdown in long-established exchange networks at the end of the European Bronze Age mentioned above. Without the stimulus of new types of exotic objects to replace those already long in use in Ireland, the practice of deliberate deposition may have lost its role as an arbiter of prestige and social standing. Alternatively this lack of novel metalwork may have meant that traditional forms maintained their significance and continued to be deposited, both as single objects and in hoards, so that the cessation may in fact be only apparent and not real. It is clear that some ceremonial objects remained in circulation for long periods, such as the cauldrons with their frequent evidence of repair (Gerloff 1986, 86–7). That there may have been a deliberate attempt at anachronism in the metalwork is suggested by the occurrence of a number of riveted spearheads with basal loops, the latter very much an archaic feature by the later stages of the Late Bronze Age (F. O'Carroll, pers. comm.). The very absence of new types makes it difficult to say when Late Bronze Age-type metalwork ceased to have importance. One of the most fascinating aspects of the period after 300 BC is that the practice of deposition of metalwork re-emerges, or perhaps simply becomes more easily dated again, emphasising anew the social and ceremonial continuity across the transition to the Early Iron Age.

10 THE IRON AGE: ENDINGS AND BEGINNINGS

The character of the evidence

The problems in trying to reconstruct the character of society and settlement in Ireland during the Iron Age are if anything more difficult than for the earlier periods in Irish prehistory. As B. Raftery (1984, 1) has put it, 'because of the virtual absence of significant associations, the paucity of burials and clearly recognisable settlements and indeed the largely selective nature of the surviving remains, there are still immense areas of uncertainty confronting the archaeologist in almost every aspect of this difficult period'. There has been a lot of recent work on the archaeological data belonging to this period, but the fundamental bias in the evidence towards unassociated metal and other objects and problematic hillfort and related sites is still a dominant feature of the Iron Age.

One aspect of the thorny question of the nature of the archaeological evidence for the Iron Age in Ireland is the considerable degree of continuity from the Late Bronze Age. This problem extends beyond the transitional period discussed in Chapter 9 to the established La Tène 'phase' of the Iron Age beginning around 300 BC. Some authors have seen the archaeological record as supporting the concept of an invasion 'by Celtic freebooters and their hangers-on' (Warner 1991, 48). But more frequently it is the limited nature of new material, its essentially Irish character and overall similarity with the Late Bronze Age that have drawn attention (e.g. B. Raftery 1991, 29).

It is worth reiterating the contrast between this evidence for continuity and the linguistic and mythological view of the introduction of the Iron Age as the result of a population intrusion (e.g. Champion 1982; MacEoin 1986, 167; Mallory 1984b; 1991c). In this context it is not surprising that rather than adhering to the tradition of the primacy of linguistic interpretation, which demanded migration to explain language change (and also assumed that the introduction of the Irish language, the coming of the Celts and the beginnings of the Iron Age were synonymous events), some archaeologists have looked for mechanisms whereby the archaeological record and linguistic developments can be reconciled without recourse to intrusions by new population groups (Renfrew 1987; Waddell 1991, 13–15). The development of the concept of 'cumulative Celticity' (after C. F. C. Hawkes 1972), suggesting that linguistic and other cultural changes could have taken place gradually as a result of continuing contact of the social élite groups with peer groups in Europe, offers one model to explain both the continuity and change seen in the Irish evidence.

The evidence for continuity has important implications and it may well be that the organisation of society and settlement in the Iron Age was along lines that had already become established in the Late Bronze Age. The appearance of high-quality La Tène metalwork which is such a visible aspect of the surviving evidence could have fulfilled a renewed demand for prestige items. Continuity can be seen in specific aspects of the archaeological evidence, for example in burial practice (B. Raftery 1981; B. O'Brien 1990). In this context the regionalisation seen in the Iron Age between a La Tène north and a largely non-La Tène south (see discussion in Caulfield 1981, 211; B. Raftery 1984, 314–19) should perhaps be examined more in the light of Late Bronze Age trends and less as being reflected in the archaeology of early historic Ireland. Indeed, it can be argued that it was at the end of the period with the introduction of Christianity that a fundamental transformation of society took place (Mytum 1992, 21) which literally brought Irish prehistory to an end.

Placing large-scale ceremonial sites in the landscape

One persistent reminder of the relevance of the past for understanding developments during the Iron Age is the deliberate location of activities and sites close to, within or surrounding existing monuments and special places in the landscape that we can suggest would already have been invested with particular cultural and social significance and meaning (e.g. Robertson 1992, 30). Excavations at Rathgall (B. Raftery 1976a), Dún Ailinne, Co. Kildare (Wailes 1976; 1990), Emain Macha (Lynn 1986), Clogher (Warner 1988) and Haughey's Fort (Mallory 1988; 1991a) and the completion of the excavation report on Ó Ríordáin's work at the Rath of the Synods, Tara (Ó Ríordáin 1965; Grogan and Caulfield, (forthcoming), have thrown light on the fact that these and other sites show signs of earlier prehistoric usage and a Late Bronze Age origin for at least some hillforts. The Iron Age features of Emain Macha, Dún Ailinne and Tara fit with the description of these sites as special ones in the early Irish literature. Hillforts continued to be used well into the first millennium AD (and even the second millennium AD) and there is evidence that some were built in the first few centuries AD, for example in the case of Clogher, although even at this site enclosure had occurred in the Late Bronze Age. These hillforts and related sites clearly stand at the apex of the settlement and social hierarchy, as indicated by their size and form, their spacing in the landscape, irregular as it may be, and their associated artifactual assemblages. One related site, albeit a relatively small one, worth mentioning is at Knowth (Eogan 1968, 355; 1991, 118–19). Here two impressive penannular ditches were dug into the main passage tomb mound to make it an enclosed settlement. Again it is interesting to record the deliberate transformation of a pre-existing, already ancient monument.

The size alone of the hillforts — the majority are between 2 and 14 hectares in area (B. Raftery 1989, 136) — might argue for their importance in the period, and what is crucial for the Irish Iron Age is their apparently ceremonial role during this period. This contrasts with the evidence for a primarily domestic role in the Late Bronze Age and large-scale settlement within the majority of excavated examples in Britain and on the Continent (e.g. Harding 1976; Collis 1984b). Excavation has demonstrated the special role of sites such as Dún Ailinne, Emain Macha, Tara and Clogher — all identified in the early historic documentation as 'royal' sites, associated in particular with the inauguration and developing status of kingship (see Wailes 1982; Warner 1988). In the early literature they are represented as the *domus* of the king also, but it is important not to assume too intimate a knowledge of the Iron Age role of the sites on the part of those scribes, writing several centuries later, who often had propaganda or myth-history in mind! The overall picture that has emerged from the recent excavations is a complex one. It appears to portray a range of activity including settlement and ceremony, the latter apparently involving considerable numbers of people, but the focus may have been an élite group or family. At Emain Macha Lynn (1992, 56) has suggested that the sequence of activity involved in the construction of the multi-ring timber structure, cairn and mound at Site B embodied themes of cosmology, social and sacred classification and territoriality.

Looking at the activities within the central foci of major site complexes like Emain Macha, there are clear indications of parallels and comparisons in structure and behaviour that stretch across the Late Bronze Age – Early Iron Age transition. Recently Lynn (1991a) has discussed a number of remarkable similarities between structures at Dún Ailinne and Site B at Emain Macha, in particular the figure-of-eight enclosures (building and yard?) with a wide funnelled approach and the large, elaborate timber structures of the final monumental stage (Fig. 10:1a and 10:1b) at each site. Lynn's (1991a) reinterpretation of the chronology at Emain Macha has already been discussed, and if this is correct it would make the sequence at this site broadly contemporary with that at Dún Ailinne (Wailes 1990). However, there appear to be some problems with this reinterpretation (see Cooney and Grogan 1991, 37). The earliest relevant phase at Dún Ailinne dates to about 300 BC while at Emain Macha, beginning in the Late Bronze Age and continuing to around 100 BC, there were six stages of construction occupying not just the same site but having the same central focus. It is this long-term continuity that would appear to be of greater significance, and if this is underlain

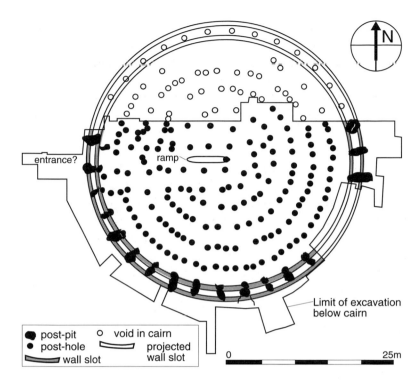

Fig. 10:1a—Plan of the large timber structure at Site B, Emain Macha, Co. Armagh (after Lynn 1986).

by a ceremonial tradition practised on important sites then it is unnecessary to have tight chronological links between specific features of this tradition as it is expressed in different regions. An examination of the Tara evidence (Fig. 10:2) lends support to this perspective as it suggests that a much broader comparison can be made between Dún Ailinne, Emain Macha and the pre-Rath of the Synods sequence of activity. At Tara some five stages, possibly beginning around the same time as Dún Ailinne, replicate many of the features of the other two sites (Grogan and Caulfield, forthcoming). Here, however, the smaller southern enclosure seems to fit between the two larger northern enclosures in the structural sequence, while the largest enclosures in the series, on the southern side of the site, represent the final phases

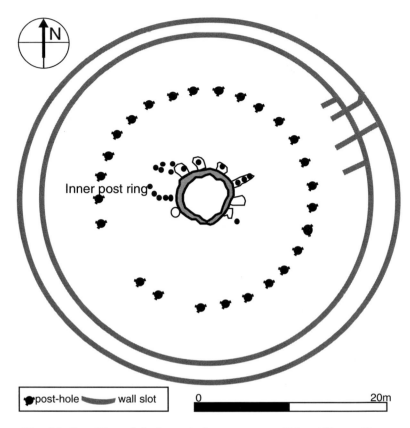

Inner post ring

post-hole ▬▬ wall slot   0   20m

*Fig. 10.1b—Plan of the large timber structure at Dún Ailinne, Co.
Kildare (after Wailes 1990).*

of this stage of activity. The juxtaposition of the ditched
settlement site and the ring-ditch of the burial complex in the
Late Bronze Age levels at Rathgall (see Fig. 8:1) offers another
possible broad parallel and support for the suggestion that the
deliberate positioning of small and large circular enclosures in
close proximity was established in the Late Bronze Age.

The wider significance of the role of these places as an arena
for ceremony is indicated by the alignment at Dún Ailinne of the
north-east-facing structures in the centre of the site with the
entranceway to the hilltop enclosure, creating an axis of
movement and activity. At Emain Macha one can see the

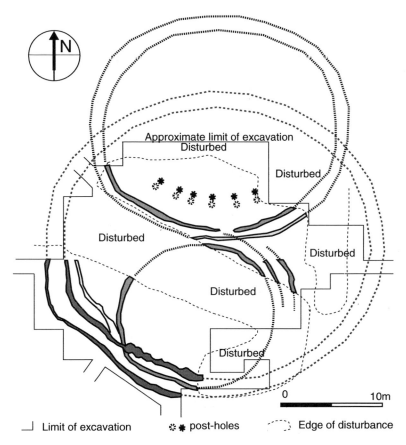

Fig. 10:2—Schematic plan of ring-slot enclosures and other features at the Rath of the Synods, Tara, Co. Meath.

monumental timber structure at Site B as having a western entrance, as is normally argued (Lynn 1992, 37), looking towards the gap in the hilltop enclosure, or alternatively aligned to the east, like the earlier structures, possibly on the line of an axis of movement with Loughnashade to the north-east of the enclosure. In the case of Tara (e.g. Swan 1978) and Rathcroghan, Co. Roscommon (Waddell 1983; Herity 1983; 1984; 1987b), the complexes of monuments of prehistoric date and varying morphology suggest a long-term ritualisation of the landscape. In

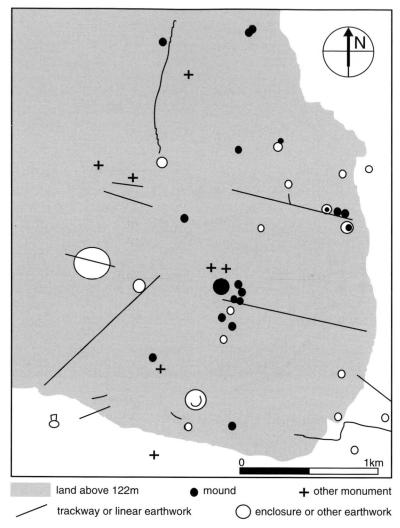

Fig. 10:3—Plan of the Rathcroghan complex, Co. Roscommon (after Waddell 1983).

the light of what has been said above regarding Emain Macha and Dún Ailinne it is possible to suggest that the spatial arrangement of sites in the Rathcroghan complex may also show a major axis of activity. Here the largest enclosure in the complex, with a maximum diameter of about 200m (Waddell 1983, 35), lies to the west of the group of monuments focused on the Rathcroghan mound (Fig. 10.3), and it may be that this spatial patterning reflects a central focus of human ceremonial movement within the complex. In the case of Tara the major alignment of monumental features follows the north–south trend of the ridge which forms the Hill of Tara.

In terms of formal ceremonial behaviour on these high-status sites this analysis indicates that we can identify similarities between individual structures and in the long-term structural sequences. There also appear to be close comparisons in the axes of activity within and outside the main enclosures which may indicate the formal route of ceremonial processions. It has been argued in Chapter 8 that a similar concept was present in the Late Bronze Age. The evidence from within the Navan complex emphasises both continuity and change from the Late Bronze Age to the Iron Age in this regard. In the Late Bronze Age there appears to have been an axis linking Haughey's Fort and the King's Stables. By the Iron Age it had shifted to the east and an axis on the same orientation and linking similar kinds of sites may have been established between Emain Macha and Loughnashade. It seems probable, however, that the hilltop at Emain Macha had already become a focal point during the Late Bronze Age and may have been enclosed at that stage (Simpson 1989b; Weir 1990), while Haughey's Fort continued to be occupied into the Iron Age (Mallory 1991b).

The wider organisation of the landscape
The construction of the large ceremonial timber structure at Emain Macha can be related in a wider context to a phase of renewed construction *c.* 100 BC of the Dorsey linear earthwork, (Lynn 1982; 1991b; Baillie 1988b; Baillie and Brown 1989), which is traditionally seen as the southern frontier of a prehistoric polity based on the Navan complex. Further west in Monaghan a 'continuation' of the Dorsey — the Black Pig's Dyke — has been dated to between 500 and 25 BC (Walsh 1987). The massive oak trackway at Corlea, Co. Longford, has been dated to 148 BC, while the nearby Derraghan track, which appears to have formed

part of the same system, has a date of 156 BC (B. Raftery 1986; 1990, 37–46). The large-scale use of oak timbers at the different sites that has made it possible to date these structures by dendrochronology also reflects the scale of organisation of human effort that was involved in the construction of these features in the landscape. In the particular case of the Ulster evidence it may indicate the growing power and cohesion of the élite who controlled the territory centred on Emain Macha, or alternatively the ceremonial activity at the site itself and the refurbishment of territorial boundaries may indicate sacred and practical responses to some exterior or interior social and political threat. The trackways and boundaries are a reminder on the one hand of the contacts between different areas and on the other of the territoriality that would have been the basis of the identity and competition of the social élites whose power was also expressed in the scale of construction of these monuments. The image portrayed in the literature of early historic Ireland having several political entities with well-defined boundaries and associated regional centres concurs at least in broad outline with the archaeological evidence from late prehistory.

Lower down the settlement hierarchy, where the horizons of the occupants are likely to have been much more localised, our evidence is very scattered. Broadly speaking it again suggests continuity from the Late Bronze Age. Small numbers of crannogs and ringfort sites may date to the period from the beginning of the Iron Age to the fourth century AD (e.g. Caulfield 1981; B. Raftery 1976a; J. Raftery 1981; Edwards 1990, 17, 36), including the trivallate site of the Rath of the Synods, Tara. But our knowledge of economic and social organisation is very limited and much of it depends on the extent to which the character of Early Christian Ireland can be projected back into the Iron Age. Lynn (1983, 56) has suggested that the ringfort complex specifically developed in the fifth and sixth centuries AD in the context of improved iron technology and agricultural developments that were introduced through increased contact with late and sub-Roman Britain. He sees these innovations as bringing about agricultural expansion and social change resulting in pressure on land and the adoption of ringforts (and crannogs) as defended farmsteads. Mytum (1992, 158, 268–9) follows the same line of argument, without the stress on defence, and further suggests that the economic expansion and material culture package associated with ringforts must be seen in the context of the ideological change associated with Christianity, including a greater role for the individual (as opposed to the kin-group) and the concept of land ownership.

One aspect of Iron Age farming practice that is worth commenting on is the increasing evidence for cereal production, both from surviving macroscopic plant remains and from querns for grinding the grain, including the introduction of rotary querns (Caulfield 1977; 1981; Monk 1985/6). This contrasts with the picture suggested by the early historic literature with its emphasis on cattle production, which may after all be a reflection of the 'macho' image and priorities of an élite section of 'Celtic' society rather than illustrating the basic food supply of the population. It might also run counter to the pollen evidence which suggests a fall-back in activity in the landscape associated with worsening climatic conditions (Mitchell 1986, 144–52). The pollen record may, however, here, as at other times, be reflecting a very gross picture in both spatial and chronological terms. Edwards (1985, 211–14) has discussed pollen evidence from several sites that show the presence of mixed agriculture throughout the Iron Age. On the other hand, Baillie (1991, 239) has suggested that the narrow growth-ring patterns exhibited by oak trees in 207 and 44 BC may reflect volcanic dust-veil effects recorded also in other northern hemisphere environmental data. These environmental events could have had a detrimental impact on agriculture and indeed settlement patterns, at least in the short term.

The material assemblage: deposition in the landscape
The paucity of associations of Late Bronze Age and Early Iron Age objects has tended to engender a sense of despair in the analysis of the transition period. Although few in number, as already discussed, they very clearly show that the use of iron was already established in the seventh century BC. The major problems become apparent in the subsequent period. The

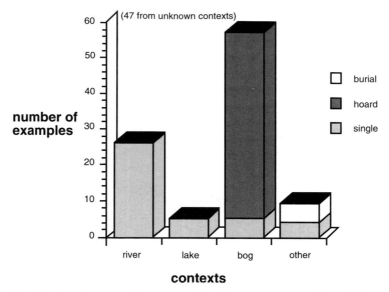

Fig. 10:5—*Context of discovery of La Tène weapons in Ireland (after B. Raftery 1983).*

with known circumstances of discovery, 90% are from wetland locations. Rivers, lakes and bogs continued to serve as repositories for what can be seen as deliberate deposits. The most spectacular example of this, perhaps taking the form of ceremonial offerings, is Lisnacrogher, which produced an array of objects, both weaponry and personal ornaments. This is a singular example of a special place within the natural environment combined with votive and probably social functions.

Lisnacrogher is not, however, entirely unique and high-status objects of the period have been recovered from specific river contexts, such as Toome on the River Bann, Banagher, Co. Offaly, on the Shannon, and at Galway on the Corrib (Rynne 1983–4). The use, during the Early Iron Age, of the small lake at Loughnashade in the Navan Complex for both exotic offerings and deposition of human skulls has already been commented on, and in that particular instance the special nature of the site is combined with a deliberate physical relationship to a major ceremonial site, the hilltop enclosure at Emain Macha to the south-west. As in the Late Bronze Age, we may be seeing then in the Navan complex the clearest example of the wider practice of deliberate deposition in small lakes or ponds. It is interesting that at another Early Iron Age site, Llyn Cerrig Bach, Anglesey, Wales (Fox 1946), the approach was, as in the case of the Navan votive sites (the King's Stables and Loughnashade), from the west and that deposition appears to have taken place from the western side of the lake, possibly with the objects being thrown out some distance into open water.

Burial practice: continuity, new trends and exotic burials

An array of elements similar to those in the latter part of the Bronze Age occur in the burials of the Iron Age. These include ring-barrows and mounds as covering features, the dominance of cremation and the presence of token burials. In contrast with the Late Bronze Age, an increased number and range of objects come from graves. The predominant grave-goods are personal ornaments. Excluding beads, which are the most common grave-good, 25% of all personal ornaments known in the Iron Age are from burial deposits. Few of these artifacts are demonstrably early, and the bulk belong to the period between 100 BC and 400 AD (B. Raftery 1981, 195–8). Few burials were accompanied by pottery, something of a contrast with the earlier period. There is, however, a very strong degree of continuity in burial practice in other aspects, notably in the nature of cremated bone deposits, sometimes token and occasionally in peripheral contexts, such as in the ditches at Oranbeg and Grannagh, Co. Galway (B. Raftery 1981, 180). The persistence of Late Bronze Age traditions, themselves firmly established in the Middle Bronze Age, can also be observed in the frequent reuse of individual sites, such as Carrowbeg North 1 and Longstone, and of funerary complexes like Cush, Carrowjames, Pollacorragune, Co. Galway, and Tara (B. Raftery 1981) which had been used in the Bronze Age. At Kiltierney in Co. Fermanagh a ditch was cut around the base of the mound of a passage tomb, and a series of small mounds, some at least covering cremated deposits, were placed outside it. Some cremation burials were also inserted into the passage tomb mound itself (Foley 1988). An Iron Age cemetery was also discovered at Knowth, close to the main passage tomb there (e.g. Eogan 1968, 365–73), and at Culleenamore 15A, Carrowmore, the crouched inhumation of a child occurred within a midden. This burial was accompanied by a glass bead and a penannular bronze ring (Burenhult 1984, 331). This is important in indicating that the child had some ascribed social status. Within the kerb of the megalithic tomb at Site 26, Carrowmore, a ring-ditch with a well-defined entrance produced a token burial of an adult female and foetus consisting mainly of skull fragments and scatters of cremated bone and pottery (Burenhult 1980, 40–9). This site seems to have been a focus of other ritual activity as well as being a place of burial.

The relatively simple nature of the funerary sites and the associated ceremony shows a persistence in the separation of statements of social standing from the final burial rite which can be observed from the Middle Bronze Age onwards. Where grave-goods occur, they are personal items rather than status symbols such as weaponry. There are a number of burials, however, that serve as exceptions to this generalisation. Barry Raftery has described these burials as intrusive (1981, 194) and it does appear that they represent the influence to a greater or lesser extent of Romano-British traditions of burial. They are also the most direct evidence of contacts between Ireland and the Roman world, particularly Britain, at this time.

The impact of the Roman world on Iron Age society

Most striking of the Roman-influenced burials are the inhumation cemetery on Lambay Island, including a warrior burial (Macalister 1929; Rynne 1976), and the cremation burial from Stoneyford, Co. Kilkenny (B. Raftery 1981, 194; Bourke 1989). The latter is a classic Roman burial in a glass cinerary urn which, as Warner points out (1976, 274), indicates the presence of a living group or community carrying out mortuary practice according to Roman fashion. Changes within the burial tradition occur towards the end of the Iron Age with the increasing incidence of inhumation. This alteration can also be observed in the gradual disappearance of above-ground monuments and burial markers. These developments are clearly associated with influence from the Roman world through the province of Britain (B. O'Brien 1990; B. Raftery 1983, 200), and the presence of an inhumation cemetery with the Roman custom of placing coins with the dead at Bray Head, Co. Wicklow, is also of interest here (K. M. Davies 1989). Small quantities of Roman material have been found in Ireland, most notably pottery, glass vessels (E. Bourke, pers. comm.), coins and some personal items (Bateson 1973; 1976), such as the iron penannular brooches from Bettystown, Co. Meath (B. Raftery 1983, 192). Within the Meath/Dublin area Roman material has come from other sites such as the Rath of the Synods ringfort at Tara, the enclosed settlement site at Knowth (Eogan 1991, 118), and in the form of gold ornaments at Newgrange (Carson and O'Kelly 1967; O'Kelly 1982, 36–7). Bateson (1973) identified two phases of Roman material in Ireland; the earlier objects date to the first and second centuries AD while the later ones belong to the fourth and fifth centuries AD. The question remains as to the broader significance of this material in Irish society during this period. This has a particular relevance because the background for the introduction of Christianity into Ireland is mainly fourth- and fifth-century Roman Britain.

Both the nature of the Roman material in Ireland and the sites where it has been found suggest that access to Roman goods and influences was primarily a preserve of social élites; indeed, this access may have become increasingly important as a marker of rank and status. Roman objects were deliberately deposited at places of sanctity, such as Newgrange. Mytum (1992, 23–36) has discussed the range of contacts that could have brought this material to Ireland, including trade, the return of Irish mercenaries who had served in Roman Britain, raiding by Irish war parties in western Britain, the movement to Ireland of refugees from Britain, and links between kin-groups. He sees the latter as the most significant process for the cultural transformation that marked the end of the Iron Age in the fourth and fifth centuries AD. The background for these kinship links across the Irish Sea was Irish migration and settlement, particularly into south-west Wales. In this context not only objects but also ideas could move along the social and kinship network, and this made for the relatively rapid and ready acceptance of a new ideology, Christianity, and the associated material and technological package (Mytum 1992, 43). On the other hand, the presence of the Stoneyford Roman burial in Ireland dating to the first century AD indicates that, contrary to Mytum's view, ideas as well as objects moved from Roman Britain to Ireland prior to the introduction of Christianity. What is clear is that the presence of Roman material from the first century AD onwards and the range of relationships between Ireland and Roman Britain were harbingers of a much more dramatic cultural change than the earlier adoption of a set of international status symbols, the La Tène metalwork, from the third century BC on.

Regional patterns in the Irish Iron Age

The northern emphasis in the distribution of La Tène material has been the inspiration of considerable speculation in the archaeological literature (Caulfield 1977; 1981; B. Raftery 1984; Rynne 1961). What is even more striking is that if this is taken in concert with the regional groupings identified by Eogan (1974) for the Dowris phase of the Late Bronze Age and the hillfort distribution (B. Raftery 1972; 1989) a clear regional pattern, spanning the whole of the later prehistoric period, emerges. The identification of similar distribution patterns is not in itself a convincing argument for continuity of population or social systems, but, when assessed in tandem with the evidence from the burials, patterns of artifact deposition, use of the material culture and ongoing occupation of settlement sites, it forms an important adjunct to the overall picture showing the persistence of Late Bronze Age traditions and social and political organisation.

For the final stages of the Bronze Age we demonstrated that two groups of high-status objects show a pattern of contrasting distribution, alongside the wide occurrence of some of the high-quality metalwork. The distinctive regional pattern of particular objects identifies core areas of consumption and deposition in the south-west and north-east, perhaps reflecting two major regionally powerful social groups. In the Iron Age the identity of

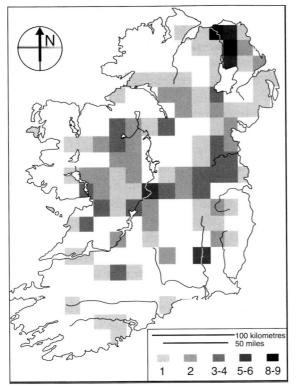

*Fig. 10:6—
Density
distribution (in
20km² blocks) of
La Tène
metalwork (based
on B. Raftery
1984).*

these areas continued, and is reflected, in particular, by the concentration and density of La Tène metalwork in the north of the country and specifically the north-east (Fig. 10:6). The relevant aspects of the material culture, the metalwork and the decorated beehive querns (B. Raftery 1983; Caulfield 1977), are largely absent from the southern part, particularly the south-west of the country. A closer look at the material reveals a more complex pattern where certain object types are concentrated in the north-cast (e.g. Lisnacrogher-type spear butts, scabbards and horns) while others are largely absent from the north-east (tubular and conical spear butts, Type 1 swords, dice and Type 4 ring-headed pins), and especially from the core area of the Bann Valley and the area to the east of it. In addition, the three main artifact categories — horsebits, pendants and beehive querns — while occurring in the north-east are concentrated in the area

witness prehistoric activity. The reliance on pollen analysis to suggest the character and effect of prehistoric farming has led to a perception and presentation of the evidence of settlement as representing phases of farming expansion alternating with regeneration of the forest cover. The difficulties of interpretation of the pollen record in landscape terms (e.g. Edwards 1979; 1982) should make us very wary of accepting a reconstruction of the course of human impact on the environment which in turn may have been influenced by views put forward in the archaeological literature. Until recently any apparent decrease in archaeological evidence was frequently taken to represent an equivalent reduction in the extent and intensity of human settlement and increasing economic difficulties (see Woodman 1992, 297). It is certainly time to recognise that gaps in the archaeological record for particular timespans, such as the so-called 'dark age' between 600 and 300 BC, do not necessarily indicate that these were periods of agricultural adversity. There are, no doubt, other instances when apparently low levels of visible archaeological evidence may mask ongoing, and perhaps intensive, settlement in a region or over a period of time. This may be the case particularly in areas which lack large-scale, high-profile monuments or exotic artifacts evident in other regions. One obvious example is the general absence of megalithic tombs in the southern half of the country — an area which is now known to have been extensively settled during the Neolithic.

We should see prehistoric settlement in the landscape not in the form of neutral dots on a distribution map but as a complex system with many components. The house would have been at the core of settlement and life; the areas used for farming, gathering and hunting on a daily basis would have been the most familiar parts of the landscape. But locations visited less frequently, for example sites where raw materials for stone or metal tool production were available or sacred places such as cemeteries, would also have been perceived as important. Changes in technology, population and social pressures, and environmental change would of course have had an influence on the ways in which the settlement pattern changed over time, but its complexity and the fact that it was set in a social matrix would have meant that there would not necessarily be a clear or direct correlation between a stress on society and the response in terms of settlement in the landscape. If human activity and settlement patterns were spread across the landscape in a complex manner, both physically and in terms of human perception, it seems unlikely that any single process, such as climatic change, would result in a widespread alteration of the settlement system.

During the course of Irish prehistory the allegiance of many communities to specific places appears to have been developing, and if there is one feature that stands out in the archaeological record it is a sense of place. We can define this as implying a sense of belonging, built upon human experience and cultural identity. At its most basic this could be expressed as the amount of time people spent in specific locations, and going right back to the Early Mesolithic site at Mount Sandel, the repeated use of the site and the journeys to and from it indicate that the group who lived there were not randomly utilising the environment but had a developed sense of their place in the landscape. Indeed, hunter-gatherer communities would have needed to have a highly developed landscape sense to mentally map and utilise the range of natural resources which they relied on as a food base, and we should not be surprised if certain landscape features were perceived as possessing a special role by these people. But it is during the Neolithic that we can more readily recognise the importance of places as the landscape was altered and transformed for both mundane and sacred purposes. Changes in the land were brought about, for example, in the agricultural sphere through the creation of field boundaries, and megalithic tombs are the best examples we have for deliberately created sacred places. One aspect of megalithic tombs that had long-term significance was the intention of their builders to create permanent structures, monuments that would remain in the landscape. Repetitive patterns of tomb siting and orientation suggest that people had specific ideas about the placement of, and approach to, these sites (see Thomas 1990), and in megalithic tomb cemeteries we can recognise for the first time the concept of a deliberately created ritual or ceremonial landscape. Landscapes like this later became focused on earthen enclosures, stone circles, cemetery mounds and barrows, although in some cases they continued to centre on a megalithic tomb. The focus of activity in these areas was not the everyday but the special or sacred, taking place at particular times of the year or important occasions. It is the organised, repetitive, ceremonial nature of human activity in these places that we can see as a link between the use of megalithic tombs and other kinds of special places that developed later in prehistory. What is interesting is that alongside the continuing focus on artificially created places such as tombs, earthen enclosures and barrow cemeteries, natural features such as rivers, bogs and lakes become increasingly important for ritual purposes, particularly from the beginning of the Early Bronze Age. We can recognise this through the deposition of objects, particularly metalwork, and one reading of this evidence is to suggest that it shows that people now were not only creating sacred sites but also linking themselves to permanent, natural places. In both cases what may have been important was that these apparently very different types of venue for ceremonial activity could be regarded as unchanging, and in this way they acted as metaphors for social continuity and stability.

What went on at these special places was of course linked to the everyday activity also. It is very often the transformation, inversion or heightening of everyday behaviour and social structure that is the basis of ceremonial action (Turner 1969, 42–3; Connerton 1989, 44–5); the latter flows from and is intimately connected to the former. What is of particular archaeological interest is that material possessions frequently appear to play a central role in these rituals and ceremonies — the ritual paraphernalia. Again, like the human activity itself, material items only have a ceremonial significance if they can be set against an everyday context. Objects may be deemed to be special in character because they are so different to what people normally use and see, or their specialness may reside in their ordinariness as reminders of the everyday. Individuals or groups may use ceremonial occasions to express and emphasise their social position and in doing so to indicate their importance in everyday life. At the same time or on different occasions the purpose of ceremony may be to demonstrate and enhance communal and social cohesion. This observation can be used as a common factor underlying the very diverse range of ceremonial activity to which the archaeological record gives witness. It is also a basis for understanding that there may be links between contemporary, but apparently different, types of ceremony. For example, we have already commented on the nature of the connection between formal burial practice and artifact deposition in the Bronze Age. In the Early Bronze Age daggers were sometimes placed with an individual in the grave as part of the funerary ceremony. Middle Bronze Age dirk/rapiers and Late Bronze Age swords, however, were not placed in graves but were often deliberately deposited in wetland, particularly rivers. This suggests that over time the ceremonial role of weapon types which had related functions altered significantly, and it indicates a changing focus from the dead to the actions of the living in ceremonial behaviour. The changing contexts of these weapon types can thus be used to suggest a linkage between what might otherwise be taken to be two unconnected types of special event. In this case it is likely that these are artifacts which most people would never have possessed. It was their rarity value that would have made them so effective as ceremonial items.

What also links formal burial and deposition is that they were carried out at specific locations. The use of cemetery areas over prolonged stretches of time has long been recognised, while the repetitive deposition of objects at places like Portora on the River Erne, Keelogue on the River Shannon and Toome on the River Bann from the Neolithic onwards has come under much less scrutiny. Lakes, such as Lough Gur, and bogs, some of which may have been lakes at the time, saw repeated episodes of deposition, as at Lagore and Ballinderry (Hencken 1942; 1950). Indeed, the question has been raised as to whether the large Late Bronze Age assemblages from bogs, such as at Dowris or the Bog of Cullen, should be regarded as examples of this kind of prolonged deposition rather than as a once-off event and hoard (Eogan 1983, 11). The same point can be made in relation to the Iron Age material from Lisnacrogher. Some of the continuity in deposition at these places has been missed in the past because detailed treatment of the data has tended to be by period or locations appears to have developed over time, as shown by periodic deposition stretching from the Early–Middle Bronze Age onwards. There is, moreover, the interesting contrast provided by a small number of very large deposits in the Shannon valley area during the Dowris phase of the Late Bronze Age. Whether one views these as single acts or prolonged episodes of deposition, as the wealth of one individual or that of a larger social unit, their nature, scale and distribution indicate that they cannot be seen simply in a local context: they have a wider regional context as well as suggesting a marked increase in social ranking. It is at this stage in the Late Bronze Age that emphasis shifted again to the construction of large earthworks, primarily in the form of hillforts and other hilltop enclosures. The scale of the monuments themselves indicates an increased population based on larger social units. There appear to have been regional differences in population density, but an overall population figure of about 500,000 can be suggested for this period and this 'guestimate' could be used for the Iron Age also, although of course population levels may have varied over the course of later prehistory.

The only comparison for the scale of monument-building in later prehistory is that of passage tombs and earthen enclosures from the developed Neolithic to the earliest stages of the Early Bronze Age. Monumentally, nothing close to the size of these classes of monuments from earlier and later prehistory was built in the thousand years of the Bronze Age that separate them. Attention has been drawn to the similarities between the earthen embanked enclosures and the enclosures at Emain Macha, Rath na Ríogh at Tara and Dún Ailinne to suggest a possibility of continuity (e.g. Wailes 1982, 21). Simpson (1989b) has speculated that the enclosing bank and ditch at Emain Macha might itself belong to the earlier tradition and date back to the final stages of the Neolithic. At a practical level we could discount any direct continuity between the earlier and later prehistoric earthworks and other structures and think instead of two major phases of monumental construction for the enclosure of, and as an arena for, ceremonial and other activity. At the level of ideology, however, it seems feasible to think of social élites emphasising their power and permanence by deliberately imitating the form of, or in some instances reusing, places that had already been in the landscape for a millennium (Robertson 1992, 30). What they have in common is a circular form which focuses attention on a central point and the care which is taken in the creation of the interior space of the monument, contrasting with the excluded exterior. In this light we can also point to the link with activities at other circular sites such as barrows and stone circles. This emphasis on the circular form of sacred places throughout the Bronze Age can be seen as the background to the emergence of larger-scale circular monuments in later prehistory.

It is of course the occurrence of human activity at different periods in prehistory that lies behind the complexity of the development of landscapes like Navan, Tara and Rathcroghan. The correlation, more deliberate than accidental we would suggest, between the location of important later prehistoric sites and earlier prehistoric activity has been noted frequently. Most commonly this involves a hilltop enclosure around an earlier burial mound. In itself this is a good landscape metaphor for the changing focus of ceremonial activity in Irish prehistory. At the end of the Neolithic, embanked enclosures similarly appear to have been deliberately sited, certainly in the Boyne Valley, to both appropriate and incorporate passage tombs and their associated meanings. Nothing like the large passage tombs were ever built again in Ireland; formal burial continued to have a role, but the dominant focus for the integration of social units became large-scale enclosures within which a variety of activities — high-status settlement, feasting, formal deposition and burial — to celebrate a social élite appear to have taken place. The idea of using the past to legitimise power in the present is something we are familiar with in more recent periods of Irish history; it should not surprise us if the same process was used in prehistory also.

What made the Late Bronze Age/Iron Age sequence of development different is that it apparently gave rise to a much more defined sense of territory and boundary than earlier social systems in Ireland. We can make sense of this when we see that expressions of communal effort and power were very much linked to at least the concept, if not the physical actuality, of defence and offence. The hillfort defences, the swords, spears and shields all suggest this emphasis and we can link this to the construction of impressive earthworks in what appear to be boundary areas, such as the Dorsey (Lynn 1991b). The other major factor that made later prehistoric developments very different to anything that had gone before is that from the first century AD there was increasing contact with the Roman world. In Wallerstein's terms (e.g. 1987, 317), a mini-social system came into contact with a world empire. In all its ramifications it was this relationship that put Irish society on a new course which was to lead to its transformation with the introduction of Christianity and which brought an end to Irish prehistory.

BIBLIOGRAPHY

Abbreviations

Antiq. J.	*Antiquaries Journal*
Archaeol. J.	*Archaeological Journal*
BAR	British Archaeological Reports
CBA Res. Reports	Council for British Archaeology Research Reports
J. Cork Hist. Archaeol. Soc.	*Journal of the Cork Historical and Archaeological Society*
J. Galway Archaeol. Hist. Soc.	*Journal of the Galway Archaeological and Historical Society*
J. Irish Archaeol.	*Journal of Irish Archaeology*
J. Kerry Archaeol. Hist. Soc.	*Journal of the Kerry Archaeological and Historical Society*
J. Kildare Archaeol. Soc.	*Journal of the Kildare Archaeological Society*
J. Roy. Soc. Antiq. Ireland	*Journal of the Royal Society of Antiquaries of Ireland*
HMSO	Her Majesty's Stationery Office
Nth Munster Antiq. J.	*North Munster Antiquarian Journal*
OPW	Office of Public Works
Proc. Prehist. Soc.	*Proceedings of the Prehistoric Society*
Proc. Roy. Irish Acad.	*Proceedings of the Royal Irish Academy*
Proc. Roy. Soc. London	*Proceedings of the Royal Society of London*
Ulster J. Archaeol.	*Ulster Journal of Archaeology*

ANDERSON, E. 1991 Kilcummer Lower. *Excavations 1990,* 16–17. Wordwell, Dublin.

ANTHONY, D.W. 1990 Migration in archeology: the baby and the bathwater. *American Anthropologist* **92,** 895–914.

APSIMON, A. 1969a An Early Neolithic house in Co. Tyrone. *J. Roy. Soc. Antiq. Ireland* **99,** 165–8.

APSIMON, A. 1969b The Earlier Bronze Age in the north of Ireland. *Ulster J. Archaeol.* **32,** 28–72.

APSIMON, A. 1976 Ballynagilly at the beginning and end of the Irish Neolithic. In S. J. de Laet (ed.), *Acculturation and continuity in Atlantic Europe,* 15–38. Dissertationes Archaeologicae Gandenses, Brugge.

APSIMON, A. 1985/6 Chronological contexts for Irish megalithic tombs. *J. Irish Archaeol.* **3,** 5–15.

ARMSTRONG, E.C.R. 1917 The Great Clare Find of 1854. *J. Roy. Soc. Antiq. Ireland* **47,** 21–36.

BAILEY, G. 1983 *Hunter-gatherer economy in prehistory.* Cambridge University Press, Cambridge.

BAILLIE, M.G.L. 1982 *Tree-ring dating and archaeology*. Croom Helm, London.

BAILLIE, M.G.L. 1985 Irish dendrochronology and radiocarbon calibration. *Ulster J. Archaeol.* **48**, 11–23.

BAILLIE, M.G.L. 1988a Irish oaks record prehistoric dust veils drama. *Archaeology Ireland* **2** (2), 71–4.

BAILLIE, M.G.L. 1988b Dating of the timbers from Navan Fort and Dorsey, Co. Armagh. *Emania* **4**, 37–42.

BAILLIE, M.G.L. 1989 Do Irish bog oaks date the Shang dynasty? *Current Archaeology* **117**, 310–13.

BAILLIE, M.G.L. 1991 Marking in marker dates; towards an archaeology with historical precision. *World Archaeology* **23**, 233–43.

BAILLIE, M.G.L. and BROWN, D.M. 1989 Further dates from the Dorsey. *Emania* **6**, 11.

BAILLIE, M.G.L. and MUNRO, M.A.R. 1988 Irish tree rings, Santorini and volcanic dust veils. *Nature* **332**, 344–6.

BARCLAY, G. 1982 Late Neolithic and Early Bronze Age burials: their treatment in salvage and rescue archaeology. *Scottish Archaeol. Review* **1**, 21–3.

BARKER, G. 1985 *Prehistoric farming in Europe*. Cambridge University Press, Cambridge.

BARRETT, J. 1988 The living, the dead and the ancestors: Neolithic and Early Bronze Age mortuary practice. In J. Barrett and I. Kinnes (eds), *The archaeology of context in the Neolithic and Bronze Age: recent trends,* 30–41. Department of Archaeology and Prehistory, University of Sheffield, Sheffield.

BARRETT, J. 1990 The monumentality of death: the character of Early Bronze Age mortuary mounds in southern Britain. *World Archaeology* **22**, 179–89.

BARRETT, J. and NEEDHAM, S. 1988 Production, circulation and exchange: problems in the interpretation of Bronze Age metalwork. In J. Barrett and I. Kinnes (eds), *The archaeology of context in the Neolithic and Bronze Age: recent trends,* 127–40. Department of Archaeology and Prehistory, University of Sheffield, Sheffield.

BATESON, J.D. 1973 Roman material from Ireland: a re-consideration. *Proc. Roy. Irish Acad.* **73C**, 21–97.

BATESON, J.D. 1976 Further finds of Roman material from Ireland. *Proc. Roy. Irish Acad.* **76C**, 171–80.

BENDER, B. 1978 Gatherer-hunter to farmer: a social perspective. *World Archaeology* **10**, 204–22.

BENGTSSON, H. and BERGH, S. 1984 The hut sites at Knocknarea North. In G. Burenhult, *The archaeology of Carrowmore: environmental archaeology and the megalithic tradition at Carrowmore, Co. Sligo, Ireland,* 216–318. Theses and Papers in North-European Archaeology 14. Institute of Archaeology, University of Stockholm, Stockholm.

BINCHY, E. 1967 Irish razors and razor-knives of the Middle Bronze Age. In E. Rynne (ed.), *North Munster Studies: Essays in commemoration of Monsignor Michael Moloney,* 43–60. Thomond Archaeological Society, Limerick.

BINFORD, L.R. 1971 Mortuary practices: their study and potential. In J.A. Brown (ed.), *Approaches to the social dimensions of mortuary practices,* 6–29. Memoirs of the Society for American Archaeology 25.

BINFORD, L.R. 1980 Willow smoke and dogs' tails: hunter-gatherer settlement systems and archaeological site form. *American Antiquity* **45**, 4–20.

BINFORD, L.R. 1983 *In pursuit of the past*. Thames and Hudson, London.

BIRD-DAVID, N. 1992 Beyond 'the original affluent society': a culturalist reformulation. *Current Anthropology* **33**, 25–47.

BLOCH, M. 1977 The past and the present in the present. *Man* 12, 278–92.

BOURKE, E. 1989 Stoneyford, a first-century Roman burial from Ireland. *Archaeology Ireland* 3 (2), 56–7.

BOWMAN, S. 1990 *Radiocarbon dating*. British Museum, London.

BRADLEY, J. 1982/3 Excavations at Moynagh Lough, Co Meath, 1980 81, interim report. *Ríocht na Midhe* 7 (2), 12–32.

BRADLEY, J. 1984 Excavations at Moynagh Lough, 1982–83, interim report. *Ríocht na Midhe* 7 (3), 86–93.

BRADLEY, J. 1985/6 Excavations at Moynagh Lough, 1984, summary report. *Ríocht na Midhe* 7 (4), 79–92.

BRADLEY, J. 1991 Excavations at Moynagh Lough, County Meath. *J. Roy. Soc. Antiq. Ireland* 121, 5–26.

BRADLEY, R. 1982a Position and possession: assemblage variation in the British Neolithic. *Oxford Journal of Archaeology* 1 (1), 27–38.

BRADLEY, R. 1982b The destruction of wealth in later prehistory. *Man* 17, 108–22.

BRADLEY, R. 1984 *The social foundations of prehistoric Britain*. Longman, London.

BRADLEY, R. 1985a *Consumption, change and the archaeological record: the archaeology of deliberate deposits*. Department of Archaeology Occasional Paper 13. University of Edinburgh, Edinburgh.

BRADLEY, R. 1985b Exchange and social distance: the structure of bronze artefact distribution. *Man* 20, 692–704.

BRADLEY, R. 1990 *The passage of arms*. Cambridge University Press, Cambridge.

BRADLEY, R. and CHAPMAN, R. 1984 Passage graves in the European Neolithic: a theory of converging evolution. In G. Burenhult, *The archaeology of Carrowmore: environmental archaeology and the megalithic tradition at Carrowmore, Co. Sligo, Ireland.*, 348–56. Theses and Papers in North-European Archaeology 14. Institute of Archaeology, University of Stockholm, Stockholm.

BRADLEY, R. and GORDON, K. 1988 Human skulls from the River Thames, their dating and significance. *Antiquity* 62, 503–9.

BRINDLEY, A.L. 1980 The Cinerary Urn tradition in Ireland—an alternative interpretation. *Proc. Roy. Irish Acad.* 80C, 197–206.

BRINDLEY, A.L. 1988 Aghnaskeagh A, County Louth: the portal dolmen and the cemetery cairn. *Co. Louth Archaeol. Hist. J.* 21, 394–7.

BRINDLEY, A.L. and LANTING, J.N. 1989/90 Radiocarbon dates for Neolithic single burials. *J. Irish Archaeol.* 5, 1–7.

BRINDLEY, A.L., LANTING, J.N. and MOOK, W.G. 1987/88 Radiocarbon dates from Moneen and Labbacallee, County Cork. *J. Irish Archaeol.* 4, 13–20.

BRINDLEY, A.L., LANTING, J.N. and MOOK, W.G. 1989/90 Radiocarbon dates from Irish fulachta fiadh and other burnt mounds. *J. Irish Archaeol.* 5, 25–33.

BRITNELL, W. 1982 The excavation of two round barrows at Trelystan, Powys. *Proc. Prehist. Soc.* 48, 133–201.

BUCKLEY, V.M. (ed.) 1990 *Burnt offerings: International contributions to burnt mound archaeology*. Wordwell, Dublin.

BUCKLEY, V.M. and SWEETMAN, P.D. 1991 *Archaeological Survey of County Louth*. OPW, Stationery Office, Dublin.

BURENHULT, G. 1980 *The archaeological excavation at Carrowmore, Co. Sligo, Ireland: excavation seasons 1977–79*. Theses and Papers in North-European Archaeology 9. Institute of Archaeology, University of Stockholm, Stockholm.

BURENHULT, G. 1984 *The archaeology of Carrowmore: environmental archaeology and the megalithic tradition at Carrowmore, Co. Sligo, Ireland*. Theses and Papers in North-European Archaeology 14. Institute of Archaeology, University of Stockholm, Stockholm.

BURGESS, C. 1974 The Bronze Age. In C. Renfrew (ed.), *British prehistory: a new outline*, 165–232. Duckworth, London.

BURGESS, C. 1976 Burials with metalwork in the Later Bronze Age in Wales and beyond. In G. Boon and J. Lewis (eds), *Welsh antiquity*, 81–104. National Museum of Wales, Cardiff.

BURGESS, C. 1980 *The age of Stonehenge*. Dent, London.

BURGESS, C. 1989 Volcanoes, catastrophe and the global crisis of the late second millennium BC. *Current Archaeology* **117**, 325–9.

BURGESS, C. and GERLOFF, S. 1981 *The dirks and rapiers of Great Britain and Ireland*. Prähistorische Bronzefunde, Abteilung IV, Band 7. C.H. Beck, Munich.

BURGESS, C. and SHENNAN, J. 1976 The Beaker phenomenon: some suggestions. In C. Burgess and R. Miket (eds), *Settlement and economy in the third and second millennia B.C.*, 309–31. BAR, Brit. Ser. 33, Oxford.

CANNON, A. 1989 The historical dimension in mortuary expressions of status and sentiment. *Current Anthropology* **30**, 437–58.

CARSON, R.A.G. and O'KELLY, C. 1967 A catalogue of the Roman coins from Newgrange, Co. Meath. *Proc. Roy. Irish Acad.* **77C**, 35–55.

CASE, H. 1969a Settlement patterns in the north Irish Neolithic. *Ulster J. Archaeol.* **32**, 3–27.

CASE, H. 1969b Neolithic explanations. *Antiquity* **43**, 176–86.

CASE, H. 1973 A ritual site in north-east Ireland. In G. Daniel and P. Kjaerum (eds), *Megalithic graves and ritual*, 173–96. Jutland Archaeological Society, Moesgard, Denmark.

CAULFIELD, S. 1977 The beehive quern in Ireland. *J. Roy. Soc. Antiq. Ireland* **107**, 104–38.

CAULFIELD, S. 1978 Neolithic fields: the Irish evidence. In H.C Bowen and P.J. Fowler (eds), *Early land allotment*, 137–44. BAR, Brit. Ser. 48, Oxford.

CAULFIELD, S. 1981 Some Celtic problems in the Irish Iron Age. In D. Ó Corráin (ed.), *Irish antiquity: essays and studies presented to Professor M. J. O'Kelly*, 205–15. Tower Books, Cork.

CAULFIELD, S. 1983 The Neolithic settlement of north Connaught. In T. Reeves-Smyth and F. Hamond (eds), *Landscape archaeology in Ireland*, 195–215. BAR, Brit. Ser. 116, Oxford.

CAULFIELD, S. 1988 *Céide Fields and Belderrig guide*. Morrigan Book Co., Killala.

CHAMPION, T.C. 1971 The end of the Irish Bronze Age. *Nth Munster Antiq. J.* **14**, 17–24.

CHAMPION, T.C. 1982 The myth of Iron Age invasions in Ireland. In B.G. Scott (ed.), *Studies on early Ireland: essays in honour of M.V. Duignan*, 39–44. Association of Young Irish Archaeologists, Belfast.

CHAMPION, T.C. 1989 From Bronze Age to Iron Age in Ireland. In M.L. Stig-Sørenson and R. Thomas (eds), *The Bronze Age–Iron Age transition in Europe*, 287–303. BAR, Int. Ser. 483, vol. 2, Oxford.

CHAMPION, T.C., GAMBLE, C.S., SHENNAN, S.J. and WHITTLE, A.W.R. 1984 *Prehistoric Europe*. Academic Press, London.

CHAPMAN, R. 1981 The emergence of formal disposal areas and the 'problem' of megalithic tombs in prehistoric Europe. In R. Chapman, I. Kinnes and K. Randsborg (eds), *The archaeology of death*, 71–81. Cambridge University Press, Cambridge.

CHAPMAN, R. and RANDSBORG, K. 1981 Approaches to the archaeology of death. In R. Chapman, I. Kinnes and K. Randsborg (eds), *The archaeology of death*, 1–24. Cambridge University Press, Cambridge.

CHAPMAN, R., KINNES, I. and RANDSBORG, K. (eds) 1981 *The archaeology of death*. Cambridge University Press, Cambridge.

CLARK, G.A. and NEELEY, M. 1987 Social differentiation in European Mesolithic burial data. In P. Rowley-Conwy, M. Zvelebil and H.P. Blankholm (eds), *Mesolithic Northwest Europe: recent trends*, 121–7. Department of Archaeology and Prehistory, University of Sheffield, Sheffield.

CLARKE, D.L. 1968 *Analytical archaeology*. Methuen, London.

CLARKE, D.L. 1976 Mesolithic Europe: the economic basis. In G. de G. Sieveking, I.H. Longworth and K.E. Wilson (eds), *Problems in economic and social archaeology*, 449–81. Duckworth, London.

CLARKE, D.V. and SHARPLES, N. 1985 Settlements and subsistence in the third millennium bc. In C. Renfrew (ed.), *The prehistory of Orkney*, 54–82. Edinburgh University Press, Edinburgh.

CLARKE, D.V., COWIE, T.G. and FOXON, A. 1985 *Symbols of power at the time of Stonehenge*. National Museum of Antiquities of Scotland, HMSO, Edinburgh.

CLEARY, R.M. 1983 The ceramic assemblage. In M.J. O'Kelly, R.M. Cleary and D. Lehane, *Newgrange, Co. Meath, Ireland: the Late Neolithic/Beaker period settlement.*, 58–117. BAR, Int. Ser. 190, Oxford.

CLEARY, R.M. and JONES, C. 1980 A cist-burial at Ballynagallagh, near Lough Gur, Co. Limerick. *Nth Munster Antiq. J.* 22, 3–7.

CLEARY, R.M., HURLEY, M.F. and TWOHIG, E.A. (eds) 1987 *Archaeological excavations on the Cork–Dublin gas pipeline (1981–82)*. Cork Archaeological Studies No. 1, University College Cork, Cork.

COLES, B. 1990 Anthropomorphic wooden figures from Britain and Ireland. *Proc. Prehist. Soc.* 56, 315–33.

COLES, J. 1963 Irish Bronze Age horns and their relations with Northern Europe. *Proc. Prehist. Soc.* 29, 326–56.

COLES, J. and HARDING, D. 1979 *The Bronze Age in Europe*. Methuen, London.

COLLINS, A.E.P. 1952 Excavations in the sandhills at Dundrum, Co. Down, 1950–1. *Ulster J. Archaeol.* 15, 2–30.

COLLINS, A.E.P. 1954 The excavation of a double horned cairn at Audleystown, Co. Down. *Ulster J. Archaeol.* 17, 7–56.

COLLINS, A.E.P. 1978 Excavations on Ballygalley Hill, County Antrim. *Ulster J. Archaeol.* 41, 15–32.

COLLINS, A.E.P. and SEABY, W.A. 1960 Structures and small finds discovered at Lough Eskragh, Co. Tyrone. *Ulster J. Archaeol.* 23, 25–37.

COLLINS, A.E.P. and WATERMAN, D.M. 1955 *Millin Bay, a Late Neolithic cairn in Co. Down*. HMSO, Belfast.

COLLIS, J. 1984a *The European Iron Age*. Batsford, London.

COLLIS, J. 1984b *Oppida: earliest towns north of the Alps*. Department of Archaeology and Prehistory, University of Sheffield, Sheffield.

COLQUHOUN, I. and BURGESS, C. 1988 *The swords of Britain*. Prähistorische Bronzefunde, Abteilung IV, Band 5. C.H. Beck, Munich.

CONDIT, T. 1990 Preliminary observations on the distribution of *fulachta fiadh* in County Kilkenny. In V. Buckley (ed.), *Burnt offerings: International contributions to burnt mound archaeology*, 18–23. Wordwell, Dublin.

CONNERTON, P. 1989 *How societies remember*. Cambridge University Press, Cambridge.

COONEY, G. 1979 Some aspects of the siting of megalithic tombs in County Leitrim. *J. Roy. Soc. Antiq. Ireland* 109, 74–91.

COONEY, G. 1983 Megalithic tombs in their environmental setting, a settlement perspective.

In T. Reeves-Smyth and F. Hamond (eds), *Landscape archaeology in Ireland*, 179–94. BAR, Brit. Ser. 116, Oxford.

COONEY, G. 1987 North Leinster in the earlier prehistoric period. Unpublished Ph.D. thesis, University College, Dublin.

COONEY, G. 1987/8 Irish Neolithic settlement and its European context. *J. Irish Archaeol.* **4**, 7–11.

COONEY, G. 1989 Stone axes of North Leinster. *Oxford Journal of Archaeology* **8**, 145–57.

COONEY, G. 1990 The place of megalithic tomb cemeteries in Ireland. *Antiquity* **64**, 741–53.

COONEY, G. 1991 Irish Neolithic landscapes and landuse systems: the implications of field systems. *Rural History* **2** (2), 123–39.

COONEY, G. 1992 Body politics and grave messages: Irish Neolithic mortuary practices. In N. Sharples and A. Sheridan (eds), *Vessels for the ancestors*, 128–42. Edinburgh University Press, Edinburgh.

COONEY, G. and GROGAN, E. 1991 An archaeological solution to the 'Irish' problem? *Emania* **9**, 33–43.

DARVILL, T. 1979 Court cairns, passage graves and social change in Ireland. *Man* **14**, 311–27.

DAVIES, K.M. 1989 A note on the location of the Roman burial site at Bray, Co. Wicklow. *Archaeology Ireland* **3** (3), 108–9.

DAVIES, O. 1936 Excavations at Dun Ruadh. *Proceedings of the Belfast Natural History and Philosophical Society* **1**, 50–75.

DAVIES, O. 1939 Excavations at the Giant's Grave, Loughash. *Ulster J. Archaeol.* **2**, 254–68.

DAVIES, O. and EVANS, E.E. 1934 Excavation of a chambered horned cairn at Ballyalton, Co. Down. *Proceedings of the Belfast Natural History and Philosophical Society* (1933–4), 79–103.

DENNELL, R. 1985 The hunter-gatherer/agricultural frontier in prehistoric temperate Europe. In S.W. Green and S.M. Perlman (eds), *The archaeology of frontiers and boundaries*, 113–39. Academic Press, London.

DE PAOR, M. 1957 Mound of the Hostages, Tara, Co. Meath. *Proc. Prehist. Soc.* **23**, 220–1.

DE VALERA, R. 1960 The court cairns of Ireland. *Proc. Roy. Irish Acad.* **60C**, 9–140.

DE VALERA, R. 1979 *Antiquities of the Irish countryside* (S.P. Ó Ríordáin: 5th edition, revised by R. de Valera). Methuen, London.

DE VALERA, R. and Ó NUALLÁIN, S. 1961 *Survey of the Megalithic Tombs of Ireland, Vol. I, Co. Clare.* Stationery Office, Dublin.

DE VALERA, R. and Ó NUALLÁIN, S. 1982 *Survey of the Megalithic Tombs of Ireland, Vol. IV, Cos Cork and Tipperary.* Stationery Office, Dublin.

DEVOY, R.J. 1983 Late Quaternary shorelines in Ireland; an assessment of their implications for isostatic land movement and relative sea level changes. In G. Smith and A.G. Dawson (eds), *Shorelines and isostasy*, 227–54. British Institute of Geographers, London.

DILLON, F. 1990 An analysis of two lithic collections. Unpublished M.A. thesis, University College, Dublin.

DOODY, M. 1987a Early Bronze Age burials, Ballyveelish 3, Co. Tipperary. In R.M. Cleary, M.F. Hurley and E.A. Twohig (eds), *Archaeological excavations on the Cork–Dublin gas pipeline (1981–82)*, 9–21. Cork Archaeological Studies No. 1, University College, Cork.

DOODY, M. 1987b Late Bronze Age settlement, Ballyveelish 2, Co. Tipperary. In R.M. Cleary, M.F. Hurley and E.A. Twohig (eds), *Archaeological excavations on the Cork–Dublin gas pipeline (1981–82)*, 22–35. Cork Archaeological Studies No 1, University College, Cork.

DOODY, M. 1987c Late Bronze Age huts at Curraghatoor, Co. Tipperary. In R.M. Cleary, M.F. Hurley and E.A. Twohig (eds), *Archaeological excavations on the Cork–Dublin gas pipeline (1981–82)*, 36–42. Cork Archaeological Studies No. 1, University College, Cork.

DOODY, M. 1988 Curraghatoor. In I. Bennett (ed.), *Excavations 1987*, 24. Wordwell, Dublin.

DOODY, M. 1989 Curraghatoor. In I. Bennett (ed.), *Excavations 1988*, 36. Wordwell, Dublin.

DOODY, M. 1990 Curraghatoor. In I. Bennett (ed.), *Excavations 1989*, 46. Wordwell, Dublin.

DOODY, M. 1991 Curraghatoor. In I. Bennett (ed.), *Excavations 1990*, 52. Wordwell, Dublin.

EDWARDS, K.J. 1979 Palynological and temporal inference in the context of prehistory with special reference to the evidence from lake and peat deposits. *Journal of Archaeological Science* **6**, 255–70.

EDWARDS, K.J. 1982 Man, space and the woodland edge—speculation on the detection and interpretation of human impact on pollen profiles. In S. Limbrey and M. Bell (eds), *Archaeological aspects of woodland ecology*, 5–22. BAR, Int. Ser. 146, Oxford.

EDWARDS, K.J. 1985 The anthropogenic factor in vegetational history. In K.J. Edwards and W.P. Warren (eds), *The Quaternary history of Ireland*, 187–220. Academic Press, London.

EDWARDS, K.J. and HIRONS, K.R. 1984 Cereal pollen grains in pre-elm decline deposits: implications for the earliest agriculture in Britain and Ireland. *Journal of Archaeological Science* **11**, 71–80.

EDWARDS, N. 1990 *The archaeology of early medieval Ireland*. Batsford, London.

EHRENBERG, M. 1989 *Women in prehistory*. British Museum, London.

EOGAN, G. 1963 A Neolithic habitation-site and megalithic tomb in Townleyhall townland, Co. Louth. *J. Roy. Soc. Antiq. Ireland* **93**, 37–81.

EOGAN, G. 1964 The Later Bronze Age in Ireland in the light of recent research. *Proc. Prehist. Soc.* **14**, 268–351.

EOGAN, G. 1965 *Catalogue of Irish bronze swords*. National Museum of Ireland, Stationery Office, Dublin.

EOGAN, G. 1968 Excavations at Knowth, Co. Meath, 1962–5. *Proc. Roy. Irish Acad.* **66C**, 299–382.

EOGAN, G. 1974 Regionale gruppierungen in der Spätbronzeit Irlands. *Archaeologisches Korrespondenzblatt* **IV**, 319–27.

EOGAN, G. 1983 *Hoards of the Irish Later Bronze Age*. University College, Dublin.

EOGAN, G. 1984 *Excavations at Knowth 1*. Royal Irish Academy Monographs in Archaeology, Dublin.

EOGAN, G. 1986 *Knowth and the passage tombs of Ireland*. Thames and Hudson, London.

EOGAN, G. 1990 Irish megalithic tombs and Iberia: comparisons and contrasts. In *Probleme der Megalithgraberforschung*, 117–37. Madrider Forschungen, Band 16. Walter de Gruyter, Berlin.

EOGAN, G. 1991 Prehistoric and Early Historic culture change at Brugh na Bóinne. *Proc. Roy. Irish Acad.* **91C**, 105–32.

EOGAN, G. and RICHARDSON, H. 1982 Two maceheads from Knowth, Co. Meath. *J. Roy. Soc. Antiq. Ireland* **112**, 123–38.

EVANS, E.E. 1935 Excavations at Aghnaskeagh, Co. Louth, Cairn A. *Co. Louth Archaeol. Hist. J.* **8**, 235–55.

EVANS, E.E. 1939 Excavations at Carnanbane, County Londonderry: a double horned cairn. *Proc. Roy. Irish Acad.* **45C**, 1–12.

EVANS, E.E. 1966 *Prehistoric and Early Christian Ireland. A guide*. Batsford, London.

EVANS, E.E. 1978 *Mourne Country: landscape and life in south Down* (3rd edn). Dundalgan Press, Dundalk.

EVANS, E.E. 1981 *The personality of Ireland* (2nd edn). Blackstaff Press, Belfast.

FAHY, E.M. 1959 A recumbent-stone circle at Drombeg, Co. Cork. *J. Cork Hist. Archaeol. Soc.* **64**, 1–27.

FAHY, E.M. 1961 A stone circle, hut and dolmen at Bohonagh, Co. Cork. *J. Cork Hist. Archaeol. Soc.* **66**, 93–104.

FAHY, E.M. 1962 A recumbent-stone circle at Reenascreena South, Co. Cork. *J. Cork Hist. Archaeol. Soc.* **67**, 59–69.

FLANAGAN, L.N.W. 1966 An unpublished flint hoard from the Braid valley, Co. Antrim. *Ulster J. Archaeol.* **29**, 82–90.

FLANAGAN, L.N W. 1976 The composition of Irish Bronze Age cemeteries. *Irish Archaeol. Research Forum* **3,** 7–20.

FLANAGAN, L.N.W. 1979 Industrial resources, production and distribution in Earlier Bronze Age Ireland. In M. Ryan (ed.), *The origins of metallurgy in Atlantic Europe*, 145–63. Stationery Office, Dublin.

FLANAGAN, L.N.W. 1982 The Earlier Irish Bronze Age industry in perspective. *J. Roy. Soc. Antiq. Ireland* **112**, 93–100.

FLEMING, A. 1987 Coaxial field systems: some questions of time and space. *Antiquity* **61**, 188–202.

FLEMING, A. 1988 *The Dartmoor Reaves*. Batsford, London.

FOLEY, C. 1988 An enigma solved: Kiltierney, Co. Fermanagh. In A. Hamlin and C. Lynn (eds), *Pieces of the past*, 24–6. HMSO, Belfast.

FOWLER, P.J. 1981 Wildscape to landscape: 'enclosure' in prehistoric Britain. In R. Mercer (ed.), *Farming practice in British prehistory*, 9–54. Edinburgh University Press, Edinburgh.

FOWLER, P.J. 1983 *The farming of prehistoric Britain*. Cambridge University Press, Cambridge.

FOX, C. 1946 *A find of the Early Iron Age from Llyn Cerrig Bach, Anglesey*. National Museum of Wales, Cardiff.

GENDEL, P.A. 1987 Socio-stylistic analysis of lithic artefacts from the Mesolithic of Northwestern Europe. In P. Rowley-Conwy, M. Zvelebil and H.P. Blankholm (eds), *Mesolithic Northwest Europe: recent trends*, 65–73. Department of Archaeology and Prehistory, University of Sheffield, Sheffield.

GENDEL, P.A. 1989 The analysis of lithic styles through distributional profiles of variation: examples from the Western European Mesolithic. In C. Bonsall (ed.), *The Mesolithic in Europe*, 40–7. John Donald, Edinburgh.

GERLOFF, S. 1986 Bronze Age Class A cauldrons: typology, origins and chronology. *J. Roy. Soc. Antiq. Ireland* **116**, 84–115.

GIBBONS, M. and HIGGINS, J. 1988 Connemara's emerging prehistory. *Archaeology Ireland* **2** (2), 63–6.

GIBSON, A.M. and SIMPSON, D.D.A. 1987 Lyles Hill, Co. Antrim. *Archaeology Ireland* **1** (2), 72–5.

GIBSON, A.M. and SIMPSON, D.D.A. 1989 Lyles Hill, Toberagnee. In I. Bennett (ed.), *Excavations 1988*, 9. Wordwell, Dublin.

GOWEN, M. 1988 *Three Irish gas pipelines: new archaeological evidence in Munster*. Wordwell, Dublin.

GOWEN, M. and TARBETT, C. 1988 A third season at Tankardstown. *Archaeology Ireland* **2** (4), 156.

GOWEN, M. and TARBETT, C. 1989 Tankardstown South Neolithic house sites. In I. Bennett (ed.), *Excavations 1988*, 38–9. Wordwell, Dublin.

GREEN, H.S. 1974 Early Bronze Age burial, territory and population in Milton Keynes, Buckinghamshire, and the Great Ouse Valley. *Archaeol. J.* **131**, 75–139.

GREEN, S.W. and ZVELEBIL, M. 1990 The Mesolithic colonisation and agricultural transition of south-east Ireland. *Proc. Prehist. Soc.* **56**, 57–88.

GREGORY, C.A. 1982 *Gifts and commodities*. Academic Press, London.

GROENMAN-VAN WAATERINGE, W. 1981 Field boundaries in Ireland. In D, Ó Corráin (ed.), *Irish antiquity: essays and studies presented to Professor M. J. O'Kelly*, 285–90. Tower Books, Cork.

GROENMAN-VAN WAATERINGE, W. 1983 The early agricultural utilisation of the Irish landscape: the last word on the elm decline?. In T. Reeves-Smyth and F. Hamond (eds), *Landscape archaeology in Ireland*, 217–32. BAR, Brit. Ser. 116, Oxford.

GROENMAN-VAN WAATERINGE, W. 1984 Appendix II: Pollen and seed analyses. In G. Eogan, *Excavations at Knowth 1*, 325–9. Royal Irish Academy Monographs in Archaeology, Dublin.

GROGAN, E. 1980 Houses of the Neolithic period in Ireland and comparative sites in Britain and on the Continent. Unpublished M.A. thesis, University College, Dublin.

GROGAN, E. 1983/4 Excavation of an Iron Age burial mound at Furness. *J. Kildare Archaeol. Soc.* **16**, 298–316.

GROGAN, E. 1988a Possible reconstructions of the (Tankardstown South) house. In M. Gowen, *Three Irish gas pipelines: new archaeological evidence in Munster*, 42. Wordwell, Dublin.

GROGAN, E. 1988b The pipeline sites and the prehistory of the Limerick area. In M. Gowen, *Three Irish gas pipelines: new archaeological evidence in Munster*, 148–57. Wordwell, Dublin.

GROGAN, E. 1989 The early prehistory of the Lough Gur region. Unpublished Ph.D. thesis, University College, Dublin.

GROGAN, E. 1990 A Bronze Age cemetery at Carrig, Blessington, Co. Wicklow. *Archaeology Ireland* **4** (4), 12–14.

GROGAN, E. and CAULFIELD, S. (forthcoming) Excavations at Tara by Seán P. Ó Ríordáin: the Rath of the Synods.

GROGAN, E. and COONEY, G. 1990 A preliminary distribution map of stone axes in Ireland. *Antiquity* **64**, 559–61.

GROGAN, E. and EOGAN, G. 1987 Lough Gur excavations by Seán P. Ó Ríordáin: further Neolithic and Beaker habitations on Knockadoon. *Proc. Roy. Irish Acad.* **87C**, 299–506.

HARBISON, P. 1968 Catalogue of Irish Early Bronze Age associated finds containing copper or bronze. *Proc. Roy. Irish Acad.* **67C**, 35–91.

HARBISON, P. 1969a *The daggers and the halberds of the Early Bronze Age in Ireland*. Prähistorische Bronzefunde, Abteilung VI, Band 1. C.H. Beck, Munich.

HARBISON, P. 1969b *The axes of the Early Bronze Age in Ireland*. Prähistorische Bronzefunde, Abteilung IX, Band 1. C.H. Beck, Munich.

HARBISON, P. 1973 The Earlier Bronze Age in Ireland. *J. Roy. Soc. Antiq. Ireland* **103**, 93–153.

HARBISON, P. 1988 *Pre-Christian Ireland*. Thames and Hudson, London.

HARRISON, R.J. 1980 *The Beaker Folk*. Thames and Hudson, London.

HARDING, A.F. and LEE, G.E. 1987 *Henge monuments and related sites in Great Britain*. BAR, Brit. Ser. 175, Oxford.

HARDING, D. 1976 *Hillforts: later prehistoric earthworks in Britain and Ireland*. Academic Press, London.

HARTNETT, P.J. 1957 Excavation of a passage grave at Fourknocks, Co. Meath. *Proc. Roy. Irish Acad.* **58C**, 197–277.

HARTNETT, P.J. 1971 The excavation of two tumuli at Fourknocks (sites II and III), Co. Meath. *Proc. Roy. Irish Acad.* **71C**, 35–89.

HARTWELL, B. 1991 Ballynahatty—a prehistoric ceremonial centre. *Archaeology Ireland* **5** (4), 12–15.

HASSAN, F. 1981 *Demographic archaeology.* Academic Press, London.

HAWKES, C.F.C. 1954 Archaeological theory and method: some suggestions from the Old World. *American Anthropologist* **56**, 155–68.

HAWKES, C.F.C. 1972 Cumulative Celticity in pre-Roman Britain. *Études Celtiques* **13**, 607–28.

HAWKES, C.F.C. and SMITH, M.A. 1957 On some buckets and cauldrons of the Bronze and Early Iron Ages. *Antiq. J.* **37**, 131–98.

HAWKES, J. 1941 Excavations of a megalithic tomb at Harristown, Co. Waterford. *J. Roy. Soc. Antiq. Ireland* **71**, 130–47.

HENCKEN, H. O'N. 1942 Ballinderry crannog No. 2. *Proc. Roy. Irish Acad.* **47C**, 1–76.

HENCKEN, H. O'N. 1950 Lagore crannog: an Irish royal residence of the 7th to 10th centuries A.D. *Proc. Roy. Irish Acad.* **53C**, 1–247.

HENCKEN, H. O'N. and MOVIUS, H.L. 1934 The cemetery cairn at Knockast. *Proc. Roy. Irish Acad.* **41C**, 232–84.

HERITY, M. 1969 Early finds of Irish antiquities. *Antiq. J.* **49**, 1–21.

HERITY, M. 1974 *Irish passage graves.* Irish University Press, Dublin.

HERITY, M. 1981 A Bronze Age farmstead at Glenree, Co. Mayo. *Popular Archaeology* **2** (9), 36–7.

HERITY, M. 1982 Irish decorated Neolithic pottery. *Proc. Roy. Irish Acad.* **82C**, 247–404.

HERITY, M. 1983 A survey of the royal site of Cruachain in Connacht, 1: introduction, the monuments and topography. *J. Roy. Soc. Antiq. Ireland* **113**, 121–42.

HERITY, M. 1984 A survey of the royal site of Cruachain in Connacht, II: prehistoric monuments. *J. Roy. Soc. Antiq. Ireland* **114**, 125–38.

HERITY, M. 1987a The finds from Irish court tombs. *Proc. Roy. Irish Acad.* **87C**, 103–281.

HERITY, M. 1987b A survey of the royal site of Cruachain in Connacht III: ringforts and ecclesiastical sites. *J. Roy. Soc. Antiq. Ireland* **117**, 125–41.

HERITY, M. and EOGAN, G. 1977 *Ireland in prehistory.* Routledge and Kegan Paul, London.

HERRING, I. 1938 The cairn excavation at Well Glass Spring, Largantea, Co. Londonderry. *Ulster J. Archaeol.* **1**, 164–88.

HIGGS, E.S. and VITA-FINZI, C. 1972 Prehistoric economies: a territorial approach. In E.S. Higgs (ed.), *Papers in economic prehistory*, 27–36. Cambridge University Press, Cambridge.

HODDER, I. 1982 *Symbols in action.* Cambridge University Press, Cambridge.

HODDER, I. 1984 Burials, houses, women and men in the European Neolithic. In D. Miller and C. Tilley (eds), *Ideology, power and prehistory*, 51–68. Cambridge University Press, Cambridge.

HODDER, I. 1986 *Reading the past..* Cambridge University Press, Cambridge.

HODDER, I. 1987 The contribution of the long-term. In I. Hodder (ed.), *Archaeology as long-term history,* 1–8. Cambridge University Press, Cambridge.

HODDER, I. 1988 Material culture texts and social change: a theoretical discussion and some archaeological examples. *Proc. Prehist. Soc.* **54**, 67–75.

HODDER, I. 1989 Post-modernism, post-structuralism and post-processual archaeology. In I. Hodder (ed.), *The meanings of things*, 64–88. Unwin Hyman, London.

HODDER, I. (ed.) 1991 *Archaeological theory in Europe.* Routledge, London.

HODGES, H. 1956 Studies in the Late Bronze Age of Ireland: 1. Stone and clay moulds and wooden models for bronze implements. *Ulster J. Archaeol.* **19**, 29–56.

HODGES, H.W.M. 1958 A hunting camp at Cullyhanna Lough, near Newtown Hamilton, County Armagh. *Ulster J. Archaeol.* **21**, 7–13.

HUNT, J. 1967 Prehistoric burials at Caherguillamore, Co. Limerick. In E. Rynne (ed.), *North Munster studies: essays in commemoration of Monsignor Michael Moloney*, 20–42. Thomond Archaeological Society, Limerick.

IVENS, R.J., SIMPSON, D.D.A. and BROWN, D. 1986 Excavations at Island MacHugh in 1985, interim report. *Ulster J. Archaeol.* **46**, 99–103.

JACOBI, R. 1979 Early Flandrian hunters in the south west. *Proc. Devon Archaeological Society* **37**, 48–93.

JENSEN, J. 1982 *The prehistory of Denmark*. Methuen, London.

JESSEN, K. and HELBAEK, H. 1944 Cereals in Great Britain and Ireland in prehistoric and Early Historic times. *Det Kongelige Danske Videnskabernes Selskab: Biologiske Skrifter* **III** (2), 1–68.

JOCHIM, M.A. 1976 *Hunter gatherer subsistence and settlement: a prehistoric model*. Academic Press, London.

JOPE, E.M. 1952 Porcellanite axes from factories in north-east Ireland: Tievebulliagh and Rathlin. *Ulster J. Archaeol.* **15**, 31–55.

KAVANAGH, R.M. 1976 Collared and Cordoned Urns in Ireland. *Proc. Roy. Irish Acad.* **76C**, 293–403.

KAVANAGH, R.M. 1991 A reconsideration of razors in the Irish Earlier Bronze Age. *J. Roy. Soc. Antiq. Ireland* **121**, 77–104.

KELLY, E.P. 1974 Aughinish stone forts. In T. Delaney (ed.), *Excavations 1974*, 21. Association of Young Irish Archaeologists, Belfast.

KELLY, E.P. 1978 A re-assessment of the dating evidence for Knockadoon Class II pottery. *Irish Archaeological Research Forum* **5**, 23–7.

KILBRIDE-JONES, H.E. 1954 The excavation of an unrecorded megalithic tomb on Kilmashogue Mountain, Co. Dublin. *Proc. Roy. Irish Acad.* **56C**, 461–79.

KILFEATHER, A. 1991 Patterns in Early Bronze Age society: a study of aceramic grave goods in Ireland. Unpublished M.A. thesis, University College, Dublin.

KINNES, I. 1988 The Cattleship Potemkin: the first Neolithic in Britain. In J. Barrett and I. Kinnes (eds), *The archaeology of context in the Neolithic and Bronze Age: recent trends*, 2–8. Department of Archaeology and Prehistory, University of Sheffield, Sheffield.

LARSSON, L. 1989 Late Mesolithic settlements and cemeteries at Skateholm, southern Sweden. In C. Bonsall (ed.), *The Mesolithic in Europe*, 367–78. John Donald, Edinburgh.

LAYTON, R. 1986 Political and territorial structures among hunter-gatherers. *Man* **21**, 18–33.

LAYTON, R., FOLEY, R. and WILLIAMS, E. 1991 The transition between hunting and gathering and the specialised husbandry of resources. *Current Anthropology* **32**, 255–74.

LEASK, H.G. and PRICE, L. 1936 The Labbacallee megalith, Co. Cork. *Proc. Roy. Irish Acad.* **43C**, 77–101.

LIVERSAGE, G.D. 1958 An island site at Lough Gur. *J. Roy. Soc. Antiq. Ireland* **88**, 67–81.

LIVERSAGE, G.D. 1960 A Neolithic site at Townleyhall, Co. Louth. *J. Roy. Soc. Antiq. Ireland* **90**, 49–60.

LIVERSAGE, G.D. 1968 Excavations at Dalkey Island, Co. Dublin, 1956–1959. *Proc. Roy. Irish Acad.* **66C**, 53–233.

LUCAS, A.T. 1960 Irish food before the Famine. *Gwerin* **3**, 1–36.

LYNCH, A. 1981 *Man and environment in south-west Ireland, 4000 BC–AD 800*. BAR, Brit. Ser. 85, Oxford.

LYNCH, A. 1988 Poulnabrone, a stone in time. *Archaeology Ireland* **2** (3), 105–7.

LYNN, C.J. 1973–4 The excavation of a ring-cairn in Carnkenny, Co. Tyrone. *Ulster J. Archaeol.* **36–7**, 17–31.

LYNN, C.J. 1977 Trial excavations of the Kings Stables, Tray Townland, County Armagh. *Ulster J. Archaeol.* **40**, 42–62.

LYNN, C.J. 1978 Early Christian period domestic structures: a change from round to rectangular. *Irish Archaeological Research Forum* **5**, 29–45.

LYNN, C.J. 1982 The Dorsey and other linear earthworks. In B. Scott (ed.), *Studies on early Ireland: essays in honour of M.V. Duignan*, 121–8. Association of Young Irish Archaeologists, Belfast.

LYNN, C.J. 1983 Some 'early' ring-forts and crannogs. *J. Irish Archaeol.* **1**, 47–58.

LYNN, C.J. 1986 Navan Fort: a draft summary of D.M. Waterman's excavations. *Emania* **1**, 11–19.

LYNN, C.J. 1988 Armagh in 3000 BC: 39–41 Scotch Street, Armagh City. In A. Hamlin and C. Lynn (eds), *Pieces of the past*, 8–10. HMSO, Belfast.

LYNN, C.J. 1991a Knockaulin (Dún Ailinne) and Navan: some architectural comparisons. *Emania* **8**, 51–6.

LYNN, C.J. 1991b Further research on the Dorsey. Supplementary note to reprint of H.G. Tempest 1930 The Dorsey. *Co. Louth Archaeol. Hist. J.* **6** (2), 187–240.

LYNN, C.J. 1992 The Iron Age mound in Navan Fort: a physical realization of Celtic religious beliefs? *Emania* **10**, 33–57.

MACALISTER, R.A.S. 1929 On some antiquities discovered upon Lambay Island. *Proc. Roy. Irish Acad.* **38C**, 240–6.

MACALISTER, R.A.S., ARMSTRONG, E.C.R. and PRAEGER, R.Ll. 1913 A Bronze Age interment with associated standing-stone and earthen ring, near Naas, Co. Kildare. *Proc. Roy. Irish Acad.* **30C**, 351–60.

MCCORMICK, F. 1985 Appendix II. The animal bones. In C. Manning, 'A Neolithic burial mound at Ashleypark, Co. Tipperary'. *Proc. Roy. Irish Acad.* **85C**, 89–94.

MCCORMICK, F. 1985/6 Animal bones from prehistoric Irish burials. *J. Irish Archaeol.* **3**, 37–48.

MCCORMICK, F. 1987 The animal bones (from Ballyveelish 2 and 3). In R.M. Cleary, M.F. Hurley and E.A. Twohig (eds), *Archaeological excavations on the Cork–Dublin gas pipeline (1981–82)*, 26–9. Cork Archaeological Studies No. 1, University College Cork, Cork.

MCCORMICK, F. 1988a The animal bones. In M. Gowen, *Three Irish gas pipelines: new archaeological evidence in Munster*, 182–4. Wordwell, Dublin.

MCCORMICK, F. 1988b Animal bones from Haughey's Fort. *Emania* **4**, 24–7.

MCCORMICK, F. 1991 The animal bones from Haughey's Fort: second report. *Emania* **8**, 27–33.

MACDERMOTT, M. 1949 Lough Gur excavations: excavation of a barrow in Cahercorney, Co. Limerick. *J. Cork Hist. Archaeol. Soc.* **54**, 101–2.

MAC EOIN, G. 1986 The Celticity of Celtic Ireland. In K.H. Schmidt (ed.), *Geschichte und Kultur der Kelten*, 161–74. Carl Winter, Universitätsverlag, Heidelberg.

MAC NIOCAILL, G. 1972 *Ireland before the Vikings*. Gill and McMillan, Dublin.

MADSEN, T. 1982 Settlement systems of early agricultural societies in East Jutland, Denmark: a regional study of change. *Journal of Anthropological Archaeology* **1**, 197–236.

MAHR, A. 1930 A wooden idol from Ireland. *Antiquity* **4**, 487.

MAHR, A. 1937 New aspects and problems in Irish prehistory. *Proc. Prehist. Soc.* **3**, 262–436.

MALINA, J. and VASICEK, Z. 1990 *Archaeology yesterday and today*. Cambridge University Press, Cambridge.

MALLORY, J.P. 1984a The Long Stone, Ballybeen, Dundonald, County Down. *Ulster J. Archaeol.* **47**, 1–4.

MALLORY, J.P. 1984b The origins of the Irish. *J. Irish Archaeol.* **2**, 65–9.

MALLORY, J.P. 1988 Trial excavations at Haughey's Fort. *Emania* **4**, 5–20.

MALLORY, J.P. 1990 Trial excavations at Tievebulliagh, Co. Antrim. *Ulster J. Archaeol.* **53**, 15–28.

MALLORY, J.P. 1991a Excavations at Haughey's Fort: 1989–1990. *Emania* **8**, 10–26.

MALLORY, J.P. 1991b Further dates from Haughey's Fort. *Emania* **9**, 64–5.

MALLORY, J.P. 1991c Two perspectives on the problem of Irish origins. *Emania* **9**, 53–8.

MALLORY, J.P. and HARTWELL, B. 1984 Donegore Hill. *Current Archaeology* **8** (9), 271–5.

MALLORY, J.P and McNEILL, T.E. 1991 *The archaeology of Ulster*. Institute of Irish Studies, Queens's University, Belfast.

MALLORY, J.P. and WARNER, R. 1988 The date of Haughey's Fort. *Emania* **5**, 36–40.

MANNING, C. 1985 A Neolithic burial mound at Ashleypark, Co. Tipperary. *Proc. Roy. Irish Acad.* **85C**, 61–100.

MAUSS, M. 1954 *The gift*. Cohen and West, London.

MEILLASSOUX, C. 1972 From reproduction to production. *Economy and Society* **1**, 93–105.

MERCER, R. (ed.) 1977 *Beakers in Britain and Europe*. BAR, Int. Ser. 26, Oxford.

MERCER, R. 1981 Excavations at Carn Brea, Illogan, Cornwall 1970–73. *Cornish Archaeology* **20**, 1–204.

MERCER, R. 1990 *Causewayed enclosures*. Shire Books, Princes Risborough.

MILLER, D. 1982 Structures and strategies: an aspect of the relationship between social hierarchy and cultural change. In I. Hodder (ed.), *Symbolic and structural archaeology*, 89–98. Cambridge University Press, Cambridge.

MITCHELL, G.F. 1940 Studies in Irish Quaternary deposits: some lacustrine deposits near Dunshaughlin, Co. Meath. *Proc. Roy. Irish Acad.* **46B**, 13–37.

MITCHELL, G.F. 1956 An early kitchen-midden at Sutton, Co. Dublin. *J. Roy. Soc. Antiq. Ireland* **86**, 1–26.

MITCHELL, G.F. 1970 Some chronological implications of the Irish Mesolithic. *Ulster J. Archaeol.* **33**, 3–14.

MITCHELL, G.F. 1972a Further investigations of the early kitchen-midden at Sutton, Co. Dublin. *J. Roy. Soc. Antiq. Ireland* **102**, 151–9.

MITCHELL, G.F. 1972b Some Ultimate Larnian sites at Lough Derravaragh, Co. Westmeath. *J. Roy. Soc. Antiq. Ireland* **102**, 160–73.

MITCHELL, G.F. 1976 *The Irish landscape*. Collins, London.

MITCHELL, G.F. 1986 *Reading the Irish landscape*. Country House, Dublin.

MITCHELL, G.F. 1989 *Man and environment in Valencia Island*. Royal Irish Academy, Dublin.

MITCHELL, G.F. and SIEVEKING, G. de G. 1972 Flint flake, probably of Palaeolithic age, from Mell townland, near Drogheda, Co. Louth, Ireland. *J. Roy. Soc. Antiq. Ireland* **102**, 174–7.

MOFFETT, L., ROBINSON, M.A. and STRAKER, V. 1989 Cereals, fruit and nuts: charred plant remains from Neolithic sites in England and Wales and the Neolithic economy. In A. Milles, D. Williams and N. Gardner (eds), *The beginnings of agriculture*, 243–61. BAR, Int. Ser. 496, Oxford.

MOGEY, J.M., THOMPSON, G.B. and PROUDFOOT, V.B. 1956 Excavation of two ring-barrows in Mullaghmore townland, Co. Down. *Ulster J. Archaeol.* **19**, 11–28.

MOHEN, J.-P. 1989 *The world of megaliths*. Cassell, London.

MOLLESON, T.I. 1985/6 New radiocarbon dates for the occupation of Kilgreany Cave, Co. Waterford. *J. Irish Archaeol.* **3**, 1–3.

MOLLOY, K. and O'CONNELL, M. 1987 The nature of the vegetational changes at about 5000 BP with particular reference to the elm decline: fresh evidence from Connemara, Western Ireland. *New Phytologist* **106**, 203–20.

MOLLOY, K. and O'CONNELL, M. 1988 Neolithic agriculture—fresh evidence from Cleggan, Connemara. *Archaeology Ireland* 2 (2), 67–70.

MOLONEY, A. 1991 Clonfinlough palisaded enclosure. In I. Bennett (ed.), *Excavations 1990*, 48–9. Wordwell, Dublin.

MONK, M.A. 1985/6 Evidence from macroscopic plant remains for crop husbandry in prehistoric and Early Historic Ireland: a review. *J. Irish Archaeol.* 3, 31–6.

MONK, M.A. 1988 Archaeobotanical study of samples from pipeline sites. In M. Gowen, *Three Irish gas pipelines: new archaeological evidence in Munster*, 185–91. Wordwell, Dublin.

MORRIS, I. 1987 *Burial and ancient society: the rise of the Greek city-state*. Cambridge University Press, Cambridge.

MOUNT, C. 1989 Early Bronze Age burials in Southern Leinster. Unpublished M.A. thesis, University College, Dublin.

MOUNT, C. 1991 Early Bronze Age burials—the social implications. *Archaeology Ireland* 5 (2), 21–3.

MOUNT, C. 1992 Animals and ritual in the Beaker period at Newgrange. *Trowel* 3, 21–6.

MOVIUS, H.L. 1942 *The Irish Stone Age; its chronology, development and relationships*. Cambridge University Press, Cambridge.

MOVIUS, H.L. 1953 Curran Point, Larne, Co. Antrim, the type site of the Irish Mesolithic. *Proc. Roy. Irish Acad.* **56C**, 1–95.

MURPHY, B. 1977 A hand axe from Dun Aonghus, Inishmore, Aran Islands, Co. Galway. *Proc. Roy. Irish Acad.* **77C**, 257–8.

MYTUM, H. 1992 *The origins of Early Christian Ireland*. Routledge, London.

O'BRIEN, B. 1990 Iron Age burial practices in Leinster: continuity and change. *Emania* **7**, 37–42.

O'BRIEN, W.F. 1990 Prehistoric copper mining in south-west Ireland: the Mount Gabriel-type mines. *Proc. Prehist. Soc.* **56**, 269–90.

O'CARROLL, F. 1986 Irish basal-looped spearheads. Unpublished M.A. thesis, University College, Dublin.

O'CONNELL, M. 1987 Early cereal-type pollen records from Connemara, western Ireland, and their possible significance. *Pollen et Spores* **29**, 207–24.

Ó DANACHAIR, C. 1981 An rí (the king): an example of traditional social organisation. *J. Roy. Soc. Antiq. Ireland* **111**, 14–28.

Ó DONNABHÁIN, B. 1988 Report on the osseous remains from sites on the Mitchelstown–Limerick and Bruff–Mallow gas pipelines. In M. Gowen, *Three Irish gas pipelines: new archaeological evidence in Munster*, 192–5. Wordwell, Dublin.

Ó FLOINN, R. 1979 Bronze axehead from a cist burial. *Ulster J. Archaeol.* **42**, 85.

Ó FLOINN, R. 1992 A Neolithic cave burial in Limerick. *Archaeology Ireland* 6 (2), 19–21.

Ó H-ICHEADHA, G. 1946 The Moylisha megalith, Co. Wicklow. *J. Roy. Soc. Antiq. Ireland* **76**, 119–28.

O'KELLY, M.J. 1951 An Early Bronze Age ringfort at Carrigillihy, Co. Cork. *J. Cork Hist. Archaeol. Soc.* **56**, 69–86.

O'KELLY, M.J. 1952 Excavation of a cairn at Moneen, Co. Cork. *Proc. Roy. Irish Acad.* **54C**, 121–59.

O'KELLY, M.J. 1958 A wedge-shaped gallery-grave at Island, Co. Cork. *J. Roy. Soc. Antiq. Ireland* **88**, 1–23.

O'KELLY, M.J. 1960 A wedge-shaped gallery grave at Baurnadomeeny, Co. Tipperary. *J. Cork Hist. Archaeol. Soc.* **65**, 85–115.

O'KELLY, M.J. 1981 The megalithic tombs of Ireland. In J.D. Evans, B. Cunliffe and C.

Renfrew (eds), *Antiquity and man: essays in honour of Glyn Daniel*, 177–90. Thames and Hudson, London.

O'KELLY, M.J. 1982 *Newgrange, archaeology, art and legend*. Thames and Hudson, London.

O'KELLY, M.J. 1983 The excavation. In M.J. O'Kelly, R.M. Cleary and D. Lehane, *Newgrange, Co. Meath, Ireland: the Late Neolithic/Beaker period settlement*, 1–57. BAR, Int. Ser. 190, Oxford.

O'KELLY, M.J. 1989 *Early Ireland, an introduction*. Cambridge University Press, Cambridge.

O'KELLY, M.J. and SHELL, C.A. 1979 Stone objects and a bronze axe from Newgrange, Co. Meath. In M. Ryan (ed.), *The origins of metallurgy in Atlantic Europe*, 127–44. Stationery Office, Dublin.

O'KELLY, M.J., CLEARY, R.M. and LEHANE, D. 1983 *Newgrange, Co. Meath, Ireland: the Late Neolithic/Beaker period settlement*. BAR, Int. Ser. 190, Oxford.

O'KELLY, M.J., LYNCH, F.M. and O'KELLY, C. 1978 Three passage graves at Newgrange, Co. Meath. *Proc. Roy. Irish Acad*. **78C**, 249–352.

Ó NUALLÁIN, S. 1972 A Neolithic house at Ballyglass near Ballycastle, Co. Mayo. *J. Roy. Soc. Antiq. Ireland* **102**, 49–57.

Ó NUALLÁIN, S. 1975 The stone circle complex of Cork and Kerry. *J. Roy. Soc. Antiq. Ireland* **105**, 83–131.

Ó NUALLÁIN, S. 1978 Boulder-burials. *Proc. Roy. Irish Acad*. **78C**, 75–100.

Ó NUALLÁIN, S. 1983 Irish portal tombs: topography, siting and distribution. *J. Roy. Soc. Antiq. Ireland* **113**, 75–105.

Ó NUALLÁIN, S. 1984a A survey of the stone circles in Cork and Kerry. *Proc. Roy. Irish Acad*. **84C**, 1–77.

Ó NUALLÁIN, S. 1984b Grouped standing stones, radial stone cairns and enclosures in the south of Ireland. *J. Roy. Soc. Antiq. Ireland* **114**, 63–79.

Ó NUALLÁIN, S. 1988 Stone rows in the south of Ireland. *Proc. Roy. Irish Acad*. **88C**, 179–256.

Ó NUALLÁIN, S. 1989 *Survey of the Megalithic Tombs of Ireland, Vol. V, Co. Sligo*. Stationery Office, Dublin.

Ó NUALLÁIN, S. and WALSH, P. 1986 A reconsideration of the Tramore passage-tombs. *Proc. Prehist. Soc*. **52**, 25–9.

Ó RÍORDÁIN, S.P. 1940 Excavations at Cush, Co. Limerick. *Proc. Roy. Irish Acad*. **45C**, 83–181.

Ó RÍORDÁIN, S.P. 1946 Prehistory in Ireland, 1937–46. *Proc. Prehist. Soc*. **12**, 142–71.

Ó RÍORDÁIN, S.P. 1947 Excavation of a barrow at Rathjordan, Co. Limerick. *J. Cork Hist. Archaeol. Soc*. **52**, 1–4.

Ó RÍORDÁIN, S.P. 1948 Further barrows at Rathjordan, Co. Limerick. *J. Cork Hist. Archaeol. Soc*. **53**, 19–31.

Ó RÍORDÁIN, S.P. 1951 Lough Gur excavations: the Great Stone Circle (B) in Grange Townland. *Proc. Roy. Irish Acad*. **54C**, 37–74.

Ó RÍORDÁIN, S.P. 1954 Lough Gur excavations: Neolithic and Bronze Age houses on Knockadoon. *Proc. Roy. Irish Acad*. **56C**, 297–459.

Ó RÍORDÁIN, S.P. 1955 A burial with faience beads at Tara. *Proc. Prehist. Soc*. **21**, 163–73.

Ó RÍORDÁIN, S.P. 1965 *Tara: the monuments on the hill* (4th edn). Dundalgan Press, Dundalk.

Ó RÍORDÁIN, S.P. and DE VALERA, R. 1952 Excavation of a megalithic tomb at Ballyedmonduff, Co. Dublin. *Proc. Roy. Irish Acad*. **55C**, 61–81.

Ó RÍORDÁIN, S.P. and Ó H-ICHEADHA, G. 1955 Lough Gur excavations: the megalithic tomb. *J. Roy. Soc. Antiq. Ireland* **85**, 34–50.

O'SULLIVAN, A. 1990 Wood in archaeology. *Archaeology Ireland* **4** (2), 69–73.

O'SULLIVAN, M. 1986 Approaches to passage tomb art. *J. Roy. Soc. Antiq. Ireland* **116**, 68–83.

O'SULLIVAN, M. 1989 A stylistic revolution in the megalithic art of the Boyne Valley. *Archaeology Ireland* **3** (4), 138–42.

PETERSON, J.D. 1990 From foraging to food production in south-east Ireland: some lithic evidence. *Proc. Prehist. Soc.* **56**, 89–99.

PILCHER, J.R. 1969 Archaeology, palaeoecology and C^{14} dating of the Beaghmore stone circle site. *Ulster J. Archaeol.* **32**, 73–90.

POLLOCK, A.J. and WATERMAN, D.M. 1964 A Bronze Age habitation site at Downpatrick. *Ulster J. Archaeol.* **27**, 31–58.

POWELL, T.G.E. 1941 Excavation of a megalithic tomb at Carriglong, Co. Waterford. *J. Cork Hist. Archaeol. Soc.* **46**, 55–62.

POWER, D. 1990 *Fulachta fiadh* in Co. Cork. In V. Buckley (ed.), *Burnt offerings: International contributions to burnt mound archaeology*, 13–17. Wordwell, Dublin.

PREECE, R.C., COXON, P. and ROBINSON, J.E. 1986 New biostratigraphic evidence of the post-glacial colonization of Ireland and for Mesolithic forest disturbance. *Journal of Biogeography* **13**, 487–509.

PRENDERGAST, E. 1959 Prehistoric burial at Rath, Co. Wicklow. *J. Roy. Soc. Antiq. Ireland* **89**, 17–29.

PRICE, T.D. 1987 The Mesolithic of Western Europe. *Journal of World Prehistory* **1**, 225–305.

PRICE, T.D. and BROWN, J.A. (eds) 1985 *Prehistoric hunter-gatherers: the emergence of cultural complexity*. Academic Press, London.

RAFTERY, B. 1972 Irish hillforts. In C. Thomas (ed.), *The Iron Age in the Irish Sea Province*, 37–58. CBA Res. Report 9, London.

RAFTERY, B. 1973 Rathgall: a Late Bronze Age burial in Ireland. *Antiquity* **47**, 293–5.

RAFTERY, B. 1974 A prehistoric burial mound at Baunogenasraid, Co. Carlow. *Proc. Roy. Irish Acad.* **74C**, 277–312.

RAFTERY, B. 1976a Rathgall and Irish hillfort problems. In D.W. Harding (ed.), *Hillforts— later prehistoric earthworks in Britain and Ireland*, 339–57. Academic Press, London.

RAFTERY, B. 1976b Dowris, Hallstatt and La Tène in Ireland: problems of the transition from bronze to iron. In S.J. de Laet (ed.), *Acculturation and continuity in Atlantic Europe*, 189–97. Dissertationes Archaeologicae Gandenses, Brugge.

RAFTERY, B. 1981 Iron Age burials in Ireland. In D. Ó Corráin (ed.), *Irish antiquity: essays and studies presented to Professor M.J. O'Kelly*, 173–204. Tower Books, Cork.

RAFTERY, B. 1983 *A catalogue of Irish Iron Age antiquities*. Veröffentlichung des Vorgeschichtlichen Seminars Marburg, Sonderband 1, Marburg.

RAFTERY, B. 1984 *La Tène in Ireland: problems of origin and chronology*. Veröffentlichung des Vorgeschichtlichen Seminars Marburg, Sonderband 2, Marburg.

RAFTERY, B. 1986 A wooden trackway of Iron Age date in Ireland. *Antiquity* **60**, 50–3.

RAFTERY, B. 1987 Some glass beads of the Later Bronze Age in Ireland. *Marburger Studien zur Vor- und Fruhgeschichte* Band **9**, 39–53.

RAFTERY, B. 1989 Barbarians to the West. In J.C. Barrett, A.P. Fitzpatrick and L. Macinnes (eds), *Barbarians and Romans in Northwest Europe*, 117–52. BAR, Int. Ser. 471, Oxford.

RAFTERY, B. 1990 *Trackways through time*. Headline Publishing, Rush.

RAFTERY, B. 1991 The Celtic Iron Age in Ireland: problems of origin. *Emania* **9**, 28–32.

RAFTERY, J. 1938–9 The tumulus cemetery of Carrowjames, Co. Mayo; Part I— Carrowjames I. *J. Galway Archaeol. Hist. Soc.* **18**, 157–67.

RAFTERY, J. 1940–1 The tumulus cemetery of Carrowjames, Co. Mayo; Part II—Carrowjames II. *J. Galway Archaeol. Hist. Soc.* **19**, 16–85.

RAFTERY, J. 1951 *Prehistoric Ireland*. Batsford, London.

RAFTERY, J. 1960 National Museum of Ireland: archaeological acquisitions in the year 1958. *J. Roy. Soc. Antiq. Ireland* **90**, 1–12.

RAFTERY, J. 1972 Iron Age and Irish Sea Province: some problems for research. In C. Thomas (ed.), *The Iron Age and the Irish Sea Province*, 1–10. CBA Res. Report 9, London.

RAFTERY, J. 1981 Concerning chronology. In D. Ó Corráin (ed.), *Irish antiquity: essays and studies presented to Professor M.J. O'Kelly*, 82–92. Tower Books, Cork.

RENFREW, C. 1973 Monuments, mobilisation and social organisation in Neolithic Wessex. In C. Renfrew (ed.), *The explanation of culture change*, 539–58. Duckworth, London.

RENFREW, C. 1976 Megaliths, territories and populations. In S.J. de Laet (ed.), *Acculturation and continuity in Atlantic Europe*, 198–220. Dissertationes Archaeologicae Gandenses, Brugge.

RENFREW, C. 1979 *Problems in European prehistory*. Edinburgh University Press, Edinburgh.

RENFREW, C. 1981 Introduction: the megalith builders of western Europe. In J.D. Evans, B. Cunliffe and C. Renfrew (eds), *Antiquity and man: essays in honour of Glyn Daniel*, 72–81. Thames and Hudson, London.

RENFREW, C. 1987 *Archaeology and language: the puzzle of Indo-European origins*. Jonathan Cape, London.

RENFREW, C. and BAHN, P. 1991 *Archaeology: theory, methods and practice*. Thames and Hudson, London.

RICHARDS, C. 1988 Altered images: a re-examination of Neolithic mortuary practices in Orkney. In J.C. Barrett and I.A. Kinnes (eds), *The archaeology of context in the Neolithic and Bronze Age: recent trends*, 42–56. Department of Archaeology and Prehistory, University of Sheffield, Sheffield.

RICHARDS, C. and THOMAS, J. 1984 Ritual activity and structured deposition in Later Neolithic Wessex. In R. Bradley and J. Gardiner (eds), *Neolithic studies*, 189–218. BAR, Brit. Ser. 133, Oxford.

ROBERTSON, D.A. 1992 The Navan Forty Metre Structure: some observations regarding the social context of an Iron Age monument. *Emania* **10**, 25–32.

ROCHE, H. 1989 Pre-tomb habitation found at Knowth, Co. Meath, Spring 1989. *Archaeology Ireland* **3** (3), 101–3.

ROPER, D. A. 1979 The method and theory of site catchment analysis: a review. In M. Schiffer (ed.), *Advances in archaeological method and theory, vol. 2*, 119–40. Academic Press, New York.

ROWLANDS, M.J. 1971 The archaeological interpretation of prehistoric metalworking. *World Archaeology* **3**, 210–14.

ROWLANDS, M.J. 1980 Kinship, alliance and exchange in the European Bronze Age. In J. Barrett and R. Bradley (eds), *Settlement and society in the British Later Bronze Age*, 15–55. BAR, Brit. Ser. 83, Oxford.

ROWLEY-CONWY, P. 1981 Slash and burn in the temperate European Neolithic. In R. Mercer (ed.), *Farming practice in British prehistory*, 85–96. Edinburgh University Press, Edinburgh.

ROWLEY-CONWY, P. 1983 Sedentary hunters: the Ertebolle example. In G. Bailey (ed.), *Hunter-gatherer economy in prehistory*, 111–26. Cambridge University Press, Cambridge.

RYAN, M. 1975 Urn burial in Killeenaghmountain townland, near Kilwatermoy, Tallow, County Waterford. *J. Roy. Soc. Antiq. Ireland* **105**, 147–9.

RYAN, M. 1980a An Early Mesolithic site in the Irish midlands. *Antiquity* **54**, 46–7.

RYAN, M. 1980b Prehistoric burials at Clane, Co. Kildare. *J. Kildare Archaeol. Soc.* **16**, 108–14.

RYAN, M. 1981 Poulawack, Co. Clare: the affinities of the central burial structure. In D. Ó Corráin (ed.), *Irish antiquity: essays and studies presented to Professor M.J. O'Kelly*, 134–46. Tower Books, Cork.

RYNNE, E. 1961 The introduction of La Tène into Ireland. In G. Bersu (ed.), *Bericht Über den V. Internationalen Kongress für Vor- und Frühgeschichte, Hamburg 1958*, 705–9. Berlin.

RYNNE, E. 1970 A Cinerary Urn from Killeenaghmountain, Co. Waterford. *J. Roy. Soc. Antiq. Ireland* **100**, 180–4.

RYNNE, E. 1976 The La Tène and Roman finds from Lambay, Co. Dublin: a reassessment. *Proc. Roy. Irish Acad.* **76C**, 231–44.

RYNNE, E. 1983–4 Military and civilian swords from the River Corrib. *J. Galway Archaeol. Hist. Soc.* **39**, 5–26.

RYNNE, E. and O'SULLIVAN, J.C. 1967 Two Urn burials from Cush, Co. Limerick. *Nth Munster Antiq. J.* **10**, 103–7.

SAHLINS, M. 1974 *Stone Age economics*. Tavistock, London.

SAHLINS, M. 1987 *Islands of history*. Tavistock, London.

SCOTT, B.G. 1979 The introduction of non-ferrous and ferrous metal technologies to Ireland: motives and mechanisms. In M. Ryan (ed.), *The origins of metallurgy in Atlantic Europe*, 189–204. Stationery Office, Dublin.

SCOTT, B.G. 1981 The origins and early development of iron use in Ireland as seen from the archaeological, linguistic and literary records. In H. Haefner (ed.), *Prähistorisches Eisen in Europa* **51–2**, 1–146.

SCOTT, B.G. 1990 *Early Irish ironworking*. Ulster Museum, Belfast.

SERVICE, E. 1971 *Primitive social organisation* (2nd edn). Random House, New York.

SHANKS, M. and TILLEY, C. 1982 Ideology, symbolic power and ritual communication: a reinterpretation of Neolithic mortuary practices. In I. Hodder (ed.), *Symbolic and structural archaeology*, 129–54. Cambridge University Press, Cambridge.

SHANKS, M. and TILLEY, C. 1987a *Re-constructing archaeology: theory and practice*. Cambridge University Press, Cambridge.

SHANKS, M. and TILLEY, C. 1987b *Social theory and archaeology*. Polity Press, London.

SHEE-TWOHIG, E. 1981 *The megalithic art of western Europe*. Clarendon Press, Oxford.

SHEE-TWOHIG, E. 1990 *Irish megalithic tombs*. Shire Books, Princes Risborough.

SHEEHAN, J. 1985 A Bronze Age cist grave near Uisneach, Co. Westmeath. *Journal of the Old Athlone Society* **2**, 89–93.

SHERIDAN, A. 1983 A reconsideration of the origins of Irish metallurgy. *J. Irish Archaeol.* **1**, 11–19.

SHERIDAN, A. 1985/6 Megaliths and megalomania: an account, and interpretation, of the development of passage tombs in Ireland. *J. Irish Archaeol.* **3**, 17–30.

SHERIDAN, A. 1986 Porcellanite artifacts: a new survey. *Ulster J. Archaeol.* **49**, 19–32.

SHERIDAN, A. 1989 Pottery production in Neolithic Ireland: a petrological and chemical study. In J. Henderson (ed.), *Scientific analysis in archaeology and its interpretation*, 112–35. Oxford University Committee for Archaeology, Monograph 19, Oxford.

SHERIDAN, A. 1991 Pottery production in Neolithic and Early Bronze Age Ireland: a petrological and chemical study. In A. Middleton and I. Freestone (eds), *Recent developments in ceramic petrology*, 305–35. Occasional Paper 81, British Museum, London.

SHERRATT, A. 1981 Plough and pastoralism: aspects of the secondary products revolution. In I. Hodder, G. Isaac and N. Hammond (eds), *Pattern of the past: studies in honour of David Clarke*, 261–305. Cambridge University Press, Cambridge.

SHERRATT, A. 1990 The genesis of megaliths; monumentality, ethnicity and social complexity in Neolithic north-west Europe. *World Archaeology* 22, 147–67.

SIMPSON, D.D.A. 1988 The stone maceheads of Ireland. *J. Roy. Soc. Antiq. Ireland* 118, 27–52.

SIMPSON, D.D.A. 1989a The stone maceheads of Ireland, part II. *J. Roy. Soc. Antiq. Ireland* 119, 113–26.

SIMPSON, D.D.A. 1989b Neolithic Navan? *Emania* 6, 31–3.

SMITH, M.A. 1955 The limitations of inference in archaeology. *Archaeological Newsletter* 6.1, 3–7.

STOUT, G. 1991 Embanked enclosures of the Boyne region. *Proc. Roy. Irish Acad.* 91C, 245–84.

STUART, A.J. 1985 Midlandian faunas. In K.J. Edwards and W.P. Warren (eds), *The Quaternary history of Ireland*, 221–33. Academic Press, London.

SWAN, D.L. 1978 The Hill of Tara, County Meath: the evidence of aerial photography. *J. Roy. Soc. Antiq. Ireland* 108, 51–66.

SWEETMAN, P.D. 1976 An earthen enclosure at Monknewtown, Slane, Co. Meath. *Proc. Roy. Irish Acad.* 76C, 25–72.

SWEETMAN, P.D. 1985 A Late Neolithic/Early Bronze Age pit circle at Newgrange, Co. Meath. *Proc. Roy. Irish Acad.* 85C, 195–221.

SWEETMAN, P.D. 1987 Excavation of a Late Neolithic/Early Bronze Age site at Newgrange, Co. Meath. *Proc. Roy. Irish Acad.* 87C, 283–98.

SYNGE, F.M. 1985 Coastal evolution. In K.J. Edwards and W.P. Warren (eds), *The Quaternary history of Ireland*, 115–31. Academic Press, London.

TAYLOR, J.J. 1970 Lunulae reconsidered. *Proc. Prehist. Soc.* 36, 38–81.

TAYLOR, J.J. 1980 *Bronze Age goldwork of the British Isles*. Cambridge University Press, Cambridge.

THOMAS, J. 1988a Neolithic explanations revisited: the Mesolithic–Neolithic transition in Britain and south Scandinavia. *Proc. Prehist. Soc.* 54, 59–66.

THOMAS, J. 1988b The social significance of Cotswold–Severn burial practices. *Man* 23, 540–59.

THOMAS, J. 1990 Monuments from the inside: the case of the Irish megalithic tombs. *World Archaeology* 22, 168–78.

THOMAS, J. 1991 *Rethinking the Neolithic*. Cambridge University Press, Cambridge.

TRIGGER, B. 1989 *A history of archaeological thought*. Cambridge University Press, Cambridge.

TURNER, V. 1969 *The ritual process: structure and anti-structure*. Cornell University Press, Ithaca, New York.

VAN WIJNGAARDEN-BAKKER, L.H. 1974 The animal remains from the Beaker settlement at Newgrange, Co. Meath: first report. *Proc. Roy. Irish Acad.* 74C, 313–83.

VAN WIJNGAARDEN-BAKKER, L.H. 1985a Littletonian faunas. In K.J. Edwards and W.P. Warren (eds), *The Quaternary history of Ireland*, 233–49. Academic Press, London.

VAN WIJNGAARDEN-BAKKER, L.H. 1985b The faunal remains. In P.C. Woodman, *Excavations at Mount Sandel 1973–77*, 71–6. HMSO, Belfast.

VAN WIJNGAARDEN-BAKKER, L.H. 1986 The animal remains from the Beaker settlement at Newgrange, Co. Meath: final report. *Proc. Roy. Irish Acad.* 86C, 17–111.

VESTERGAARD, E. 1987 The perpetual reconstruction of the past. In I. Hodder (ed.), *Archaeology as long-term history*, 63–7. Cambridge University Press, Cambridge.

VUEROLA, I. 1973 Relative pollen rain around ploughed fields. *Acta Botanica Fennica* 102, 1–27.

WADDELL, J. 1970 Irish Bronze Age cists: a survey. *J. Roy. Soc. Antiq. Ireland* **100**, 91–139.

WADDELL, J. 1978 The invasion hypothesis in Irish prehistory. *Antiquity* **52**, 121–8.

WADDELL, J. 1981 The antique order of the dead. In D. Ó Corráin (ed.), *Irish antiquity: essays and studies presented to Professor M.J. O'Kelly*, 163-72. Tower Books, Cork.

WADDELL, J. 1983 Rathcroghan—a royal site in Connacht. *J. Irish Archaeol.* **1**, 21–46.

WADDELL, J. 1984 Bronzes and bones. *J. Irish Archaeol.* **2**, 71–2.

WADDELL, J. 1990a *The Bronze Age burials of Ireland.* Galway University Press, Galway.

WADDELL, J. 1990b Past imperfect: women in ancient Europe. *Archaeology Ireland* **4** (3), 12–14.

WADDELL, J. 1991 The question of the Celticization of Ireland. *Emania* **9**, 5–16.

WAILES, B. 1976 Dún Ailinne: an interim report. In D.W. Harding (ed.), *Hillforts—later prehistoric earthworks in Britain and Ireland*, 319–38. Academic Press, London.

WAILES, B. 1982 The Irish 'Royal Sites' in history and archaeology. *Cambridge Medieval Celtic Studies* **3**, 1–29.

WAILES, B. 1990 Dún Ailinne: a summary excavation report. *Emania* **7**, 10–21.

WAINWRIGHT, G. L. 1989 *The henge monuments.* Thames and Hudson, London.

WALLACE, P.F. 1977 A prehistoric burial cairn at Ardcrony, Nenagh, Co. Tipperary. *Nth Munster Antiq. J.* **19**, 3–20.

WALLERSTEIN, I. 1987 World-systems analysis. In A. Giddens and J. Turner (eds), *Social theory today,* 309–24. Polity Press, London.

WALSH, A. 1987 Excavating the Black Pig's Dyke. *Emania* **3**, 4–11.

WARNER, R. 1976 Some observations on the context and importation of exotic material in Ireland, from the first century BC to the second century AD. *Proc. Roy. Irish Acad.* **76C**, 267–92.

WARNER, R. 1986 Preliminary schedules of sites and stray finds in the Navan Complex. *Emania* **1**, 5–9.

WARNER, R. 1988 The archaeology of early historic Irish kingship. In S.T. Driscoll and M.R. Nieke (eds), *Power and politics in early medieval Britain and Ireland*, 47–68. Edinburgh University Press, Edinburgh.

WARNER, R. 1991 Cultural intrusions in the Early Iron Age: some notes. *Emania* **9**, 44–52.

WARNER, R., MALLORY, J. and BAILLIE, M. 1990 Irish Early Iron Age sites: a provisional map of absolute dated sites. *Emania* **7**, 46–50.

WATERMAN, D. 1965 The court cairn at Annaghmare, Co. Armagh. *Ulster J. Archaeol.* **28**, 3–46.

WATERMAN, D. 1968 Cordoned Urn burials and ring-ditch at Urbalreagh, Co. Antrim. *Ulster J. Archaeol.* **31**, 25–32.

WATERMAN, D. 1978 The excavation of a court cairn at Tully, Co. Fermanagh. *Ulster J. Archaeol.* **41**, 3–14.

WEIR, D. 1987 Palynology and the environmental history of the Navan area. *Emania* **3**, 34–43.

WEIR, D. 1990 A radiocarbon date from the ditch of Navan Fort. *Emania* **6**, 34–5.

WEISS, K.M. 1973 *Demographic models for anthropology.* Memoirs of the Society for American Archaeology 27.

WHEELER, A. 1977 The origin and distribution of the freshwater fishes of the British Isles. *Journal of Biogeography* **4**, 1–24.

WHITTLE, A. 1985 *Neolithic Europe: a survey.* Cambridge University Press, Cambridge.

WHITTLE, A. 1988 *Problems in Neolithic archaeology.* Cambridge University Press, Cambridge.

WHITTLE, A. 1990 Prolegomena to the study of the Mesolithic–Neolithic transition in

Britain and Ireland. In D. Cahen and M. Otte (eds), *Rubane et Cardial*, 209–27. ERAUL 39, Liège.

WILDE, W. 1861 *A descriptive catalogue of the animal materials and bronze in the Museum of the Royal Irish Academy*. Hodges Smith, Dublin.

WILLIAMS, B.B. 1978 Excavations at Lough Eskragh, Co. Tyrone. *Ulster J. Archaeol.* **41**, 37–48.

WILLIAMS, B.B. 1986 Excavations at Altanagh, County Tyrone. *Ulster J. Archaeol.* **49**, 33–88.

WILLIAMS, B.B. and WILKINSON, J.L. 1988 Excavation of a Bronze Age cist at Knockroe, Co. Tyrone. *Ulster J. Archaeol.* **51**, 85–90.

WILLIAMS, E. 1989 Dating the introduction of food production into Britain and Ireland. *Antiquity* **63**, 510–21.

WOBST, H.M. 1974 Boundary conditions for Palaeolithic social systems: a simulation approach. *American Antiquity* **39**, 147–78.

WOODMAN, P.C. 1967 A flint hoard from Killybeg. *Ulster J. Archaeol.* **30**, 8–14.

WOODMAN, P.C. 1973/4 Settlement patterns of the Irish Mesolithic. *Ulster J. Archaeol.* **37**, 1–16.

WOODMAN, P.C. 1976 The Irish Mesolithic/Neolithic transition. In S.J. de Laet (ed.), *Acculturation and continuity in Atlantic Europe*, 296–309. Dissertationes Archaeologicae Gandenses, Brugge.

WOODMAN, P.C. 1977 Recent excavations at Newferry, Co. Antrim. *Proc. Prehist. Soc.* **43**, 155–200.

WOODMAN, P.C. 1978 *The Mesolithic in Ireland*. BAR, Brit. Ser. 58, Oxford.

WOODMAN, P.C. 1981 The post-glacial colonisation of Ireland: the human factors. In D. Ó Corráin (ed.), *Irish antiquity: essays and studies presented to Professor M.J. O'Kelly*, 93–100. Tower Books, Cork.

WOODMAN, P.C. 1983 The Glencloy Project in perspective. In T. Reeves-Smyth and F. Hamond (eds), *Landscape archaeology in Ireland*, 25–34. BAR, Brit. Ser. 116, Oxford.

WOODMAN, P.C. 1984 The early prehistory of Munster. *J. Cork Hist. Archaeol. Soc.* **89**, 1–11.

WOODMAN, P.C. 1985a *Excavations at Mount Sandel 1973–77*. HMSO, Belfast.

WOODMAN, P.C. 1985b Prehistoric settlement and environment. In K.J. Edwards and W.P. Warren (eds), *The Quaternary history of Ireland*, 251–78. Academic Press, London.

WOODMAN, P.C. 1985c Mobility in the Mesolithic of northwestern Europe: an alternative explanation. In T.D. Price and J.A. Brown (eds), *Prehistoric hunter-gatherers: the emergence of cultural complexity*, 325–39. Academic Press, London.

WOODMAN, P.C. 1985d Excavations at Glendhu, Co. Down. *Ulster J. Archaeol.* **48**, 31–40.

WOODMAN, P.C. 1986a Why not an Irish Upper Palaeolithic? In D. Roe (ed.), *Studies in the Upper Palaeolithic of Britain and North West Europe*, 43–54. BAR, Int. Ser. 296, Oxford.

WOODMAN, P.C. 1986b Problems in the colonisation of Ireland. *Ulster J. Archaeol.* **49**, 7–17.

WOODMAN, P.C. 1987 The impact of resource availability on lithic industrial traditions in prehistoric Ireland. In P. Rowley-Conwy, M. Zvelebil and H.P. Blankholm (eds), *Mesolithic Northwest Europe: recent trends*, 138–46. Department of Archaeology and Prehistory, University of Sheffield, Sheffield.

WOODMAN, P.C. 1989 The Mesolithic of Munster: a preliminary assessment. In C. Bonsall (ed.), *The Mesolithic in Europe*, 116–24. John Donald, Edinburgh.

WOODMAN, P.C. 1992 Filling in the spaces in Irish prehistory. *Antiquity* **66**, 295–314.

WOODMAN, P.C. and ANDERSON, E. 1990 The Irish Later Mesolithic: a partial picture. In P.M. Vermeersch and P. Van Peer (eds), *Contributions to the Mesolithic in Europe*, 377–87. Leuven University Press, Leuven.

WOODMAN, P.C., DUGGAN, M.A. and MCCARTHY, A. 1984 Excavations at Ferriter's Cove. *J. Kerry Archaeol. Hist. Soc.* **17**, 4–9.

ZVELEBIL, M. and ROWLEY-CONWY, P. 1984 Transition to farming in northern Europe: a hunter-gatherer's perspective. *Norwegian Archaeological Review* **17**, 104–28.

ZVELEBIL, M. and ROWLEY-CONWY, P. 1986 Foragers and farmers in Atlantic Europe. In M. Zvelebil (ed.), *Hunters in transition*, 67–96. Cambridge University Press, Cambridge.

ZVELEBIL, M., MOORE, J., GREEN, S.W. and HENSON, D. 1987 Regional survey and analysis of lithic scatters: a case study from south-east Ireland. In P. Rowley-Conwy, M. Zvelebil and H.P. Blankholm (eds), *Mesolithic Northwest Europe: recent trends*, 9–32. Department of Archaeology and Prehistory, University of Sheffield, Sheffield.

INDEX